The Reader in the Writer

Centre for Language
clpe
in Primary Education

Acknowledgements

We thank the head teachers of the following schools for their support and
commitment to the KS2 Literature and Writing Project over the project year:

Manor Park Primary School
Thomas Becket Primary School
Alfred Salter Primary School
Cayley Primary School
John Donne Primary School

We offer heartfelt thanks to the following class teachers:

Anne Thomas
Carol Kirwan
Noreen Manion
Justine Whelan-Cox
Lizzie Steeds
Jane Wood

for their collaboration, enthusiasm and willingness to explore unfamiliar texts and new territory
during the project year, despite the work involved in the introduction of the NLS during the
same year. We are grateful for their generosity and openness in welcoming us into their
classrooms and sharing their practice with us and with the readers of this book.

We are indebted to the young writers whose texts are included in this book – and especially to
the case study children, for sharing their ideas and thoughts about literacy and literature with us
and for teaching us so much about writing.

We thank the teaching staff of CLPE, especially Sue Ellis, Olivia O'Sullivan and
Deborah Nicholson. As members of the research committee for the project they did much to
shape its course and to analyse its findings. We also thank other experts in this field, including
Janet White of QCA and Ted Chittenden of ETS, for helpfully extending our thinking. We owe
a particular debt of thanks to Margaret Meek Spencer, a true critical friend, who gave us so
much of her time and energy and who provided the kind of experienced guidance that all
researchers need. We thank Ann Lazim for her proofreading and her work on the bibliography,
and Brenda Hockley and Iris Scott for their help with the administration of the project and
their work on the manuscript.

We thank the following schools for allowing us to use photographs of their classrooms:

Manor Park Primary School
Thomas Becket Primary School
Alfred Salter Primary School
St Augustine's RC Primary School
Cardwell Primary School
Good Shepherd Primary School

Extracts from *Fire, Bed and Bone*© 1997 by Henrietta Branford.
Reproduced by permission of the publisher Walker Books Limited, London.
Extracts from *The Green Children*© 1994 by Kevin Crossley-Holland.
Reproduced by permission of Oxford University Press.
Extract from *The Midnight Fox*© 1970 by Betsy Byars.
Reproduced by permission of the publisher Faber and Faber.

The Reader in the Writer

The links between the study of literature and writing development at Key Stage 2

Myra Barrs and Valerie Cork

With a Preface by Margaret Meek Spencer

CLPE

Centre for Language in Primary Education

Webber Street

London SE1 8QW

©CLPE/LBSouthwark 2001

ISBN 1872267 25 4

Published by:
Centre for Language in Primary Education (LB Southwark)
Webber Street
London SE1 8QW
Tel: 020 7401 3382/3 020 7633 0840
Fax: 020 7928 4624

email: info@clpe.co.uk
www.clpe.co.uk
Editor: Myra Barrs

Photography: Phil Polglaze
Printed by: William Caple, Leicester, UK
Design: Chris Hyde

CONTENTS

'I think I see good reading as the best way of encouraging, and making possible, good writing.'

A.S.Byatt
On History and Stories

PREFACE

Margaret Meek Spencer

We need only try to imagine the enormous changes in the cultural development of children that occur as the result of mastery of written language and the ability to read and of thus becoming aware of everything that human genius has created in the realm of the written word.

L.S. Vygotsky

This Research Report is about writing and reading: how they came together in the literacy work of teachers and their pupils in five London primary schools in the course of the school year, 1998-99. That year also saw the formal beginning of the National Literacy Strategy, and the programme of events associated with the National Year of Reading, both of which reflected the current public determination to promote 'a literate nation'. In contrast to these official, widespread projects, this small-scale inquiry was designed to focus intently, and in some depth, on the effect on children's writing of books of perceived literary quality.

The importance of this endeavour is made plain by the report of Ofsted HMI on the first year of the much-debated Literacy Strategy, which was implemented in most primary schools in England. 'The Strategy has so far been much more successful with the teaching of reading than writing' (OFSTED 1999). Thus, this study of children's writing at Key Stage 2 is, as the authors say, 'timely'. It fills an obvious gap in writing research by highlighting a significant number of aspects of writing that have not hitherto been part of assessment procedures in school. In addition, there are discussions of what counts as being a successful writer at age ten or eleven.

One conundrum of introducing this research and making clear its significance is how to query what appears to be obvious. Most people who talk about children 'learning to read and write' seem to assume a relationship between these two activities that can be taken for granted. Indeed, those who practise writing as a profession - novelists, poets and journalists - often say that they read in order to write. This kind of 'everybody knows' assumption lurks in the teaching of writing in school. The evidence that children who are confident and competent readers appear to write without too much difficulty upholds it. But exactly how making texts mean by reading is linked to the written expression of personal meanings in writing has not, until now, been examined in depth.

Writing

Writing comes before reading, much of it anonymously. Someone composes the words on notices, train tickets, newspaper headlines, acts of Parliament. Behind every TV programme are bundles of papers the viewers never see, all hand-written by successful literates. Authors are named writers; readers feel they know them. Texts are composed writings where writers and readers meet, with different degrees of proximity and power.

In the very early stages of learning to write, children move from drawing 'maps of play' (Barrs 1988) to drawing letters. Besides attempting to write, little children practise being writers. Not long after, the confident pencil-to-page beginning becomes hesitant. More is at risk as composing becomes the multiconscious manoeuvring of content and form. In the best writing lessons, children discover, as they did when they learned to speak and to read, that progress lies in trying out what adult writers invite you to do so as to be like them. But learning to write is slower than learning to read. The complementary nature of each process is often ignored when children learn them separately. In their early school years, apprentice writers are scriveners, copyists. With patient practice and tolerant understanding on the part of adults, the difficulties of balancing the intent to communicate with the snags of orthography and syntax become fewer, and meanings become legible. Good teachers know how to reach children's emergent ideas in their first drafts of continuous text, but these are sometimes puzzling for the uninitiated.

Talk and drama

Writing is not speech written down. It can encompass a variety of tonalities and sentence construction, but the rhetorical forms of speeches that begin as writing are rarely found in conversation. However, the importance of talk and discussion in supporting writing has been professionally acknowledged at least since the Bullock Report in 1975. In this new inquiry we have included drama as a contributor to children's understanding of writing. The heightening of awareness of stylistic forms and of different ways of saying things is clearly relevant to descriptions of pupils' progress.

To bring a text into being, the writer has to address a reader whose existence is presumed or imagined. In school, the most obvious reader is the teacher. When young writers believe that their teacher is interested, really interested, in what they want to communicate, they will do their best to get their meaning across, especially if they are sure they will be given more than one chance to explain themselves. In a helpful environment, the difficulties that all apprentices encounter can become instances of creative learning, rather than what Harold Rosen once called 'a forced march through enemy territory'. One of the impressive things in this research is the reciprocity of teacher-pupil relations evident in most of the reported exemplars. We see the teachers learning *with* the children how to acquire a sense of the unseen, implied reader.

When they write, the young draw on the same resources as adults: background knowledge, linguistic patterns and rhythms, samples from books of things that are transcribable, including feelings and emotions. We see them discovering what a writing task can be like, and how to get help from their peers who become 'response partners'. Recorded more than once in the text of this report is the observation that children's increasing knowledge of writing styles supports and extends both their writing and their reading. But, while reading seems to disappear into the mind or the memory, in writing the ideas are there to be seen. Words appear from under the writers' fingers on a page or a screen as they balance fluency and control, ideas and technique. Their media are language and imagination; their models are other writers.

Children's progress varies; it cannot be clearly predicted, nor winched into place by short exercises. A forceful impression, derived from watching the events and effects of this work, is that enthusiastic inexperienced writers seem to press against the words they use to make them yield the expressive meanings they want to convey. The less confident write less; the risks are seen as too great. Those whose reading appears in their writing of *continuous* text have discovered a different kind of consciousness.

There is, of course, 'hard' evidence of what *counts* as progress in writing. The National Curriculum charts progress in terms of planning and drafting, spelling, morphology, handwriting and 'standard' English. Varieties of sentences, language structures and organizational features also 'count'; they are part of the anatomy of textual presentation. But the writing from 'inside', the desire to tell a story or to communicate thinking, to experiment with forms and literary styles such as in parody, and to discover the force and beauty of metaphor are other features of learning to be a writer, and these are difficult for young writers to take from their reading; the hard work, in fact.

The evidence in this report shows young writers balancing fluency and control in the production of texts that reflect what they have read. Their progress is visible, but it is not all of a piece. When young writers take on new writing responsibilities and concentrate on what they want to say in the way they want to say it, their clerical skills may lapse. We have considered a number of different facets of children's writing, such as tonality, the sense of a reader, and literary turns of phrase, all of which come from their experience of reading and provide evidence of their understanding beyond the surface structures of texts. Assessment of writing has now to take account of many different kinds of evidence beyond spelling, handwriting and sentence construction, evidence that relates more directly to the writers' purposes and intentions in meaning making. It has become clear that this transitional stage in children's schooling coincides with the pupils' growing confidence of themselves as writers. They are also coming to understand that the mastery of meaning making in linear writing involves them in more difficult thinking.

Partly as the result of deliberate interventions by skilled drama teachers, partly as a response to what the children in the study were trying to do in their meaning making, features of dramatic role-play appeared in their writing, especially when the writer adopted a different role as the narrator. It is important to note that this is not the same activity as writing in the first person. Most apprentice writers can be encouraged to become authors by generating a text about themselves (Hall 1989). To write as someone else is to accomplish a kind of reflexivity, 'me, yet not me', peculiar to authors.

Reading

No one writes about children's learning to read without some ulterior motive. For some time now, reading has been the focus of literacy 'standards'. The drive for improvement may have diverted attention from the ways in which reading and writing can interact to support children's progress as competent and experienced literates.

There is abundant evidence that 'Reading is indeed learned and taught; it is done well or it is done badly, but it has too much in it of art or craft to yield entirely – or even largely – to methodization' (Scholes 1989). The children in this study had at least five years of school reading before the research began. In their early days they would have learned the relation of the 'big shapes' of stories to the 'little shapes' of letters, words and sentences. Their lessons would have included what they taught themselves from texts in the world, television and other sources of print. As their fluency increased they were probably expected to read on their own, to choose books from libraries and to demonstrate the competences required in class. Their reading experiences are firmly located in a specific history of education, individual and collective, in particular languages and authors, as well as in the cultural commodities of late twentieth century childhood.

Now they stand on the cusp of their schooling. Soon they will make choices about the uses of their literacy, and choices will be made for them according to the results of standardized assessments. What counts as reading at KS2 is more than being able to read aloud fluently without making miscues. Called 'comprehension' in school, *interpretive* reading is a complex extension of earlier meaning making and the orchestration of knowledge about written language, which learners have gathered both in school and outside it.

These understandings include what readers learn from writers and texts rather than as formal lessons: how the beginning of a story is related to the end; when words do not mean what they say; how to 'do the voices' of characters so that their personalities and moods become clear, and how to distinguish the author from the narrator. The dialogic imagination is a feature of reading stories for oneself. Readers who discover that some writers please them more than others wonder if they are bound to believe all that they are told. Writing in a reading diary shared with a trusted teacher may be a way to learn how to explore these things.

Good teachers read aloud when they want to engage pupils with texts they might not choose for themselves: stories with unfamiliar contexts, denser argumentative prose, newspaper articles or older, less familiar forms of poetry and narrative. In the last two years of primary school, teachers may not read aloud regularly to a whole class for the pleasure of it. 'Just reading to them' is sometimes regarded as an escape from more strenuous textual encounters, such as asking questions. There seems to be no reason why the spellbinding of reading to a class should cease before Year 6.

Many new voices in books are begging to be heard by the young. 'Tuning the page' is still a series of important lessons when young readers begin to sense that there is more to the meaning of what they are reading than they fully understand. For example, to read a fable by Aesop is not a difficult feat for ten year-olds, but to realize the full import of the story in terms of human behaviour is more demanding. Another reading lesson, learned in some detail by the children in this research, is that there may even be too much meaning in a text for the reader to grasp entirely at the first attempt.

Although most children who have had good teaching and enough practice are able to read by themselves before they leave primary school, the interpretation of texts is not straightforward where the reader's understanding depends on knowledge of cultural codes. *What is being taken for granted* is a recurrent perplexity for children for whom English is an additional language, and especially so if the textual references are located in a different period of literary history. Michael Foreman's picture book *War Boy: A Country Childhood* needs more explanation now of its autobiographical details even than it did when it first appeared in 1989. The same is true of many 'multilayered' texts in books for the young.

Children bring to texts their own understandings and their awareness of themselves. In the short period that is childhood some of these processes change in ways that teachers and other adults are not always aware of. Victor Watson tells how a boy in Year 6 was prompted 'to explain without any embarrassment' that John Burningham's *Granpa* 'made him feel like crying' – though he had read it in an infant class without being upset by it – and he knew that this was because a much-loved member of his family had recently died. This young reader knew about death and grief; and he also saw – and talked about – the connection between his life and his reading.' Watson continues 'It is not quite sufficient to say simply that '*Granpa* has another layer of significance'; it is that this young reader had a new and sensitive readiness for recognition, a new potential for engaged responsiveness'(Watson 1993). During the year of this research, we have seen this kind of reading in classrooms where teachers have taken time to probe, with their pupils, the texts that make this degree of complex, sensitive understanding possible.

But reading at KS2 is even more complicated than the 'searching' that teachers encourage children to do when they engage in discussions of complex meanings. Some readers seem to grasp quite complicated things instantly so that they are given credit for having thought about them. Others see in texts details that adults have missed. This is often the case when the text includes pictures, which children seem, from time to time, to read differently from adults. We are not very good at discovering what children think they are doing when they read, but if we ask them, they tell us things that we, as their teachers, might never have thought of. 'It's like having someone to guide you through your dreams', or, 'you know the book is there, but you're looking at something else besides the words'. We could tell them what the writers say:

> '*Now and then there are readings which make the hairs on the neck, the non-existent pelt, stand on end and tremble, when every word burns and shines so hard and clear and infinite, and exact, like stones of fire like points in the dark'.*
> (Byatt 1990)

Looking to the future where her pupils will encounter a different kind of discourse in each lesson on the secondary school timetable and an extended series of writing tasks, a skilled primary school teacher has to effect a balance between wide reading over a range of written genres and reading a single literary text in some depth. Keep in mind that, in response to the content of books, children's feelings may run ahead of their ability to put them into words, so that when authors do that for them, their attention is doubly engaged.

Children's literature
The programme of study for English at KS2 in the National Curriculum is based on the assumption, and, indeed, on the evidence, that an outstanding

literature for children already exists and is continuously being added to as material to extend and enhance children's reading experience. How else could the curriculum makers have determined that children and teachers should read 'modern fiction by significant children's authors, long-established children's fiction, a range of good quality modern poetry, texts drawn from a variety of cultures and traditions, myths and legends, traditional stories and playscripts'. Even if we query fractious aesthetic subtleties and other criteria implied in 'good', 'significant' and 'classic', we know that this list is clearly meant to emphasize texts where the authors are concerned with their craft, their artistry and the importance of their themes. The books the children read in this inquiry certainly encourage the reader's engagement with these kinds of texts, probably for more than one reading.

The chosen books are mostly narratives; storying is the ground base of children's literature in primary school, and, more generally, 'the fundamental means of organizing our experience along the dimension of time' (Fox 1993). Narrative content and structures appear early in children's language development. In school, reading and writing stories begin with a plain sequence of events, as in traditional tales, and move to more complex forms of narration and more sophisticated subject matter. The details of this progress and the matching literary texts to form a 'structured approach to using books within the reading curriculum' are mapped in CLPE's *The Core Book* (Ellis & Barrs 1996).

The paradox of children's literature is the fact that it is created, produced, distributed, sold, bought and read by adults and children come in at the last as readers. The texts of children's books are obviously short, with the result that adults tend to read them quickly, especially picture books and early books with chapters. But this simplicity is, in fact, the result of skilful artistry strenuously exposed, as in Bach's 'Inventions' for young pianists. Children's literature is never really simple at any age or stage. Picture books for young children address both adult and child readers in the same text. Writers of books for young competent readers concentrate on making worlds for them to enter and explore, where they meet the deep matters of meaning making: being and becoming, love and loss, doubt and despair, the psychological realities presented as people and events.

In current children's books, the creation of texts in both writing and pictures is of a very high order. Writers, artists, promoters, and a long train of prize sponsors know that children's literature no longer has to be excused as something childish. Informed criticism and historical studies abound. The gap between books for children and those for adults may even seem to be closing because adults now don't mind being seen with *Harry Potter*. This *rapprochement* may be due in part to increased parental interest in what their children read with evident delight. However, the evidence suggests that children's and adults' interpretation of books with literary value differs not simply as a matter of reading, more as a generational gap in the culture, now much wider than at any time in the past.

The dominant theme in children's literature is *childhood*. Adult memories of childhood and what they read when young often get in the way of their understanding what children read now in order to *explore* childhood, their actual experience. To extend their encounters with the world of their time (even if the story is set in the past), writers teach children how to reflect on 'what happens' as a way of anticipating the future. Peter Hollindale who has examined this habit of exploratory anticipation in detail, has this to say about definitions of children's literature. 'The only secure grounds for definition are those that rest in the exchange between adult author and child reader of complex constructions of childhood'. In Hollindale's view, 'the adult children's author is always obsolete. He or she can never inhabit the presentness of childhood' (Hollindale 1997).

Literary competences

As you will soon see, the children whose part in this inquiry is examined in detail demonstrate growing literary competences in their writing over the year during which they were observed. For the most part, these are the conventions by which a writer signals to a reader the particular nature of the text and how it is to be read. In the case of narrative, the first page of a book alerts the reader to the kind of world the writer has created and to who is telling the story.

To discover the literary features at work in children's texts, teachers have to read them slowly so as not to miss the experimental nature of their writing and its links with other texts (intertextuality), especially those which 'everybody knows'. In the last two years of primary school, readers are also being invited to be more aware of 'how the author does it' in new texts, or to re-examine texts they know well. I think of John Burningham's *Come Away from the Water, Shirley*, where the reader has to become aware of two sets of literary conventions simultaneously, the realism of the everyday and the heroine's book-inspired imaginary exploits with pirates. A definitively English characteristic in children's literature is the embedding of books in other books. As in *The Jolly Postman*, this is a reading game with rules and surprises through a whole series of discourse kinds. Reading the jokes in this book successfully - the witch's advertising flyer, for example - implies knowing the context, the references and the tricks of language. Discerning irony is a sophisticated social as well as a reading competence. Again reading aloud helps the inexperienced to catch the tone.

Careful reading reveals the experimental nature, in both form and content, of what the maturing writer is taking from models discovered in books. Straightforward examples include: how a story develops; how the end changes what happens at the start; how dialogue works on a page. Who is the reader to think well of, whom to distrust? In an earlier generation, Enid Blyton's texts made these things clear as rules for writing. Roald Dahl subverted them. At another level of awareness young writers like young readers have to learn to 'tune' the page. It is difficult to describe the composing process without references to musical scores, with their devices of time, rhythm, key, tune, pitch, sounds and echoes. The word used in *The Reading Book* and in *Inquiry into Meaning* that best describes the complexity of what is involved in meaning making in reading and writing is *orchestration*. Writers shift their awareness back and forth from their writing to the reader. Having a voice in writing and working out how it will be heard are extensions of an early important reading lesson; how to become both the teller and the told. These and other literary competences are rarely taught deliberately.

The two books chosen as 'standard' texts which were used in this research for shared reading by the teacher and the pupils and for close analysis of subsequent writing were *The Green Children*, a story from the older tradition of oral tales retold by Kevin Crossley-Holland and illustrated by Alan Marks (OUP 1994) and *Fire, Bed and Bone* by Henrietta Branford (Walker 1997). Crossley-Holland tells his readers that the story was 'twice written down seven hundred years ago'. His retelling strips the narrative to its bare bones so that the dramatic and emotive impact of the language is immediate. The narrator, a girl who keeps her name a secret till the end, is the elder of two entirely green children (the other is her brother), discovered in a wolfpit by children from a nearby village.

Readers must interpret the actions and responses of the village children as described by the narrator:

> *There was one girl taller than the others: she stepped towards us,*
> *half-a-step, and she sang some words.*
> *What do they mean?' asked my brother.*
> *'I don't know', I said. 'I've never heard those words. They sound all right'.*
> *Then I asked the girl, 'You, all of you, who are you?'*
> *The tall girl smacked her mouth. She made her eyes dark and wide.*
> *'Why aren't you green?' I asked her. 'What is this place?'*
> *She gave me her back and whispered with all the children.*
> *Then she beckoned, and my brother and I followed her.*

'She gave me her back', 'smacked her mouth' and other phrases that describe actions the green children have never seen went straight into the wordhoard of the listening-reading children. As the story goes on, people, language and food are held in a double vision of familiarity and difference. (The pictures support and extend this.) The strangeness proves too strenuous for the boy and he dies. The girl endures derision as the sorrow lingers, asking, "Where do I belong?' until she is loved enough to want to stay. The strong emotional charge, completely unsentimental as is the direct way of traditional tales, came from a clear narrative outline, dramatic dialogue exchanges, specific details, especially of colours, so that the research children not only learned to fill the gaps in the texts, but also to feel that they were working with the storyteller. The details of the effects of this text on the children's writing are in the case studies.

It may be worth noting in passing that there is a different retelling of this story by Crossley-Holland in his book, *The Old Stories* (1997). Here the protagonists are the puzzled, anxious villagers and their sympathetic Lord of the Manor. The storyteller takes up his more traditional place, outside the action of the tale, which is a dun-coloured rendering of events with an emphasis on food. The language has very little tune, nothing bardic about it, not so clear, so exposed, as the version the children read, where the girl, who keeps her name a secret until almost the last page, narrates the events.

> *When we reached the town, the fair-people started to forefinger and shout..*
> *'Look at that one!'*
> *'All green!'*
> *'She's a freak!'*
> *'Has she gone rotten?'*
> *'Clear off' shouted Guy. 'She's normal!'*
> *'How much does she cost'? they yelled 'How much?*
> *Has she got hooves? Has she got nails or claws?'*
> *'Let her be,' shouted Guy. 'She's just the same as you and me.'*
> *I ran away then. I ran out of the town and did not stop*
> *running for a long time.*
> *Even then, on my own, the voices of the fair people jeered and*
> *hooted and screamed inside my head.*

In his discussion of how storytelling works, Crossley-Holland says: 'the telling of tales revolving around conflict-resolution and tolerance and even delight in differences is valuable work…there may be a case for reflecting this in the form of the retelling… simply by telling the tale in the first person, from the viewpoint of the central character.' (Cliff Hodges et al, 2000) This writing in role is what the children were invited to do, with powerful results.

Fire, Bed and Bone is a historical novel about the events that led to the Peasants' Revolt at the end of the fourteenth century. It is also one of the triumphs of contemporary writing for children of the age we are concerned with. The first chapter opens more windows on understanding reading and writing than almost any other children's book I know or have read with children. Its only difficulty is that it seems simple to adults who are used to seeing challenging texts in terms of dense prose and over-complicated plots. Here the text is both straightforward in the telling and deeply complex in its import, yielding increased significance with each re-reading. The voice is strong, clear and unsentimental. In my view, this story fits young readers' needs and longings for narrative adventure and adventurous reading in a way they recognise better than adults can describe.

The narrative is classic in shape: home - away from home - back home. In between there has been an unsuccessful revolution of poor farmers against the greed of their overlords. While nothing has been changed structurally, nothing will ever be the same again. Here the unfamiliar medieval world of the story is more actual in its details than that of *The Green Children*; the implications have to be read more closely. The author writes in role; the narrator is a hunting dog, whose pups are due. She describes the family and the animals asleep around the fire in the farmhouse, then tells in a rising tone, how she is 'a creature of several worlds', leading the reader to scan the scene outside and beyond the farmhouse, and anticipate its implications. The peace of the family scene is already threatened by the tone of the first sentence:

> *The wolves came down to the farm last night.*
> *They spoke to me of freedom*

At this point the less experienced reader moves on to sort out the characters, setting and action of 'what happens next?'. The more experienced one suspects that the writer means more than is said. Wolves are a threat to humans; whom did they speak to? Who is the 'me,' so close to the reader, who tells about the wolves before the reader has time to ask 'who says'? Short sentences, short breaths for whoever reads this aloud; impossible to say the words without menace. Why should wolves speak of freedom? What kind of freedom? The safe quiet of the sleeping family is about to be disturbed. It is freedom that is threatened. The first page of a novel is where the writer makes a pact with the reader, that the text will make reading part of the experience of the tale. The significant literary competence that the text teaches the reader is the next step in becoming a writer.

Afterword

This inquiry began as a concern about children's writing at that point in their education when expectations about their ability to compose texts of various kinds move to the fore in the assessment of their literacy. The focus on the links between the study of literature and writing development at Key Stage 2 of the National Curriculum, carried out over a school year, allowed the researchers to report the activities in school, detailed empirical observations of classroom contexts and project activities, teachers' pedagogies and, particularly, children's reading of quality literature, talk, drama and writing, all of which serve as evidence. To this are added forms of assessment and detailed case studies of individual children. These carefully considered data show how the children grew in competence and understanding as writers of narrative. In addition, however, there is a deal of evidence, both quantitative and qualitative, that the literary quality of the texts the children encountered not only played a large part in their success, but also showed them how to enjoy continuous reading and writing as something they could do because they wanted to.

Margaret Meek Spencer

CHAPTER

1

Where the Project Began

When the improvement of standards of writing is discussed, the issue is sometimes considered in a vacuum without reference to one of the key potential influences on children's writing – their reading. Although most people do assume that children's reading influences their writing and makes a difference to their progress, there has been very little research into the links between children's reading and their writing. In 1997 the Centre for Language in Primary Education began to plan a small-scale research study into the relationship between children's reading of literature and their writing development at Key Stage 2.

This was timely since, in recent years, with an emphatic government commitment to raising standards at KS2, there has been a very close focus indeed on children's attainments in reading and writing at age 11. It is clear from National Curriculum assessment statistics that there is an imbalance between children's reading and their writing at this stage of the school. Children's progress in reading runs ahead of their writing and scores in the KS2 reading SATs are considerably higher than those in the writing SATs. Fewer than 60% of 11 year olds reach the target of level 4 in NC tests of writing. This figure hides a marked difference between girls and boys: almost two thirds of girls reached level 4 in 1999, compared with only 49% of boys. Writing is now a major priority and funds are being provided to train all teachers of 10 and 11 year olds in the teaching of writing.

In some ways of course, this disparity between reading and writing is not very surprising. Up until recent years, children's progress in reading was always the aspect of English that was most carefully monitored, scrutinised and reported on. Until National Curriculum testing put an equal emphasis on writing, this aspect of English was less frequently seen as a measure of children's progress in English. The widespread assessment of writing in the primary school is a relatively new development.

Writing assessments make many demands of pupils, testing their ability to control several different aspects of a text and to do so under unfamiliar conditions. Children are often working at the very limits of their ability, attempting to organise their writing in a relatively short time, without an opportunity to discuss and work on their drafts in the way that the National Curriculum acknowledges is important (its section on planning writing at KS2 requires children to have experience of planning, drafting, revising, and finally proofreading their writing).

There is great interest now in the teaching of writing and how it can be improved. Our research was therefore topical. We wanted to explore the changes which took place in children's writing when the teacher introduced them to challenging literature and provided time for the study and discussion of literature.

The context of the research year

The research began in September 1998. It was conceived as a small-scale study, to be carried out within a single school year. At the time that the study began, the teaching of literacy was (and continues to be) very high up on the educational agenda, with the Government's determination to drive up standards being exemplified by the introduction of a National Literacy Strategy and the implementation of a Literacy Hour for every child at KS1 and KS2. The year of our research was also the year of implementation of the National Literacy Strategy and of the National Year of Reading, and schools' responses to the NLS became a strand in our enquiry.

At about that same time, the report was published of a Teacher Training Agency-funded research project into *Effective Teachers of Literacy* (Medwell, Wray, Poulson & Fox,1998). As part of this study, the researchers conducted an enquiry into the links between teachers' belief systems about the teaching of literacy and their practice in the classroom. One of the team's key findings about the teachers identified as effective teachers of literacy was that these teachers believed that 'the *creation of meaning* in literacy (our italics) was fundamental'. This was reflected in teachers' practice in the classroom where they 'prioritised the creation of meaning in their literacy teaching' and placed great emphasis on children understanding *why* they should read and write, focusing attention first of all on the content of texts and on composition.

This emphasis on the creation of meaning as central to literacy learning was of great interest to us. We hoped, in our research, to be able to observe the ways that children at KS2 created and communicated their own personal meanings in their writing, and the ways in which teachers focused on meaning in teaching writing. But we also wanted to track the influence on children's writing of the literature that they read and studied. In doing this, we wanted to look not only at how challenging literary texts influenced their writing *stylistically*, but also at how they affected their deeper understanding of the way in which meanings can be explored, developed and communicated through writing.

In this research project we set out to examine these relationships in depth; to discover how teachers used literary texts in the classroom, how they linked the study of literary texts with what they taught children about writing narrative, what kinds of teaching practices and learning experiences enabled children to develop their literary competence, and how their progress as readers was linked to their progress as writers.

This project was originally planned before the National Literacy Strategy began, and the introduction of the Strategy changed the context of the project considerably. However, the strong focus on texts in the NLS, together with growing evidence of the imbalance between progress in reading and progress in writing at KS2, meant that our research topic continued to be an important area for schools to address. The timing of the project also enabled us to work closely with a group of teachers during this introductory year, to support their work, and to observe the way in which they accommodated their practice to NLS requirements.

Project aims

The main aims of the project over the year were to examine, through observation and collection of case study data, any changes that take place in children's writing when they study challenging literature, and to help teachers to develop their practice in teaching literature and writing at KS2. A further aim, formed during the initial stages as we began to consider the possibility of introducing some standard texts across all the classrooms, was to help teachers to develop a literature programme for their Year 5 classes (always working within the context of the National Literacy Strategy).

Partners in the Project

The schools

The project was based in five primary schools within four Greater London Authorities. The following information about the schools was collected in the Autumn term:

1. School A, London Borough of Croydon
The school has 434 pupils on roll in fifteen classes (two form entry with the exception of Year 2, which is three-form entry). 25.3% of the pupils have Special Educational Needs and 4.8% are bilingual learners.

2. School B, London Borough of Sutton
The school has 370 pupils on roll in thirteen classes (in the process of becoming two-form entry). 10.9% of the pupils have Special Educational Needs and 3.4% are bilingual learners.

3. School C, London Borough of Tower Hamlets
The school has 380 pupils on roll in fourteen classes (two-form entry) plus a nursery with 25 full-time children. 23% of pupils have Special Educational Needs and 92% are bilingual learners.

4. School D, London Borough of Southwark

The school has 320 pupils on roll in fourteen classes (two-form entry) plus a nursery with 40 full-time children. 36.4% of the pupils have Special Educational Needs and 25.6% are bilingual learners.

5. School E, London Borough of Southwark

The school has 288 pupils on roll, in eleven classes (in the process of becoming three-form entry), plus a nursery with 25 full-time and 48 part-time children. 27.7% of the pupils have Special Educational Needs and 8% are bilingual learners.

Participating teachers and classes

In each school there was one teacher involved in the project, each of whom had a Year 5 class, with the exception of School E where there were two teachers, both with mixed Year 5/6 classes. In School A the Deputy Head also taught the class for one day a week. At the beginning of the project all the teachers had at least four years experience of classroom practice; only one was an English Coordinator.

The fact that all of the participating teachers were teaching Year 5 was not a planned aspect of the study, but a fortunate coincidence. Although it obviously meant that we were not able to look at children's writing across the whole of KS2, this focus on Y5 did enable us to compare children's work across all of the project schools much more easily. The Y5 focus also meant that, because of the introduction of the National Literacy Strategy, all of the participating teachers were working to the same general objectives. This lent an element of standardisation to the study, which proved helpful when we began to draw conclusions about the children's progress as writers.

The teachers' experience ranged from four to twenty-five years in teaching, but most had been teaching for between seven and ten years. None of the teachers in the project had studied English or Literacy at Higher Education level, although two had followed ten-day INSET courses at CLPE.

Case Study Children

Each class teacher was asked to identify three pupils to be followed throughout the Project as case studies. Initially there were 18 case study pupils in the Project: eight girls and ten boys. Seven of these pupils were bilingual children at different stages of learning English. In the course of the year this initial cohort was narrowed down to six children – three boys and three girls including two bilingual children. The writing from all these children was collected during the course of the year. The six 'core' case study children were interviewed about their reading and writing and their writing samples were analysed in detail.

The Project Coordinator

The work in the schools was undertaken by an advisory teacher as Project Coordinator. The advisory teacher, Val Cork, was an English Coordinator from a Croydon primary school who was seconded to CLPE for one year in order to carry out the research and contribute to the Centre's teaching programme. She had previously participated in the Croydon Reading Project, a teachers' action research project directed by Lynda Graham, which had focused on raising standards of reading at KS2.

The Research Committee

The information gathered by the Project Coordinator was considered and evaluated at several points in the year by the staff of CLPE, who formed the research committee which devised, planned and guided the research. On two occasions during the year the research committee hosted meetings for the participating teachers, when interim findings were fed back and discussed.

Margaret Meek Spencer was part of the research committee, and served as a consultant throughout the project, providing advice and editorial help.

'Standard' texts studied across the schools

Although it was clear that all the classes being visited were already involving children with high quality literature, we nevertheless wanted to introduce an element of commonality across all six classes, so as to see whether particular literary experiences might influence children's later writing, and how far we could detect common patterns across the classrooms where the same choice of texts had been used. With this in mind, we selected two 'standard' texts to be studied; one in the Spring term and one in the Summer term.

In the Spring term, following a drama workshop for teachers with Susanna Steele, the teachers and their classes were introduced to the folktale *The Green Children* by Kevin Crossley-Holland. This text was chosen partly because it fitted well into the NLS Framework for that term, which requires Y5 children to study legends and explore the differences between oral and written storytelling. Two drama consultants – Susanna Steele and Fiona Collins – worked with three classes each to introduce the children to the story through drama and storytelling. We hoped that these experiences would help the children and teachers to explore the world of this folktale more fully, to interpret the text through drama before coming to write, and to take on more of the language of Kevin Crossley-Holland's retelling.

In the Summer term, all the teachers were introduced to the novel *Fire, Bed and Bone* by Henrietta Branford, during a workshop run by Margaret Meek Spencer. This striking book is written in first person as by an old faithful dog; the story is set in the fourteenth century at the time of the Peasants' Revolt. This first person narrative again fitted well with the objectives of the National Literacy Strategy Framework, which requires children to look at the 'viewpoint from which stories are told' during this term. The language and style of the story are powerful and we hoped that this might influence children's own writing, and that these influences would be detectable.

The Research Questions

Three main research questions emerged during the course of the project. These questions did not exist in this form at the beginning of the project but became clarified and refined as the data collection gathered pace. They were:

1. What do children take from their reading of literary texts and what evidence could we find of influences in their writing?

This was our main focus throughout the project: we were attempting to track the way in which children's experience of literature might be affecting and influencing the way they wrote themselves. Sometimes this learning from literature would be informal; sometimes it would take the form of more conscious imitation or would be more directly encouraged by the teacher. To investigate this question our enquiry focused on the analysis of children's writing. After examining many samples of writing, we developed a pro forma (see appendix 2) to help us to describe those features of children's writing which seemed to reflect definite influences from their reading, including such aspects as genre, viewpoint, and language and style. Although our focus was on children's reading of literary texts, we sometimes also had to take into account the influences of children's reading of media texts, when these formed a significant element of their home reading.

2. How far do certain classroom practices support children in learning about writing from literary texts?

For this research to be useful to teachers it was also important to us to focus on pedagogy and to describe the more effective practices that we could identify in the project schools. To investigate the second question our enquiry focused on the analysis of classroom observations of literacy sessions. With the help of another pro forma (see appendix 2) we observed the different classroom contexts in which the teachers and children were working and tried to characterise those learning experiences which were most enabling to children in developing as reflective readers and confident writers. All the teachers in the project were working within the context of the Literacy Hour and therefore part of our enquiry examined the impact of this model on teaching and learning and its influences and constraints on teachers' practice.

3. Are the experiences which enable children to develop as readers the same as those which enable them to develop as writers?

If reading and writing are both aspects of learning written language, and if development in one aspect supports development in the other, we would expect to find some relationship between improvements in children's writing and improvements in their reading. To explore the third question, we again considered the role of classroom practices and teaching approaches, particularly in relation to shared text work, but we focused on selected case study children, whose development as readers as well as writers was being closely followed. Samples of their reading as well as their writing were taken, and their progress in reading and writing was assessed by their teachers.

Towards the end of the research year we added a fourth question to those we had already framed:

4. What kinds of literary texts are particularly supportive to KS2 children who are learning writing?

Most teachers know from their own experience that certain texts speak powerfully to a wide range of children and can be important influences on their literary development. In this category we might include Ted Hughes' classic, *The Iron Man*. We wanted to take note of the kinds of texts which were having most influence on children's writing, including the standard texts that we had chosen to introduce into the project schools, and to see what it was about these texts that children were picking up on and using in their writing. We trawled through the research evidence for texts which appeared to have been especially important in this respect and looked closely at their features.

Implicit in the background of this research were the assumptions that the children would enjoy the reading they were asked to do, and that they and their teachers would gain more experience and knowledge of modern literature for young readers. From the outset it was clear that we could not define in advance, or characterise in detail, what would 'count' as evidence of the influence of children's reading on their writing. We expected and hoped to be surprised by some of what we found. The children's and teachers' interactions, interpretations and reflections on a wide range of literary texts in the context of quite different classrooms, formed a complex site for our study. It was a time when the teachers' practice in their classrooms was coming under very close scrutiny. We knew that collecting potential evidence would entail different kinds of watchfulness in the researchers, including the ability to reflect on and reconsider their own readings of literary texts, and their experience of classrooms.

CHAPTER

2

Learning Written Language

This research project took as its starting point a very generally held assumption — that what children write reflects the nature and quality of their reading — and set out to test this assumption. We wanted first to gather evidence of the effects of children's literary experiences on their writing and then to consider the most effective pedagogical approaches to the use of literature in the teaching of writing.

We were surprised to find that very few relevant studies existed which dealt in any way directly with these kinds of questions. Although our basic assumption could well have been thought of as a truism, and is indeed a central premise of the National Literacy Strategy, there was hardly any genuinely relevant research identified in our initial search of research literature. Among the few studies which we felt to have a direct bearing on our topic was Carol Fox's *At the Very Edge of the Forest,* which is a study of children's oral storytelling. In referring to the many examples of direct quotation from books they know well in the children's stories that she collected, Fox expresses her gratitude for this 'demonstrable and verifiable evidence that books were sometimes major models for the children's stories'. But she also suggests that there are other less obvious signs to be found of the deep relationship between children's narrative and literary competences and their experiences of books and written language. We too wanted to trace these kinds of relationships and were grateful for the important and pioneering work that Fox had done. The analytic systems that she had used in exploring the structure of children's oral stories were to prove extremely helpful to us in analysing our own examples of children's writing.

Texts that teach

We could of course have chosen to look more widely at the way in which all kinds of texts that children read influence their writing. But we had a particular interest in the reading of literature in the primary school, and especially at KS2, partly because we believed that this was an area which was in real need of further development in schools. We also thought that certain kinds of texts might have a particular role to play in influencing children's developing writing — that they might be, for young writers, what Margaret Meek, in talking about reading, terms 'texts that teach' (Meek 1988).

The special mark of a literary work, according to Louise Rosenblatt, is that it can be 'lived through' by the reader, who is then 'absorbed in the quality and structure of the experience engendered by the text' (Rosenblatt 1978). Powerful literary experiences can thus engage children in the fictional worlds of texts and also make them more aware that 'language is constitutive of reality, it creates by describing' (Bruner 1986). Children who have had these kinds of literary experiences are more likely to realise that, in Frank Smith's words 'language offers a particularly powerful way....to create worlds.' (Smith 1984) This of course is a lesson both in reading and in writing.

Aesthetic reading

Rosenblatt (1978) also suggests that aesthetic experiences are characterised by a 'heightened awareness' in readers both of their own responses and of the language of the text. The 'aesthetic stance' towards a text makes readers more attentive not only to meanings but also to the words themselves, their sounds, patterns, and nuances. Certain texts, she considers, are more likely to produce these kinds of aesthetic responses in a reader, they simply have more 'potentiality for qualitative response'. These are the kinds of texts which teachers usually look for in compiling a literature programme; although there might be disagreement about exactly what to include in such a programme, we do generally recognise that certain texts lend themselves particularly well to discussion, reflective reading and creative interpretation (Ellis & Barrs 1996).

All of this suggests that 'texts that teach' are ones which challenge and make demands on readers; they require readers to become active and involved in the world of the text. They also hold more potential interest for readers who are becoming attuned to their own responses. Iser (1978) suggests that 'literary texts initiate "performances" of meaning' – that is, their readers are led to recreate or reenact the text or to picture the text as they read, finding new patterns and establishing new interpretations through these (inner) performances.

Similarly, Bruner (1986) argues that, as readers make literary texts their own, they construct a 'virtual text' which is not the actual text, 'but the text which the reader has constructed under its sway'. Texts with literary power are ones that are told with sufficient 'subjunctivity', or openness to possible meanings, to engage the reader in this way. In this way readers become co-authors with the writer. Bruner continues:

> *Like Barthes, I believe that the writer's greatest gift to a reader is to help him become a writer.*

We, of course, are arguing that this is literally true; it is precisely this kind of engagement with a text that enables apprentice writers (of any age) to observe how writers go about affecting them in this way.

The role of folktales

In considering how children are best introduced to this kind of aesthetic reading, we found ourselves agreeing strongly with Carol Fox's view that folktales have a particularly important role to play in children's narrative education. Such stories link the oral tradition of narration with the language of writing and with literary devices, styles and rhythms.

Literary devices, such as iterative structures, have their origins, as Walter Ong (1982) suggests, in the narrative devices of oral cultures, and came about originally as ways of patterning memory. David Olson, in *The World on Paper* (1996), has also explored the way that 'cultures without writing systems for preserving wording' employed 'poetic devices including symbolic devices such as homophony, metonymy and metaphor to make information memorable by preserving the verbal form'.

Folktales, which derive closely from the oral tradition, foreground these kinds of devices; readers of (and listeners to) folktales meet many of the tunes, patterns and rhythms which have also come to characterise literary texts. Fox suggests that folktales, and stories that use folktale traditions in their writing, provide 'a perfect bridge from oracy to literacy' for children, because of the way in which they demonstrate the tunes and patterns of this kind of memorable language. One of the major tasks for early years educators is to help children to cross the oracy-literacy bridge and to recognise that written language has, hidden within its dense rows of print, familiar stories, pleasurable rhythms and expressive voices.

The tune on the page

The role of large-scale holistic structures, such as tunes and rhythms, in learning language – including written language – has yet to be generally given its full importance. As Bussis et al (1985) suggest in their study of learning to read:

> *Whereas young children's knowledge of language sounds and grammar is well documented, their knowledge of writing styles as a support for reading is barely mentioned in the research literature.*

Ground-breaking studies like *Inquiry into Meaning* have, however, shown how children learning to read are helped by texts with strong literary styles and rhythms. The authors attribute this to the fact that:

> *artful writing entails the creation of truly rhythmic language, and rhythmic structures are easier to anticipate than the choppy and stilted prose typical of so many books for beginners.*

They quote from a study of early reading programmes by E. Bartlett (1979) which hypothesised that the larger written discourse structures of literature, such as rhyme structures or cumulative narrative structures, may serve as cognitive organisations that help to order the reading process for young children, as they begin to come to terms with the written code and the information contained in the print.

There is now a growing body of work on the importance of tunes and rhythms in children's literacy learning. A number of writers on language in education have argued the importance of these large scale structures or 'big shapes' in learning to read and in learning to write. Young children, they argue, first become aware of the way texts sound, and pick up on these tunes and patterns before they start to pay more conscious attention to the detail of texts.

Evidence from a number of different sources suggests that language learners begin by attending to the large scale organising structures before learning to attend to more detailed features of language. In a study from the 1930s involving a series of retelling experiments, the psychologist researcher found that his subjects always worked from whole to part; from a general impression of the whole towards the construction of the details. 'A step by step story recall was rare...*the overall organization of a story* persisted in the memory' (Fox p. 68, our italics).

Among other psychologists who have addressed this question, the cognitive psychologist Ulric Neisser has drawn attention to the fact that 'rhythmic structure is a powerful facilitator of verbal memory' (Neisser, 1967) and has suggested that all internal representations of language are likely to be auditory in character. Stories with strong and memorable 'tunes' are therefore likely to be especially helpful to children who are beginning to learn written language. In the same way young writers, who are learning how to make their own texts sound for a reader, are likely to echo the tunes and patterns of stories they have encountered. When a six year old girl writes –

> *The circus was coming and the animals had babies. But one animal did not have a baby. She looked high and low for a baby to suit her. But no, she did not find her.*

– we recognise the signs of a writer learning to mark the tune of a story for her readers, and drawing on her own experience of literary styles and rhythms (Barrs, 1992).

Reading aloud

The recognition that we learn the large-scale structures of written language above all by learning to listen to its tunes and rhythms, and that these become part of our auditory memory, helps to explain why hearing texts read aloud is such an important experience for young language learners. Performative reading brings out the tunes of a text and emphasises them. Listening to an expressive reading of a text helps young readers to understand how written language can be brought to life. They see how (in the words of Henrietta Dombey) readers can 'lift the words off the page'. One of the children interviewed for this research said, in explaining why listening to a text read aloud helped him with his own writing, 'You get the idea of how it *sounds.*'

Reading aloud is a major way in which teachers engage children with texts. Where reading aloud is effective, it is often strongly performative and dramatic in character, with teachers taking on the voices of the characters and bringing the world of the text to life. Such reading provides an important way into unfamiliar texts for inexperienced readers.

In our research we became particularly interested in the way in which teachers reading aloud to children helped them to attend to the tunes of literary texts. Their reading enlarged the text for children, helping them to hear the author's voice and characteristic stylistic rhythms – the chatty contemporary speech-like rhythms of Betsy Byars, the spare poeticised speech of Kevin Crossley-Holland's prose.

But such readings also helped children by enabling them to attend more closely to the language of the text. Reading aloud does this partly, of course, by slowing the experience of reading down from the more rapid pace of silent reading. In reading aloud, text cannot be scanned or skipped over; the full effect of the text as it is written must be experienced and given voice. The reading-aloud pace enables readers not only to read to get at the meaning, but also to take in many more of the subtleties of the writing: to register the effect of the 'particular words in their particular order' (Rosenblatt 1978).

Through artful and expressive reading aloud these teachers framed the 'reading event' which is the encounter between the reader and the text. Their reading drew children's attention to the 'particular pattern of words during the period of actual reading', thus engaging them in the kind of attention to their own responses which Rosenblatt regards as characteristic of aesthetic reading.

Learning listening

The point has often been made that reading aloud is a form of interpretation: we speak, in fact, of a 'reading' of a text. (The parallel is even clearer in music, where performances are always regarded as interpretations of the 'text'.) Reading aloud always involves a reader in many decisions about the appropriate ways to render the multiple aspects of a text, decisions which are often taken at a relatively unconscious level.

Similarly, listening to a text read aloud can be seen as a way of internalising these interpretations of multiple aspects of the text, and doing so at a level beyond conscious analysis. Aspects of the text such as its genre, tone, register, style, voice, rhythm, and tune are taken in holistically, as children learn to 'read through their ears' (Manguel 1996). As children hear stories read aloud in this way they are learning a kind of attuned and responsive listening to written language which mirrors the listening that was part of their learning of spoken language (Pradl 1988).

The development of an ear for language is one of a writer's (and a reader's) most valuable attributes, and this 'inner ear' is likely to be developed above all by such aural experiences of language. James Britton considered that the store of language that children internalise is acquired 'through reading and being read to'. He argued that in this way we build up a store of written language forms on which we draw as writers:

> the developed writing process (is) one of hearing an inner voice dictating forms of the written language appropriate to a task in hand.
> (Britton 1982, quoted in Pradl 1988)

By the end of this research we had identified skilful reading aloud as a key feature of the teaching of the especially effective teachers in our sample. The children in these teachers' classes were regularly involved in listening to their teachers' performances of literary texts. These readings were a source of intense interest and enjoyment, engaging children with new texts and providing them with dramatic interpretations of familiar texts. Their responsiveness to the language of these texts became apparent in their writing. When Yossif wrote:

> I ran away because I was scared of the people. Guy found me and put a flower in my hand. He made me warm, comfortable and confident. We went back home and we danced together.

he is clearly echoing the tune and patterns of the Kevin Crossley-Holland text, but creating entirely new structures in this mould, without using the words of the original. Reading aloud and re-reading was an especially notable feature of Yossif's teacher's approach to teaching reading and writing; he had had many experiences of hearing *The Green Children* read and of reading it for himself, and was steeped in its rhythms. Listening to texts read aloud in this way is likely to be a particularly important language experience for children like Yossif, who are learning English as a second language.

Listening to one's own text

It is clear that the interplay between reading and writing in learning to write is likely to be constant, and that the teaching of writing needs continually to foster and emphasise this interplay. Reading aloud is a way of encouraging children to listen to their own texts, as well as those of others.

We were interested in the way in which some experienced teachers help children to hear their own text by reading it aloud to them, and by encouraging them to read their own texts aloud.

Manguel observes that 'when you read your own text aloud you can feel the weakest part'. The creation of opportunities for children to hear their texts read and to read them aloud themselves, sometimes to a writing partner, is often an effective way of enabling them to see how they can revise and improve their texts. In 'learning to listen to their own texts' (Barrs 1992) children are also learning to become their own 'first reader' and to develop the kind of 'ear' for written language which will be an important resource in their reading and their writing. This kind of practice was characteristic of the most effective teachers in our sample.

Discussing reading

Closely linked to the reading aloud and re-reading of texts, in the classrooms we visited, was the discussion of texts and of children's responses to those texts. Discussions of this kind are a central part of a literature programme, and help to illuminate 'problems of perception and interpretation' (Harding 1963) for inexperienced readers. But such discussions also enlarge and demonstrate to children what it is that readers take from a literary experience, how they respond to a text, and what it is that goes on as they read. They can also make them more conscious of, and observant of, their own reactions: the 'moment by moment reactions during a reading event' which Rosenblatt sees as the hallmark of aesthetic reading (Rosenblatt, op. cit.).

Discussion may raise many different kinds of issues. One fundamental area of response for discussion will be the readers' responses to the content of the text. Children in our sample responded to *Fire, Bed and Bone* in a markedly empathetic manner, clearly identifying with the dog-narrator and the plight of the family in the book. In discussion children made links between the text and their own experiences, often moving from 'text to life'.

But discussions of texts also lead to a more developed sense of how readers interpret texts, and of the 'multiple perspectives' present in a rich text, its 'polyphonic' (Iser 1978) character. By sharing and discussing responses, children begin to appreciate that other readers might read the same text somewhat differently, and to search for evidence of how their own interpretation is supported by the text. Discussions of this kind extend children's awareness of their own responses to the text.

Learning to write reading

Our research supposed that reading and writing are, as Vygotsky suggests, two halves of the same process: that of 'mastering written language' (Vygotsky 1978). We expected to find young writers, in James Britton's words, 'shuttling between spoken resources and an increasing store of forms internalised from their reading' (Britton 1982). We were fascinated to observe this happening as we tracked the ways in which the two 'standard' texts that we introduced directly influenced children's writing.

But young writers are not simply learning to use written language structures, they are also learning to 'write reading' and to shape a reader's response. This is always a difficult thing to do for, as David Olson (1996) points out, written text 'preserves the words, not the voice'. The problematic task for a writer is to decide how to render what Olson terms the 'illocutionary force' of an utterance – such features of spoken language as stress, pause, tone, pitch and intonation, which do so much to affect the meaning. Alberto Manguel describes *public reading* as a form of publishing and suggests that it offers the writer an important opportunity to 'give the text a tone', something which, he implies, it is difficult to do through the written words alone.

Olson suggests that 'writing modern prose is nothing more than the attempt to control how the reader takes the text'. While we must acknowledge that this is never completely possible, we also know that good writers develop a wide repertoire of means of representing these 'illocutionary' aspects of text, ranging from the precise choice of words and the word order to the use of all the resources of punctuation and layout. It will be Rosenblatt's kind of attentive 'aesthetic' reading that will help to alert young writers to the way these features are used.

In developing their own resources, an apprentice writer's main assets will therefore be their reading and their growing sense of how experienced writers work, which skilful teaching will help them to develop. As children become more aware of themselves as both writers and readers, they begin to learn to 'read like writers' and to 'write like readers'. D. W. Harding (1963) underlines the importance of this constant movement between reading and writing when he writes:

> The writer invokes the presence of the reader as he writes, the reader invokes
> the presence of the writer as he reads.

The internalised 'sense of a reader' is a major support to a writer in shaping a text and influences many of the choices that need to be made, from the overall style and register to the precise ordering of the material.

Conclusion

As we embarked on our investigation, we hoped to bring to bear on the evidence we gathered from classrooms, the insights from the writers and thinkers quoted above. We felt that they offered a challenging and complex account of what was involved in learning to be a responsive reader and accomplished writer of narrative.

There emerges from these sources a view of learning to write which sees it as an extension of learning spoken language. In this view, young writers become more closely attuned to the rhythms and patterns of literary language as they apprentice themselves to the experienced writers of challenging and powerful texts. Aesthetic reading helps them to attend to their own responses and to their experience of the text as a whole, as well as to its local features. Teachers develop children's responses at all of these levels, initially by their interpretations of the text as they read it aloud, and then through their orchestration of discussions of the text, which draw on the multiple responses present in any group.

This picture of what happens when we read literature in classrooms, and how these experiences can form part of the writing curriculum, foregrounds different aspects of writing narrative from those commonly emphasised in books about learning to write. It demonstrates the narrowness of preoccupations with plot, character and setting – important as these elements of narrative are. It places more emphasis on the way a story is told, on the communication of meaning, on the development of an ear for written language, and on the interaction between the writer and the reader. As we framed our research questions, planned the project, and began to interrogate the evidence, our view of the process that we were trying to track was therefore informed by the kinds of questions raised by literary theorists, as well as psychologists, educational thinkers, and experts on literacy.

BETSY BYARS
Bingo Brown,
Gypsy Lover

Bingo's eyes rolled up into the top of his head. Not only did he have to come up with a gift! Not only did the gift have to be something nice! This gift had to be worthy of a gypsy lover!

Bingo Brown is twelve and has a reputation to keep up. He has been declared more dashing than Romondo, the gypsy hero of a best-selling romance! But being a gypsy lover is fraught with problems, for how can Bingo find the perfect Christmas present for girlfriend Melissa when he is suffering from 'shopper's block'? And how can he put a gentlemanly end to the mixed-sex conversations on the phone with a lady admirer called Boots?

The irresistible Bingo Brown is back in this third touching and hilariously funny story which follows on *The Burning Questions of Bingo Brown* and *Bingo Brown and the Language of Love*.

... paced novel, readers will find ... out loud. Byars is pure gold' – ... blishers Weekly

... disappoint you' – *Guardian*

... ation by *Julie Douglas*

N BOOK   ISBN 0-14-034765-8

U.K. £2.99   9 780140 347654   90101

CHAPTER

3

The Project Year

This chapter gives an overview of the project year. It describes how the Project Coordinator worked in the schools, and details the kinds of evidence which she collected from classrooms. It provides a term-by-term account of the progress of the enquiry, and of the kinds of activities in which the project teachers participated. It explains how the evidence gathered from the project, and the analysis of this evidence, has been drawn on in the chapters that follow.

Autumn Term 1998

The project began in the Autumn term with sixteen half day visits to schools and nine after-school meetings. During this time relationships were established with the participating teachers and their classes, as the Project Coordinator built up a picture of each classroom. It was important to try to collect as much information as possible about the school, home and community contexts in which case study pupils were learning, although resources necessarily limited the inquiry to what was manageable. For instance, it was not possible to carry out any home visits, although some of the case study pupils' parents were able to meet the Project Coordinator at the school.

Baseline information and Project Documentation

At the beginning of the project, basic information was collected about the schools, the teachers, and the case study pupils. Several kinds of information were collected in the first term of the project:

1. Factual information

Headteachers provided information about their school, including the number of pupils on roll, the number of children receiving free school meals, the number of children with Special Educational Needs, the number of bilingual learners, the percentage of pupils who achieved Level 4 and above in their SATs in July 1998, and their NLS targets for July 1999 for Year 6 (see appendix 2, Data from schools).

Class teachers provided information about case study pupils' individual attainments in reading and writing (see appendix 2).

2. Questionnaire and interview with teachers

Each class teacher completed a questionnaire at the beginning of the project to enable them to reflect on their practice in the teaching of literature and writing, and to provide a framework for discussion in the interview (see appendix 3). Following the completion of the questionnaire, each teacher was interviewed in the Autumn term about their classroom practice and their planning of work around texts.

3. Structured observations of classroom activities

Each class teacher was observed teaching at least four language and literacy sessions in the first term, and this pattern was repeated in subsequent terms. In almost all cases, the sessions took the format of a Literacy Hour. To record these observations a pro-forma was completed (see appendix 3) and detailed field-notes were kept. These notes were used as a basis for informal discussion with the teachers after the sessions.

4. Interview with case study pupils

Each of the case study pupils was interviewed during the Autumn term about their reading and writing history. Each pupil was asked questions about their attitudes to reading and writing, their own writing process, and their favourite texts (see appendix 3).

5. Reading and writing samples

All the teachers were asked to complete a reading sample and a writing sample form (see appendix 3) with each of the case study pupils. Some of the teachers were familiar with this way of recording. Class teachers also provided a wide range of samples of writing from each of the case study pupils that reflected the work programme each term. These samples of writing formed part of the data collection that went on throughout the project and their features were analysed by the research committee.

All of the evidence from questionnaires, interviews and classroom observations that was gathered in the autumn term informed the account of classroom contexts that is incorporated in Chapter 4 of this report.

Spring Term 1999

During the Spring term, data collection continued with 27 half day visits to schools, including meetings with teachers. During this term all 18 case study children were interviewed about their reading and writing histories, their reading preferences, and about aspects of writing that they enjoyed or found difficult. Some of the children were tape recorded reading their stories and poems and talking about them to the Project Coordinator.

In January all the teachers met with the members of the research committee at CLPE for a one-day seminar and workshop, where the Project Coordinator reported on the interim findings of the research from the Autumn term. The teachers discussed texts which they felt had particularly influenced children's writing and described their ways of working within the Literacy Hour. They also worked in small groups with CLPE staff examining children's writing samples, to identify the features of those pieces of writing which they agreed were of high quality. They took part in a workshop by drama consultant Susanna Steele, who introduced teachers to ways of working with a text through role play in a way that could lead to writing.

During the Spring term each class was introduced to a standard text (*The Green Children* by Kevin Crossley-Holland) through a drama/storytelling workshop run by Susanna Steele or Fiona Collins, another drama consultant. These consultants each visited three classrooms for a one-hour session (working within the time allowed for the Literacy Hour). On four of these occasions they were accompanied by the Project Coordinator who made field notes during the sessions. (See appendix 1 for an account of the drama work on *The Green Children*.)

Towards the end of this term the research committee began to look in more detail at the samples of writing that were being collected. They developed a pro forma to enable key features of the case study children's writing to be described and compared (see appendix 3).

At the same time the research committee considered the Project Coordinator's observations, and other evidence from classrooms about patterns of teaching literature and writing, and developed a featural analysis of the most effective kinds of practice in classrooms, that is to say the kind of teaching approaches which seemed to be helping children to make marked progress in writing. This analysis of pedagogy now forms the basis of Chapter 5 of this report.

Summer Term 1999
During the first week of the Summer term the teachers met with the research committee and the drama consultants for a whole day at CLPE to look at the work arising from the study of *The Green Children*. They described their classes' responses to the text and discussed how they had planned for writing after the drama/storytelling input. They showed samples of children's work, and discussed how the text had influenced the quality of their writing. Later in the day they were introduced to a second standard text (*Fire, Bed and Bone*) by Margaret Meek Spencer and worked with CLPE staff on some initial planning around this text.

During this term the Project Coordinator visited each class for a further half day, and interviewed case study children about their views of themselves as readers and writers. Data collection continued and towards the end of the term the Project Coordinator began to write up the observations of six of the case study children.

Towards the end of the term, teachers were asked to complete an evaluation questionnaire about the impact of the Project on their practice. Some of the questions related to the influence of the Literacy Strategy on their ways of working, and some teachers were also interviewed about their responses to the Literacy Strategy. The analysis of their responses, and of the Project Coordinator's observations of Literacy Hours in the project classrooms, is incorporated in Chapter 4 of this report, which deals with classroom contexts.

Case studies and data analysis

In the course of the project six case study children were selected as the subject of in-depth analysis. These children's progress as readers and writers was tracked, using their teachers' termly records and their assessments of children on the CLPE reading and writing scales in October 1998 and July 1999, together with any information from standardised tests that was available. The children's samples of writing were also analysed in detail, from their baseline samples to the final samples in the Summer term. These samples, together with information from interviews with children and teachers, formed the basis of the case studies.

In addition, three samples from each child (one from each term) were selected for particularly careful analysis. These samples were assessed against a range of indicators, which could be counted or scored. It was clear that the data analysis would have to focus on the quality of children's writing and on the changes in their writing in the course of the year. This analysis included an examination of how the writing was influenced by the reading of literary texts, particularly of the 'standard texts' which were read in all project classrooms.

The completed case studies form the basis of Chapter 6 of this report, while the work on data analysis is reported on in Chapter 7.

Conclusion

This was a small-scale research project which aimed to take a close look at practice in the teaching of literature and writing in a few London classrooms. We began without many preconceptions about what would count as convincing evidence of the links between children's reading of literature and their development in writing. With the exception of Carol Fox's *At the Very Edge of the Forest*, there were few studies which provided us with any real precedents for the kind of analysis which we wanted to do. We used the research as a time of genuine enquiry, developing pro formas and observational frameworks to enable us to collect the data more systematically as we went along, and then looking for patterns emerging from the data.

We were working during the very year when the most ambitious government initiative in literacy that had ever been devised, the National Literacy Strategy, was being introduced right across the country. This initiative foregrounded some of the very questions that we were most interested in and assumed a close relationship between children's reading and their writing. A sub-theme of our investigation became the impact of this initiative on patterns of practice and an evaluation of teachers' responses to its opportunities and constraints.

In our analysis of the data emerging from the project, we tried to keep a number of different things in view at the same time: the evidence emerging from children's writing samples across the whole project year; the evidence from detailed case studies of individual children; and the evidence from observation of patterns of teaching and learning in the different project classrooms. In this way we were able to arrive at modest and tentative conclusions about teaching, about learning and about the particular features of children's texts which mark their progress as writers.

4

Teachers, Children and Texts

Our research set out to document the contexts and the teaching approaches which might enable children to use their experiences of literature most effectively in their learning of writing. In this chapter we begin our account by examining the classroom contexts in which the case study children were learning. We give a broad picture of these contexts as we observed them at the beginning of the project, in the autumn term of 1998. We consider the views of the people in these classrooms, the teachers and children themselves, and explore their attitudes to reading and writing, drawing on the evidence available from our questionnaires and interviews. Next, we review the resources that were available in the project school classrooms: the provision, organisation and management of these resources and the kinds of literary texts that were chosen for close study. Finally we discuss the influence on these classrooms of the National Literacy Strategy, the government initiative on the teaching of literacy in primary schools which was introduced during the project year.

Later in this report, in Chapter 5, we go on to describe in more detail the teaching approaches observed in these classrooms, and to analyse effective patterns of practice.

Teachers

The six teachers who took part in the project all had a particular interest in the research topic. Some knew the work of the Centre for Language in Primary Education and two had attended courses at CLPE. Several felt interested in learning more about the teaching of writing, and in looking closely at individual children's progress through the case studies. Teachers were attracted to the possibility of extending their knowledge of literary texts and of trying out new approaches to using literature in teaching writing. Some appreciated the possibility of extra advice and support during the introduction of the National Literacy Strategy. They welcomed the opportunity of being part of a project which might potentially have important implications for the teaching of English at KS2.

Initial training and professional development in literacy

The teachers came to this research project with very different experiences. Three of the six had specialised in English during their initial training, although none of these felt that they had received sufficient training at this stage in the teaching of literacy. One teacher who had specialised in teaching in the junior school (KS2) said that there had been no direct input on reading on her course, as it was assumed that children could read by this stage of the school. In general the teachers did not think that their training had given them enough of an introduction into the teaching of writing, except for some input on starting-points for writing.

None of these teachers had followed an HE course with an English or literacy focus and their experiences of professional development in literacy at LEA level had been widely different. Three had followed substantial (ten-day) courses in literacy which had required them to complete an investigation into some aspect of literacy in their own classrooms. Two had received no training at all, while one had been part of the National Literacy Project and had therefore had five days of LEA-based training.

At school level, all of the teachers had taken part in some school-based INSET on literacy, one had received training in the moderation of writing samples, and one teacher was an in-service provider for her colleagues in her role as English Coordinator. Throughout the project year all of the teachers were involved in school-based INSET meetings on the National Literacy Strategy.

Teachers' views of teaching and learning
All the teachers in the project were interviewed about their ideas of teaching and learning, their views about how children developed as readers and writers, and the classroom practices which they used to promote progress in writing. They responded to questions such as:

a) How do you promote literacy through the way you organise the classroom?
Teachers described how they emphasised literacy, and writing in particular, through planning and organising the environment of the classroom. All the teachers stressed the importance of well organised resources in the book corner and the writing area. They believed that the attractive display of a variety of quality texts was important in motivating children to read and inspiring them to become authors. Teachers had other effective ways of promoting reading; in one classroom the teacher kept a 'waiting list' for books read aloud to the class and children signed up to read these books. Displaying children's writing and including their publications in the book corner were viewed as important ways of valuing and promoting writing.

b) How do you link children's reading with their writing?
Teachers described ways in which they used texts as a starting point for writing. The following activities had been especially successsful: retelling or continuing the story or writing a different ending; writing the story from a different viewpoint (eg in role as a character other than the narrator); writing a diary or letter as a character in the story. Some teachers used journal writing as a way of enabling children to record their personal responses to texts. Journals might include: reflections on texts read, notes of the 'good bits' children had enjoyed in books, or dialogues with the teacher.

c) Which classroom practices are most effective for teaching writing?

Most teachers organised regular extended writing sessions, during which children used a range of writing skills. These sessions often took the form of 'writers' workshops' where children could conference with the teacher and each other about their work in progress. This approach allowed teachers to focus on different aspects of the process of writing – sharing ideas, composing, redrafting, editing or proofreading – with the whole class, groups or individuals.

d) How do you respond to children's writing?

Teachers described how they responded to children's writing and encouraged children to reflect on their writing. They had found the following types of response particularly effective: conferencing with children while they were redrafting their texts; target setting, where teachers suggested an area for development for individual children; written comments on children's work – which could include praise of particular aspects and questions to encourage thinking about the structure, content, or use of language.

e) How do you track and monitor progress and development in writing?

The teachers found the following ways helpful in planning the next steps for individuals and groups: regular marking - highlighting significant achievements; looking at samples of children's writing to assess strengths and weaknesses; individual or group writing conferences; reviewing and celebrating achievement in plenary sessions.

f) What do you think are the most important influences on children as writers?

Among the factors teachers highlighted were: exposure to a wide range of quality texts; the valuing of children's writing in the school community; the provision of genuine purposes for writing in school; the use of response partners, in which children work with each other in pairs to develop their texts.

g) How would you define an experienced writer?

Teachers defined an experienced writer as someone: who is self-motivated; who enjoys writing and chooses to write; who writes extended pieces; who is confident and independent in making choices; who has a strong sense of a reader and can engage an audience; who is able to structure narrative and non-narrative texts; who uses a variety of ideas and styles and draws on models from a range of sources; who is able to edit and proof-read their own work and knows that they can always improve their writing.

These responses from teachers helped us as we framed the research questions, and also began to contribute to a picture of what was involved in the effective teaching of writing.

Children

In the first term of the study all 18 children in the initial sample were interviewed about their preferences and attitudes towards reading and writing, and about their views of themselves as readers and writers.

Reading for enjoyment and pleasure

Children's enjoyment of their reading seemed closely linked to their teacher's enthusiasm for a text. In this way, a teacher's personal choice and knowledge of what they read to children was a crucially important factor in motivating children to read for pleasure. Where teachers promoted the texts they had studied with their classes as part of an attractive and inviting display in their class libraries, children were more likely to choose to read these texts for themselves or to try others by the same authors. For example Fiona said that she had 'got into diaries like Anne Frank' because there was a collection in her classroom.

Where children had discussed features of texts (for example the author's use of language, literary style and characterisation) with their teachers as part of a Literacy Hour, they often mentioned these texts as being among their favourite reading. For example, Sian said that she liked books by the author Anne Fine, and that two of her favourite stories were *The Afterdark Princess* and *The Midnight Fox*. All these were texts that her teacher had introduced her class to during Literacy Hours in the Autumn term.

Children's favourite texts included ones encountered at home. Some children mentioned texts that they listened to at home in their home language. Rukshana said that she liked listening to stories about the prophets in Bengali and Walid said that he read from the Koran for half an hour every day. Many children mentioned nursery rhymes, fairy tales, Bible stories, Disney videos, poetry, as well as books by Shirley Hughes and Janet and Allan Ahlberg.

All the children interviewed in the case studies mentioned poetry, especially funny poetry such as Michael Rosen's and rhyming poetry, in their lists of preferred reading material. Rhymes are important in children's early literacy development and it was interesting that they still wanted to hear these kinds of poems at KS2.

Children also mentioned their enjoyment of texts other than books such as newspapers, comics, magazines, computer games, CD-ROMS, TV and non-fiction (eg encyclopedias and atlases). Many children were enjoying a wide range of material and reading different kinds of texts at the same time. Rojina said that she liked reading nature books like *The King Cobra*, stories by Roald Dahl and Dick King-Smith and Tony Ross. She said that she regularly read her brother's comics 'about mutants who have special powers'. She watched *Eastenders* and *The Simpsons*.

Favourite genres

Almost all the children said that they enjoyed writing stories: mystery and adventure stories had a special mention. Most children also said that they enjoyed writing poetry and one or two preferred this form of writing to story.

Some children said that they liked to write letters; one mentioned sending e-mails to his friend in Iceland. Several girls wrote diaries; Ellie said that she kept a 'secret diary' on her computer at home and Fiona said that she liked to write down her own personal thoughts and feelings.

More of the boys than the girls said that they enjoyed factual writing and mentioned topics such as history, maths, science and technology.

Content of writing

The children were asked what kinds of topics they liked to write about. Many said that they liked to write about animals. Some liked to write about their families or school and a few of the boys mentioned specific subjects like war, space, Henry VIII or football.

Some of the children liked retelling stories that they knew either from books or films, for example, Rukshana said she liked to write about 'stories I know' - *Rapunzel*, *The Three Little Pigs* and *The Prince and the Pauper* which she said that she 'read in my aunty's house'.

The writing process

Children were asked which parts of the writing process they enjoyed most. Almost all said that they liked their work to be recognised by an audience, either by having it on display for others to read or by reading it aloud themselves to their class, to parents or teachers. Many enjoyed making a best copy and some mentioned the use of the computer to enhance presentation. Some liked to illustrate their work and make books. A few children enjoyed planning and redrafting.

Children were also asked which parts of the writing process they didn't enjoy or found particularly difficult. Most initially interpreted this as a question about transcription and said that they found spelling or punctuation difficult. A few children said that they did not enjoy planning. One child said that he disliked it 'because when you begin to write you often have better ideas and you have to go back and put them on your plan.' Some children said that they found redrafting difficult. One child said that this was 'because even if you've put your heart into it, you have to do it all over again.' Another said that he didn't like redrafting 'because I find it hard to improve my ideas.'

Linking reading and writing

All the children said that reading helped them with their writing in various ways. They enjoyed retelling stories and writing in particular styles, sometimes imitating texts that they had read or heard. One boy said that reading aloud helped his writing: 'You get the idea of how it sounds'. When children had been led to discuss the language of books, this sometimes influenced what they wrote. Some children were used to keeping notes of the 'good bits' in books they read. Having a visit from a writer had made an impact on all those who had experience of it; these children seemed to remember everything they had been told about writing by their visiting writer.

Texts and the organisation of resources

Teachers' personal knowledge of texts is fundamental to the planning of literacy activities in the classroom. All the teachers in the project shared a belief in the importance of choosing the right kind of texts, which were suitable for children to study. Our research set out to discover how the teachers actually used these literary texts in the classroom, and how they built on this experience in teaching children about writing. Inevitably, in the project year, their choice was heavily influenced by the requirements of the National Literacy Strategy.

Text choices and the NLS

Because this was the first year of the introduction of the National Literacy Strategy, all the teachers in the project had planned their literature curriculum from the range of texts suggested for each term in the National Literacy Framework. Each term, teachers chose texts to match this range and there was therefore some similarity in the particular texts which the pupils encountered across the project schools.

Different emphases

However, although there were similarities across these classrooms, there were also marked differences, which probably reflected the tastes and preferences of the teachers and their view of the appropriate choices of texts for their particular classes. The texts teachers chose for their read-aloud programme over the year exemplified these different emphases and also showed how different teachers interpreted the guidance available in the NLS Framework differently.

For instance, in the Y5 classroom at School B there was a particular emphasis on poetry and myths. In the course of the year the teacher introduced the children to texts and authors such as Grace Nichols' *Can I Buy a Slice of Sky*, James Berry's *Classic Poems to Read Aloud*, Michael Morpurgo's *The Wreck of the Zanzibar* and Betsy Byars' *The Midnight Fox*. The class also met versions of the stories of Daedalus and Icarus and Orpheus and Eurydice.

At School A, the teacher chose relatively little poetry but focused heavily on modern novels with some emphasis also on traditional tales and folktales. She introduced texts such as Joan Aiken's *The Moon's Revenge*, Annie Dalton's *The Afterdark Princess*, Betsy Byars' *The Midnight Fox*, and several books by Jon Scieszka, including *The True Story of the Three Little Pigs*.

At School E, the two teachers chose mainly fantasy and classic texts for their Year 5/6 classes. These included *Tom's Midnight Garden*, *The Wind in the Willows*, *East o' the Sun and West o' the Moon*, Anne Frank's Diary and Tennyson's *The Lady of Shalott*.

Other teachers put a particular emphasis on folktales, poetry, and the work of certain authors such as Roald Dahl.

Organisation of resources for literacy

All the teachers in the project had mentioned an inviting book corner as an important factor in promoting children's interest in books. Some of their classrooms had more space and better shelving for book display, but all gave children opportunities to browse, choose and revisit texts in a comfortable space. Resources for writing were either centrally located or stored in children's individual trays. Some classes used exercise books for their initial drafting, while others used a writing folder. Most children used pencil for initial drafts of writing and pen for final copies.

Every classroom was equipped with at least one computer. Four teachers regularly had children using the computer for word processing during literacy sessions. Two classrooms were significantly better resourced for IT than the others and children in these classes were confident in using computers for their writing. The children in these classes also had the use of an IT suite in school and pocket book computers that they could borrow to use at home. In these classes, although the use of IT significantly enhanced the quality of presentation of the work and the children's motivation to write, it did not necessarily affect the quality of their composition, although it did sometimes seem to be resulting in longer texts.

Displays of children's writing

In some classrooms the display of children's writing was given a high priority, often as part of the book display. For example, in School E where the children were studying a topic on 'Britain since the 1930s' the display provided a rich resource for children to draw on in their writing. The book corners in both classrooms at this school featured information texts on war, posters, and artefacts such as gas masks and medals. Copies of the literary texts being studied, such as *Goodnight Mr. Tom*, *The Lion and the Unicorn* and *The Diary of Anne Frank*, were displayed, as well as a selection of war poetry and a class book of diary entries written by the children.

On the surrounding walls, children's poetry and art work were given prominence alongside commercially produced texts and much attention was paid to the quality of presentation. The publication of children's writing was viewed as an important part of writing, allowing children to see themselves as authors *and* as the audience for each other's work.

The Literacy Hour

The relatively new classroom context in which all the teachers and children were working was that of the National Literacy Strategy and the implementation of the Literacy Hour. All the schools in the project had begun to implement the Strategy, in part or as a whole, throughout their classes from

September. Most of our classroom observations were made during Literacy Hour sessions and as the year progressed a picture was beginning to emerge of the influences of the Literacy Hour on teaching and learning practices, as well as certain constraints that it introduced. The Literacy Hour foregrounded two key issues which were at the very heart of this research:

- the range, quality and provision of literary texts
- the opportunities for extended writing at the top end of KS2, including opportunities to engage more consciously with the process of writing

Teachers felt that NLS framework had helped them in planning a literature curriculum for each term, and in particular a read-aloud programme which would ensure that children met a variety of different types of texts across the course of the year. They felt that their awareness was raised of particular authors and poets and genres of fiction and that this would influence their future choices of texts for their classrooms.

However the kinds of texts that teachers wanted to use were not always readily available to them. There was a notable difference in the amount, quality and suitability of texts available across the classrooms. Where school budget and extra NLS money had been allocated for resources, teachers could choose from a good stock within the school, but if resources were not available in school they had to borrow books, for instance from their local teachers' centre libraries.

Range, quality and provision of Literary Texts

In all six classrooms the teachers planned their literature curriculum from the range of texts suggested by the National Literacy Strategy Framework document for their year group. Every teacher selected texts for each term to fit in with the range for Year 5, except for the two teachers at School E with mixed Year 5/6 classes who also included texts from the Year 6 range.

For instance, in the second term in Year 5 the range of fiction that pupils were to study included 'traditional stories, myths, legends' and 'fables from a range of cultures'. Across the schools, under these categories, teachers chose to study books and stories such as: *Cric-Crac Stories*; Anansi stories; *Aladdin*; *Aesop's Fables*; *Psyche and Eros*; *Hansel and Gretel*; *Cinderella*; *The Seal Woman*; *Ishtar and Tammuz*; *The Mean Pear Seller* and *Roasted Peanuts Don't Grow*.

Problems of extracts

One of the features of the weekly planning exemplars in the NLS documents was the number of extracts from texts that children were apparently expected to study during the course of the five Literacy Hours per week. The need to 'cover' a wide range of genres and text-types meant that depth was being sacrificed to breadth. In the course of the first term of the project, the teachers in the project schools became concerned that children were not being given the opportunity to read a *whole* text through from beginning to end. All felt that this was not only detrimental to children's enjoyment and understanding of story, but also led to a disjointed impression of texts. At a more general level they were concerned that the literature curriculum was becoming fragmented and lacking in continuity.

In view of this, some teachers amended their planning to develop activities around a core text that they read to their classes. It soon became apparent that where teachers focused on one particular story or poem in depth over a number of weeks, as the stimulus for both reading and writing, children were better able to produce writing which took on some of the qualities of the text being studied.

A focus on form rather than content in writing

The teachers mainly welcomed the guidance available in the NLS, its focus on texts and text-types, and its linking of reading and writing. However, several teachers in the project felt that the NLS Framework was too tightly focused on *forms* of writing and that issues of *content* were getting lost. While all the teachers wanted to extend children's range as writers, they were also concerned to keep a focus on meaning, and not to present learning to write as a series of exercises in different genres. They therefore tried to foreground the content of the writing and to ensure that children were, wherever possible, writing for a purpose. This was not always easy, because of the issues of coverage already discussed.

The project teachers were also concerned that the need to give children practice in writing in different genres meant that, in writing as in reading, schools were often resorting to extensive use of worksheets in the Literacy Hour.

Management of the Literacy Hour

Groupings

Teachers found the management of five or six ability groups, during the independent activities part of the hour, problematic. Some groups of children were unable to work independently in a productive way. In all six classes children were seated around tables in groups; some of these groupings, specifically for literacy sessions, were initially organised by ability. In some cases children stayed in these groups for the whole literacy session, in others they moved into the groups for part of the session only – eg for guided reading or literature circles.

As the year progressed, some of the teachers abandoned the practice of grouping by ability (suggested by the National Literacy Strategy Framework) as they felt that it was not helping with the management of the class. They expressed the view that lower attaining children needed to be with more experienced and competent children, both for social reasons, and in order to learn from their experience. One teacher regrouped her children into mixed ability groups for group reading in literature circles, as she had found that this created a better learning atmosphere.

Teachers also adapted groupings in the independent activity time, so that the majority of the class were working on independent or paired writing tasks differentiated by outcome, whilst they themselves worked with one particular group for guided reading or writing. Where classroom assistants were available it was possible for a second group of children to receive close support.

Timings
At first teachers tried out the prescribed format of the Literacy Hour with its timed components of whole class shared reading and writing, group and independent activities followed by a plenary session. However, as the year progressed, teachers found that it was difficult to achieve their objectives in the time allocated for each section.

One of the main difficulties was in the area of the word and sentence level work. All the teachers found that this part of the hour broke the continuity between shared text work and group or independent writing activities. The majority of the teachers changed this aspect of their planning. Two teachers dealt with word level work once a week only, making a separate time for it. They felt that text level work led naturally into writing, and that this sequence was interrupted by word level work. They also thought that ten to fifteen minutes was too short a time to deal in depth with, for example, word study.

Most teachers found that they could incorporate word and sentence level work into a shared reading or writing session, by focusing on aspects of the language and structure of the text they were studying (rather than a separate focus on 'adjectives' for example). One teacher chose to move the word and sentence level work to the beginning of the hour, sometimes (but not always) drawing this work from the text being studied. After this initial fifteen minutes she was then able to move into shared reading or writing and link this straight into group or independent writing tasks.

The need to stop work for a final plenary was also felt to be breaking up the time available for extended writing. In the course of the year the final plenary was often omitted from the Literacy Hours observed.

Extended Writing

During the first term of implementing the Literacy Hour all the teachers in the project began to voice the same major concern. They found that their children did not have enough time to work on longer narratives and that many pieces of writing were being left unfinished at the first draft stage. There was a danger of pieces of writing being 'left behind' as the focus of attention moved on to other kinds of texts, and teachers were having to devise ways of providing 'catch-up' time. However, this often meant that concentration was broken, and children found it hard to pick up the threads of their writing.

The whole practice of a writers' workshop, where attention could be given to the process of writing and to the development of children's texts, was being eroded, and the work in writing was becoming 'bitty'. Some children complained because they had too little time to write. Several teachers, with extensive experience of teaching writing, felt that the standard of children's writing was suffering and that they were producing less work, which was of lower quality, in comparison with other classes in previous years.

As a result of these concerns, five of the teachers decided to extend the time for literacy to one and a half hours a day and one teacher began to use two sessions a week for extended writing. Teachers also maximised opportunities for writing across the curriculum, for instance in science and history. By the end of the project, therefore, all of the participating teachers had adapted the Literacy Hour in some way or other, most especially to allow time for extended writing.

One year later: evaluating the Literacy Hour

By the autumn term of 1999, most of the teachers involved in the project felt that they had got the Literacy Hour into perspective. They had found ways of making more time for writing, often by providing writing workshops once or twice a week. They were continuing to foreground other practices (such as reading aloud) which they felt to be essential. They welcomed the NLS Framework, with its detailed guidance on word and sentence level work, but were adapting the way in which these aspects of texts were taught, often incorporating them into their study of whole texts. Their overall feeling was that flexibility was the key to making a success of the Literacy Hour, and they were using their own judgement and experience to guide the way in which they incorporated its features in their practice.

However, the project teachers were aware that not all teachers in their own schools, or in other schools, were as confident and experienced as themselves, and they were concerned about some of the practice that they saw around them. Young teachers who had only been teaching for a year or two did not have the breadth of experience to be able to to adapt the NLS guidance for their own classrooms. They followed the planning formats provided closely, instead of regarding them as examples, and were often over-reliant on worksheets. The Literacy Hour was often being cited by teachers as a reason why some valuable experiences (eg drama) could not be 'fitted in'. Often the attitude of the LEA affected how far schools felt free to take a flexible approach to the Literacy Hour.

Several teachers expressed concern about the spread of worksheets and the widespread use of published books of extracts in KS2 classes. They felt that it was essential that children should experience whole texts and that they should be introduced to texts of high quality. Their experience within the project had convinced them further of the importance of this kind of emphasis on whole texts. Where schools had spent money wisely, making a long-term investment in a range of children's literature and in sets of books for group work, children were obviously meeting a much wider range of reading than before. But where there had been a short-term policy of stocking up for the Literacy Hour by making bulk purchases of published schemes of extracts, or where there was a heavy reliance on worksheets to structure group work, results were less positive.

CHAPTER

5

Pedagogies

In this research project we were interested in observing above all how teachers introduced literary texts to children, how they made links between reading and writing in their teaching, and how they furthered children's progress and development as writers, especially writers of stories and poems. In this chapter we describe the teaching styles and practices observed in the six project classrooms and the ways in which the teachers introduced and used literature to develop children's understanding, knowledge and skills about writing. We analyse the pedagogical processes we observed during the project year and reflect on the quality of interactions between pupils and teachers, focusing particularly on those interchanges which seemed to develop children's writing most effectively.

Introducing children to texts

All the teachers in the project introduced their whole classes to new texts as part of their read-aloud programme and during the shared reading part of the Literacy Hour. In two of the classrooms this session took place on the carpet away from the children's tables. In the other four classrooms, where space or the arrangement of furniture did not permit this, children remained at their tables. The teaching styles observed during these sessions were mixed. Teachers often read aloud to the children from the text in the book or from the text projected on a screen from an OHP. Sometimes children read aloud *with* the teacher, either as a whole class or in groups taking turns to read sections. Teachers used some or all of these practices within one session, according to the objectives they were focusing on.

A striking example of effective practice in discussing a new text was observed in Anne's classroom at School B, where the class were studying *The Stove Haunting* by Bel Mooney. The story is set in the West Country. A boy, Daniel, moves to a new house with his parents, only to find himself travelling back to the time of the Tolpuddle Martyrs. Anne began the session by asking her children to discuss, in pairs, how they saw what had happened in the story so far. Then she read them part of the text and went on to summarise the next chapter, checking that the children understood the social and political issues about workers fighting for the right to form a union. This regular practice of *summarising and telling* part of the story allowed Anne to use the shared reading time economically and draw her children into further discussion about the issues in the story. It also meant that she could focus their attention on a particular piece of text that she wanted to read aloud, perhaps as preparation for a writing task – without omitting any part of the story.

The teacher as a performative reader

Reading texts aloud to children was a fundamental part of all the teachers' classroom practice. All read aloud in their most expressive voices, to bring the text alive and engage their children in a reading 'performance'. Some gave multiple readings, or reread certain passages or verses that they wished to focus on – perhaps to illustrate the way in which a writer used language to convey atmosphere or build up suspense, or to demonstrate how the writer used dialogue as part of characterisation.

This social act of bringing the text alive and lifting it off the page, with the pupils, at first, as listeners, meant that the language and the 'voice' of the author or poet was strongly present in the classroom. It provided an important background for children's own reading of the text, whenever they reread it individually. It seemed likely that this expressive reading would echo in the children's memories, helping them to internalise some of the language of the text. Certainly this seemed to be the case with some children, whose writing showed strong influences of texts that they had heard, but not yet read independently.

The teacher as orchestrator of discussion

Within the shared reading session, all the teachers in the project orchestrated some kind of general discussion about the text, in order to deepen children's understanding, to encourage some sort of personal response, and to reflect on particular literary qualities in the text. In most cases teachers concentrated initially on establishing the meaning of the text, by asking open-ended questions, often about characters, their predicaments and their motives. This led children to make connections with their own worlds and experiences, and this kind of 'text-to-life' response was encouraged.

From here, the teachers generally moved the discussion on to a closer reading of the text, focusing on individual words or phrases. They drew children's attention to features of the author's language, their *style, imagery* or the *characterisation* present in *description* or *dialogue*. In some cases children were encouraged to use this kind of metalanguage to talk about features of the text.

A particularly clear example of this kind of discussion was observed in Justine's class at School E, where the children were reading an extract from *The Green Children* which describes the green girl's visit to the great fair. Her appearance provoked taunts and jeers from the fair people, which made her run away from the fair and brought home to her the fact that she would never belong.

Justine used this passage to draw the children's attention to the contrasting feelings of the green girl before and after the fair. She encouraged the children to empathise with the character. She asked them to close their eyes and imagine they were the green girl, while she reread the insults of the fair-people to them again. She then invited the children to say how the words made them feel. Some of the children responded at a personal level, but some responded on a deeper level to one of the key issues of the story – that of otherness and being different – linking this to questions of race and colour:

> Ollie: 'I hate being green.'
> Mofe: 'I don't want to be different.'
> Fiona: She feels depressed because she thought that the white people were kind.
> Kelly: She feels that wherever she goes she is going to be called names.
> Harry: Maybe she thinks they are going to harm her.

Multiple readings of the text and exploratory conversations such as these allowed young writers to reflect on their own interpretations of a particular text and consider those of others. They also gave children the opportunity to explore issues in stories, such as the racial prejudice in *The Green Children, before* writing. After this, children were in a better position to write with more knowledge and understanding, from *inside* the story world.

Using texts as models for writing

All the teachers in the project planned writing activities from the texts which they had read to their classes. Sometimes texts were used as a basis for children to generate their own ideas – which could obviously lead them away from the text. At other times the texts were offered as a direct model for children to imitate: for instance the task might be to write the next chapter of a story in the style of the author.

A good example of this was when Anne, at School B, asked her class to write a follow-on chapter of Dick King-Smith's *Lady Daisy*. This story is about a boy called Ned who discovers a Victorian doll in his grandmother's attic. The doll, Lady Daisy, speaks to Ned and through her he learns about life in Victorian times. One day a dog runs off with the doll and, just as Ned catches up with her, he bumps into an antique dealer:

> " 'A remarkable specimen,' said the man after a while. 'And the clothes – exquisite. No harm done, it seems – she just needs a wash and brush up. By the way, let me introduce myself. My name is Mr. Merryweather-Jones, and I am an antique dealer.'"
> Extract from 'Lady Daisy', p103

Anne invited her class to write the next chapter of the story. Here is an extract from Sophie's chapter:

> 'Ned's mum went to bed while Ned's dad was reading the paper, it wasn't long before the door bell rang. Ned's dad answered it.

In came Mr. Merryweather-Jones. "I wondered if you had any valuable antiques which are worth a lot of money," said Mr. Merryweather-Jones in a normal voice. "Hang on" said Ned's dad as he hurried into Ned's bedroom he picked up the doll and took it back into the living room.
"Here you are Sir" said Ned's dad. Mr. Merryweather-Jones gave Ned's dad a large pile of money.
"Thank you" replied Ned's dad.
"That's ok. I enjoyed doing business with you," said Mr. Merryweather-Jones.'

Sophie has picked up on the easy but superior manner which characterises the antique dealer and has demonstrated her understanding of his role and his motives.

Texts offered to children in this way as models for writing not only provided a store of ideas and language but also served as supportive narrative structures. Children were able to draw on the tone and style of a story in creating their own texts. They built on the frameworks stories provided, sometimes retelling the events from a different viewpoint, taking the story further, or writing a completely new version of a story.

Shared Writing and Editing

In the sessions observed, the teachers usually led the discussion towards a writing task, generally moving from shared reading to shared writing. In most cases the shared writing simply took the form of a brainstorm, with children exchanging ideas and teachers extending their thinking. Sometimes these ideas were recorded by the teacher on a board, flipchart or OHP. Sometimes the children made their own notes of ideas, and these notes often became their planning.

On a relatively few occasions the teachers engaged the children in actual shared writing - collaborative composition with the whole class, where the teacher acted as scribe. This strategy, often used at earlier stages in KS1 to demonstrate both composition and transcription, can also support older children in beginning, developing, revising or editing their work. Although most of the teachers in the project helped children to revise their writing at their tables, either in pairs, small groups or one to one, this was also something which was occasionally done as a whole class. It was the kind of intervention which could be used at any point during the writers' workshop.

In Noreen's class at School A, she used a child's text to demonstrate the process of revision. Grace needed some help in redrafting her poem, which had been inspired by the study of *The Green Children*. Noreen gathered the children together on the carpet and wrote a verse of Grace's poem on a large sheet of paper. Here is a brief transcription of the conversation that followed:

> Noreen: *Let's look at the second verse - the flower swayed in the cold breeze - a lovely image. Would you change this in any way, Grace?*
> Grace: *I would move 'the' to the next line.*
> Noreen: *Yes, this makes us pause doesn't it? So it makes sense to move it to the next line. Now this verse is also about the breeze…. is there anything we might want to change about the language?*
> Annette: *I would change 'cold breeze' to maybe 'cold rushing breeze'.*
> Bill: *I think that 'rushing' makes it too windy.*
> Noreen: *Okay, what else might you have?*
> Eve: *I would put floaty breeze.*
> Child: *I would put flowing breeze.*

In this way Noreen and the class helped Grace to make choices about the language and layout of her poem. The children were encouraged to reread the poem several times to check that the sense of the piece was maintained. They focused on the rhythm and experimented with changing the length of lines. The whole class benefited from this discussion and the writer learned that she had a wider range of options to choose from – but that in the end she had control over her decisions.

Task-setting and planning

During whole class discussions, teachers moved into setting the writing task and planning it with the whole class. Sometimes the brainstorming and recording of ideas during discussions around a text became the plan which children used for their writing.

There were notable differences between the teachers in their ways of setting the writing tasks. These differences seemed to be determining the way that children worked and helping to shape their writing. We observed three distinct forms of planning or preparation which teachers and children engaged in before writing:

- informal planning, in which jottings were made of interesting ideas, words or phrases and sketches of characters, or where possibilities for plot events were noted and captioned (as in a storyboard)
- formal planning, such as a writing frame (either commercially produced or teacher invented) or 'link boxes', where a plan of the successive episodes of the story is expressed as a flow diagram
- indirect planning – where little was written down but where there were extensive opportunities for talking and thinking about ideas and directions before writing.

Informal planning

In three of the classrooms the teachers used this method of supporting children. Sometimes they wrote key words or phrases on the board, flipchart or OHP, and left them there for children to see as they began their writing. Some of the children started to compose their first draft from this point, while others made a personal selection of some of the key words or phrases that they might want to use and copied them into their draft books. These ideas were then sometimes assimilated into the writing as the draft took shape.

In a lesson in Carol's class, at School D, the children were studying traditional tales from a variety of cultures. Carol read a Chinese story, *The Mean Pear Seller,* to the children. During shared writing, Carol asked if there were any special words that they might need when writing their own retelling of the story. In the course of a discussion, the children suggested: *China, customer, trader, magic, pears, customary, travellers, disappear, beggars, cunning, poor,* and *admiration.* Carol wrote all these words up on the overhead projector for children to see and some of them copied the words into their draft books.

This type of informal planning led to a variety of starting points in individual children's writing – a key factor being that they could *choose* whether to include ideas or language from the discussion. They were encouraged to make these choices and regarded as being in control of their own writing. The teacher's influence was supportive. but not limiting. The writing task was not differentiated according to ability; the whole class did the same task.

Formal planning

In two of the classrooms observed the teachers had demonstrated, early in the year, a set planning format for story writing, and one for poetry writing. In the course of the year children became very familiar with these invariable planning formats and used them regularly before their initial drafting. The format for story planning took the form of 'link' or plot boxes, which were used to help children to link events into a coherent plot. The format for poetry writing took the form of a 'web' of ideas which was constructed around the idea of using the five senses. Children posed themselves questions such as 'If I were an animal what would I be? If I were a colour what would I be?' in relation to the topic of their poem.

This type of planning meant that there was less room for children to deviate from the plan and often resulted in them redrafting their work several times in order to stick to their initial plan. The use of the poetry plan often seemed to lead children further away from the text that they were studying and away from the class discussion. Many of the ideas they had talked about in response to the text could not be incorporated into their writing. Overuse of these invariable planning formats seemed to be less than helpful and sometimes resulted in writing where form took precedence over meaning.

In another classroom children were always given a 'writing frame' – often a list of words, phrases or starter sentences printed on an A4 sheet as a lead into the writing. Sometimes the frame was commercially produced and sometimes it was designed by the teacher around a particular text. Whilst this strategy can be useful in scaffolding writing for some children, it did seem to limit children's confidence in taking control of the writing. They were not in a position to choose their own ways of beginning, and yet their writing did not always take off from the standard beginning provided.

Indirect planning – talking and thinking before writing

Children in all six classrooms would sometimes begin to compose their first drafts following on from an in-depth discussion of a text that had been read, without any form of written plan. Where this happened, the text itself, performed during the reading aloud and revisited during the discussion, often became a scaffold or support for children's writing. All the children in the project were given opportunities to write in this way, sometimes using first person narrative as they wrote in role. For example, in School D during the drama and storytelling work on *The Green Children*, Lizzy's class wrote a first draft of first person narrative whilst still 'in role' as one of the characters in the story. Later, the children worked their drafts up into a final copy, but first they revisited the text. Here is a short extract from the talking and thinking that took place:

> *Lizzy: Now we're going to look at the beginning of the story and* how *it begins. Do you think it's a good beginning and why? How does it draw us into the story and how does the author get us involved?*

(Lizzy reads the first two paragraphs of the story from an OHP)
Robert: I don't think you get any information about the green children.
Joe: I disagree because I think that where the lamb has slipped into the cave is the link to the events.
Kerry: It makes me think - what happened? - I want to know.
Aren: I like it because it leads you into suspense because you don't know what's happened.
Morris: I think it's good because it gets you involved in the story and later she (the green girl) tells you about her world.
Lizzy: Is that important because we know it's the character who's speaking?
Tim: It's like someone is retelling the story.
Geraldine: I like the way it gets straight to the point - 'one of our lambs skipped in'.
Alan: For me I think that something interesting is going to happen when they set off to rescue the lamb. Also 'from our home country.'

Noticeable in this discussion was how little the teacher talked, thereby giving space to the children to express their ideas. Lizzy encouraged exploratory talk, orchestrating children's responses. The children were confident in drawing inferences, often quoting parts of the text to support their views. In this way they spoke the language of the text aloud, and these were the phrases which seemed to stay with them when they came to write.

This kind of talking and thinking about literary texts before writing enables young writers to build up a fund of ideas and language to use in their own writing. It can therefore be seen as a form of indirect planning. Some of the most successful writing in the project came about after a particularly involving discussion when children had generated plenty of initial ideas for writing. In these circumstances they wrote readily, and their first drafts showed how absorbed they had been in the fictional world.

Teachers' interventions during the writing process
The teachers all shared the belief that children should be enabled to reflect on the different stages of the process of writing, and in all the classes the children drafted, redrafted, edited, proof-read, and published their work. Obviously it was not possible or even desirable for children to go through all of these stages for every piece of writing, but it was important that they were frequently given time to see a piece of writing through to the finished product.

It was interesting to observe that different teachers placed more emphasis on some aspects of the writing process than on others, and gave time for talk at different points in the process. Two teachers emphasised planning and talking *before* writing, and redrafting and publishing of final drafts. In these classrooms, children generally began writing on their own and then worked with a partner or the teacher to edit their work when it was finished. In these classrooms the display of children's writing was a very high priority. Children often used IT to enhance the quality of their final drafts and time was spent on presentation.

Two of the teachers prioritised talk *in between* draftings. This talk took several forms: the teacher's response to individual children's writing; whole class revising and editing; children talking to each other in pairs as 'response partners'. In these classrooms children often began writing collaboratively and then moved towards independent writing. There was less emphasis on the presentation and display of children's writing. The writing was usually shared, with either teacher or children reading drafts to the whole class. This sharing often took place during the plenary part of the Literacy Hour, which was not always fixed at the end of the lesson. A notable feature of these plenary sessions between redrafts was the teachers' practice of revisiting the literary text which had been the starting point for the writing.

Another teacher placed most emphasis on independent writing activities following on from an initial discussion of the text. In this class, the writing task was differentiated for each ability group. This was unlike the other five classes, where the work was differentiated either by outcome or by giving some children extra support.

Finally, one teacher placed most emphasis on initial drafting following shared reading, without any structured kind of planning. She responded to children's texts in whole class sessions which followed this initial drafting. She also prioritised the display and publication of children's work.

All of the teachers helped to shape children's writing, by responding orally or in writing to their texts at various stages during the writing process. Teacher intervention *between* children's drafts, however, appeared to be especially effective in encouraging them to develop their texts. It seemed to provide children with an audience and with the kind of immediate feedback which encouraged them to take their ideas further. Teachers could then go on to help children to work through any revision problems. Four of the teachers consciously modelled this process for the whole class, so that children could take on a supportive role themselves in writers' workshop sessions, working as 'response partners'.

Response partners
Four of the teachers regularly planned writing workshop sessions so that children could respond to each other's work, working in pairs. Children either had fixed partners or chose someone to work with for that particu-

lar session. In pairs, they helped each other with redrafting, editing or proof reading. Some children wrote comments on another's work; others discussed ways of making their writing better.

Response partners provided these young authors with an immediate audience for their work and encouraged children to become readers of each other's work. The social nature of writing was stressed and children were enabled to work more independently on their texts. However, for this time to be productively used, it was essential that teachers should demonstrate this process regularly and monitor what was going on. One teacher devised a useful set of 'conference cards' that children could use as prompts to remind them of the things they needed to look at, either as editors or proof-readers. Once children had used these cards several times, they no longer needed them as prompts for working together.

Conclusions

Within these classroom contexts children were gaining experience in different parts of the writing process. Common to all the classrooms was the role of the literary text as a source and as an inspiration for writing. But how the text was used in teaching children more about writing varied across the project classrooms. Some of these variations seemed to be linked to differences in what children were able to do in their own writing.

Three key factors in the way in which the reading of literary texts was closely linked to the teaching of writing seemed to emerge from the observations made across these classrooms during the project year. These factors, which often seemed to be positively associated with high quality in children's writing, related to:

- reading aloud and rereading, which helped children to take on the language and style of texts
- indirect planning, which prepared children for writing through multiple readings of the text and in-depth discussions
- teachers intervening and responding to children's texts during the process of writing, and reading their work aloud to them.

Reading aloud and rereading

In classrooms where the teachers knew the text well and gave *powerful readings*, often revisiting certain passages or verses and reading them over again for children to listen to and comment on, children seemed more ready to take on the rhythms, structures and style of the language of the text being studied. In these classrooms, during the reading aloud sessions, teachers also led the class into sustained discussion of particular aspects of the author's way of writing, and of the literary features of the text. These aspects could often be detected in children's subsequent writing, but were well integrated into what they wrote, showing that they had thoroughly internalised these features of style and were not simply 'parroting' back what they had been led to observe.

Indirect planning

In classrooms where the writing task was thoroughly prepared for through multiple readings of the text and through discussion, children were able to draw on ideas and language from the text as starting points for their writing. In these situations, the writing task was usually relatively open-ended. The texts that had been read provided a model, but did not limit what children did with their own material. They were being invited to learn from the text and to draw on its features to structure and shape their own writing.

Teachers' interventions during the writing process

Teachers' interventions were especially effective when they responded to children's writing between drafts. These interventions seemed to be reflected in what children were able to go on to do independently. These teachers often read the children's writing back to them aloud, before posing questions, ideas and suggestions which enabled them to develop their ideas further. Where these things happened, children seemed better able to participate in discussions of the features of their writing and how it might be improved.

This sensitive form of intervention enabled teachers to demonstrate to children how their texts 'sounded'. All writers need to develop a strong sense of an internalised reader; this practice helped children anticipate the effect their writing would have on a reader. They were learning to listen to their own texts and developing a critical ear for their writing.

Teachers who intervened effectively in children's work and helped them to improve the quality of their writing usually expected them to make the final decisions about their texts. They encouraged them to work constructively on their own texts and to improve them, using the feedback that they had received. Where teachers had these expectations, children were more likely to retain control of their writing and to be able to explain how and why they had changed and developed their texts.

CHAPTER

6

Case Studies

Introduction to Case Studies

Although children are increasingly measured against common standards, it is only when we come to look in some depth and detail at individual instances of learning that we can observe what children are making of their teaching. We need to slow our pace to see how different children internalise both the taught lessons in writing provided by their teachers and the 'untaught lessons' provided by the texts they read. In this chapter therefore, we move into close-up for a series of case studies of individual children from four of the schools that took part in the project. Through this study of six learners from five classrooms we hope to be able to look more closely at the texture of learning, and to see what happens as these pupils begin to find new voices in their writing.

Initially the five class teachers in the project selected a total of 18 as possible case studies. They focused especially on those children who, while they were independent and enthusiastic readers (including some bilingual children who were independent readers in their first language), were less experienced as writers. The reading and writing of all these children was sampled, and they were assessed in relation to the CLPE reading and writing scales.

Following initial interviews with all 18 children, the Project Coordinator selected six 'core' case study children, from four classes, to follow more closely. All of the children in this core group were Y5 pupils; three were in Y5 classes and three were in mixed Y5/6 classes. (A full account of the classroom contexts in which the children were learning is given in Chapter 4.) The children made up a balanced sample of three girls and three boys. Two children were bilingual, at very different stages of English learning (one fully fluent and one who was still becoming familiar with English after only one year in the UK). All of the children chosen were ready and able to discuss their reading and writing and all enjoyed writing as an activity, although some were much more technically competent than others. In the sections that follow we tell the story of how their writing developed during the project year and what influenced their development.

During the year all eighteen case study children made marked progress in their reading and writing, while the six core case study children made slightly more progress. These results are reported in chapter 8 (General

Conclusions). It will be apparent from the following sections that the writing development of certain children was particularly remarkable. Their progress was closely related to the opportunities and teaching available in their classrooms.

In compiling the case studies of the six core case study children, we surveyed all of the writing done during the year by a particular child using a feature analysis pro forma that we developed in the course of the year (see appendix 3). Not all of the texts composed by the children are included in this chapter, but all were considered during the analysis of their work. In the space available here, we have tried to represent the particular strengths and outstanding features of individual children's writing, as well as show something of its range. Spelling has been regularised in all the pieces of writing included, but punctuation remains as in the originals.

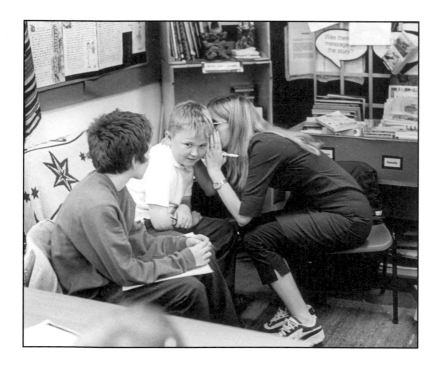

Sophie

Sophie is in year 5 at School B. She lives with her parents and her younger sister, who is in Year 3 at the school. Her mother is a governor of the school. At home, Sophie is surrounded by books and is an avid reader. Once she has discovered an author she likes, she often becomes hooked and sets out to read everything by him or her. Sophie's list of favourite authors so far includes: Jean Ure, Bel Mooney, Enid Blyton, Roald Dahl, Anthony Browne, Michael Morpurgo, Jacqueline Wilson, Lucy Daniels, Michael Coleman and Anne Fine. This list shows that Sophie is a competent and experienced reader, and reveals her wide-ranging tastes in children's fiction.

A story written by Sophie at the beginning of the year illustrates her ability to write a family adventure. The story was composed without any initial input or intervention by her teacher; it was set as an unaided task, with just a choice of titles given, in much the same way as the writing task for the SAT.

> ### An Adventure in Spain
> "Hurry up" I shouted "We'll miss the plane"
> "Sorry we're coming" said Georgia and Hollie giggling. We climbed up on to the plane and we all sat down tiredly. Georgia, Hollie, Millie and Baby Allysia were all fast asleep. The aeroplane landed we all got off the plane and made our way to the villa. The next morning we all put our swim suits on grabbed the pool key and a towel and we dived in the lovely swimming pool outside our villa. A strange man appeared at the swimming pool gate put his hand through the gate got our pool key and ran off with it.
> "Lets follow him" shouted Georgia we grabbed our towels. I grabbed and put her on my back and ran too up with the others. We saw the man go into a villa right beside ours. "I'm going back and telling Daddy" said Millie so we all made our way back to the villa and told my Uncle David all about it. David phoned the Police and came round and broke into the villa grabbed the strange looking man gave us the key and they went off. "Everything's back to normal" I said.
> "But where's Millie?" said Georgia "oh no" I said "Here I am" she said as she jumped up from behind the bench!

A story beginning

Without a particular literary model for the story, 'Adventure in Spain', Sophie draws on her own experience of family outings and on her private reading of many Enid Blyton adventure stories. At the beginning of her story we hear a sense of adventure in Sophie's narrating voice:

'"Hurry up" I shouted "We'll miss the plane".'

The story begins, as some of Sophie's other work does, with dialogue. There is an Enid Blytonish element in the situation and a sense of urgency; Sophie is keen to get on with the introduction and take the reader off on a plane with the characters. There is a strong sense of forward movement and narrative drive. But what starts out as a safe holiday will turn into something potentially more dangerous.

Introducing characters

Sophie introduces us to the characters so that we can move straight into the action:

We climbed onto the plane and we all sat down tiredly. Georgia, Hollie, Millie and Baby Allysia were all fast asleep.

There is a sense of togetherness conveyed by the repetition of 'all', which is repeated again in the next two sentences as the family 'all got off the plane' and 'all put our swimsuits on'.

Sophie is writing as herself, drawing upon family experiences and real life events. But her story is a mixture of reality and fantasy, as Sophie introduces an intruder into the family's comfortable world. This transition occurs rather abruptly in the first paragraph:

....we dived into the lovely swimming pool outside our villa. A strange man appeared at the swimming pool gate got our pool key and ran off with it.

In what follows, there is no indication of the characters' feelings nor any suggestion that they might be upset by what has happened, there is simply a straightforward response of heroism and bravery in a manner strongly reminiscent of an Enid Blyton story:

'Let's follow him' shouted Georgia.

But unlike Enid Blyton's children, who face dangers and solve their own problems, emerging as heroes, the children in Sophie's story quickly raise the alarm and the adults in authority, an uncle and the police, are the ones to save the day and take control.

Ending

In this story, Sophie seems to be struggling with the ending. No sooner is the story's problem introduced than it is resolved; but this is rather unsatisfactorily done – the reader is left with all sorts of questions unanswered about 'the strange man' and about who broke into the villa. Sophie seems unsure about how to develop the situation; she returns as swiftly as possible to the familiar and cosy world of the family:

"Everything's back to normal" I said.

And at the very end of the story, she uses humour to make light of the whole episode:

> *"But where's Millie?" said Georgia.*
> *"Oh no" I said.*
> *"Here I am" she said as she jumped up from behind the bench.*

This text suggests that the writer has not yet learnt how to construct a story in a way that fully makes sense to the reader. The narrative is incomplete; it is all 'beginning'; plot elements are not fully developed. As narrator, Sophie does not comment on the events but merely records them. Without any particular input from her teacher, or influence from literary models, Sophie draws on what she knows best – her personal experience of being part of a family and her memories of holidays – as her subject matter.

Writing in role

Later in the year, Sophie wrote some narratives which were prompted by studying literary texts in class. Two letters, written in role as characters from *The Midnight Fox* which Anne had read to her class in the Spring term, show how well Sophie can take on the style of a text that she has heard.

Sophie has taken the whole of the content of this letter from Betsy Byars' story, which was read aloud in the class. She heard the text read, but did not read it independently. Comparing the content of the letter with some passages from the book, we can see that Sophie must have listened intently, as she has recalled many small details. She uses these to give authenticity to the letter, demonstrating how far she has been able to enter the world of the story.

Sophie's letter

Dear Petie

How are you? I am really lonely and fed up Aunt Millie has been annoying because at supper time she forced me to eat a pimento cheese sandwich.

I didn't want to hurt her feelings so I hid some of them in my pocket so she thought I had eaten some of them.

The thing I could do with is one of your special scrumptious sandwiches.

My room is really creepy because there is a gun hanging on the wall and a stuffed squirrel and a small drawer full of bullets – very scary!

Also there is a large tree right outside the window and Aunt Millie doesn't trust me. She thinks I want to climb down it, well I know one thing for sure she will never catch me down that tree! I can't stand heights!

Could I ask you a favour please check on the eggs
Your best friend Tom
PS have you found a good place to hide the doll?

Extracts from The Midnight Fox

I sat there holding the crumpled sandwich in my hand.
It was pimento cheese..........her boys' favourites.........When I heard that, I had tried even harder to get one down but I just couldn't.

Finally I had managed to hide some food in my pocket so she would think I had eaten something.

Petie was a great eater and he got an idea for a new food invention. It was called the Petie Burkis Special........The only thing in all the world I could have eaten right then was a Petie Burkis Special.........

Just one glance at me and anyone would know that I had never shouldered the shotgun on the rack, that I had never stuffed the squirrel in the bookcase, ...

Auntie Millie was saying, "I...I know how boys love to climb out their windows late at night. Come here."
I went over and she pointed to the huge tree beside the window..........

Sophie has caught the tone of Betsy Byars' original really well. Of course she is writing here as an American boy and, writing as Tom, her tone is very different from her normal voice.

Following the writing of this first letter, Anne collected the letters in, put them in envelopes, and distributed them around the class. She felt that receiving a 'real' letter would help the children to reply convincingly in role. This was a very successful idea and most of the class responded enthusiastically. Sophie's second letter was therefore written in role as Petie writing back to Tom.

In the second letter, Sophie still draws on her knowledge of the content from the text, but this time she switches from a conventional style of letter writing and imitates the unconventional style of 'Petie's' letters. She includes funny headlines, such as had appeared in Petie's letters in the book ('Here's the story: BOY FALLS DOWN BANK WHILE GIRL ONLOOKERS CHEER') and a mock questionnaire, such as the boys send to each other ('1. If you found a whole box of candy bars, would you (a) sell them (b) eat them (c) try to find the owner'). This second letter is longer and livelier than the first one; responding to an actual letter seems to have helped Sophie to get into the swing of things and to write confidently in role.

In both letters Sophie has included descriptions of the events and details of the characters' situations. She has conveyed the relationship between the two male characters and caught the teasing tone in the 'in' jokes that they share. These letters show Sophie's ability to take on an author's style and tune, and reveal what close attention she has paid to detail in listening to the text. They also show how, by creating a real audience (with the children responding to each other's letters in role), Anne has enabled Sophie to find a stronger voice, one which reflects Betsy Byars' style but which is also a genuine communication in role.

Talking about texts

This kind of detailed writing would not have happened without the kind of discussion around texts that goes on in Sophie's classroom. To prepare the children for writing in role, her teacher encourages her class to reflect on what they have heard in the part of the story she has read to them.

In the following extract from a classroom observation of a literature session, Anne initiates a discussion about the character of Petie in *The Midnight Fox*. She encourages the children to recall details from the text, but first asks them to use their imagination to fill in the picture of the character's physical description, which Betsy Byars has not supplied:

Anne: What do you think Petie looks like?

Kady: Tall, with brown hair and blue eyes.

Anne: What would he wear?

Jamie: A t-shirt and a coat like people on the news.

Charlotte: Jeans and a polo shirt.

Natalie: I think he'd wear Adidas and Reebok.

Paula: Navy jeans and a checked shirt.

Anne: In my mind, he's got glasses. So you've got your picture in your mind, now what does Petie do?

Peter: Reporting.

Charles: He makes up news stories from titles.

Anne: Yes, when he cut up headlines like 'CITY BOY CHASED BY PIG'.

Jamie: I think he's a wild boy who runs about a lot - he's adventurous. He's close to the wildlife and he goes out a lot.

Sindri: Like Jamie, I think he likes nature because he's watching the birds.

Anne: But was Tom an outdoor person because he liked nature?

Christina: No, he liked making models.

Anne: What did they get up to ?

Charles: They hid the doll's head.

Anne: What else did they make up together?

Paul: A questionnaire.

Anne: What do they often talk about?

Charles: What's on TV adverts.

Anne: What kind of adverts?

Jamie: The room spray.

Sophie: Deodorant.

Anne: So they do seem to watch a lot of TV so they can't be that outdoors. Now what might you, Petie, tell your friend Tom?

Anastasia: The latest ads.

Christina: If anything new has happened, like one of their friends who broke a leg.

Matthew: He could tell Tom how the eggs are doing.

Christina: He might ask Tom some questions.

Sindri: You might say 'do you remember?'

What is it about this kind of discussion that has enabled Sophie and the other children in her class to write convincingly in role as the characters? It seems significant that, when Anne is asking the children to imagine, she allows them to do most of the talking. She wants them to have a clear idea of the characters, and suggests that they do that by imagining them physically. She listens to what they offer and accepts their ideas, always encouraging them to create their own pictures in their minds.

When she is asking for evidence from the text, however, Anne asks more searching questions, pushing the children to recall details. This combination of effective questioning and responsive listening by the teacher allows young writers like Sophie to explore a text and build up their knowledge of the characters' motives and intentions, so as to be able to become them in their imagination.

By responding to each other's letters, the children become both author and reader, and this makes more explicit to them the purposes of writing. In their historical analysis of the movements in reading and writing over the last thirty years, Nelson and Calfee (1998) emphasise that the main feature of a discourse community is the social construction of meaning as a group, with an emphasis on speaking and listening as the language modes which knit together the processes of reading and writing:

> This community conception has done much to unify reading, writing, and the oral uses of language.... A community is seen as constructing a body of knowledge as its members read one another's texts and build upon one another's work in producing one's own – thus blending the roles of author and audience.

Anne's class is such a community. She herself suggested that it was particularly important to work on providing an audience for children's writing, saying:

> 'Often children find audience difficult because the audience is often the teacher. They find it difficult to imagine that the audience could be anyone but you.'

Creating audiences is one of the ways that teachers can give children the feeling that their writing is really going somewhere and must communicate with a reader.

The tunes of stories

Another piece of writing which illustrates Sophie's ability to adopt the style of an author is 'The Day of the Turtle'. Anne had read them *The Wreck of the Zanzibar* by Michael Morpurgo, which is written the whole way through as a diary kept by the central character, Laura, now old, looking back at her life on the Scilly Isles. The first two paragraphs demonstrate how carefully Sophie has listened to the tune of Michael Morpurgo's text.

> I realized that he didn't have the strength to move. I knew I couldn't save the turtle on my own. I looked around and saw the Gulls had gone but I knew they would be back. I covered the turtle in seaweed and driftwood. I slowly walked away.
> This evening I walked down to Rushey bay, but this time Granny May secretly followed me. I sat down and heard Granny May's kind voice saying: Laura it's me Granny May what are you doing out here?"
> "Er just out watching the tide" I said.

Although they are not conventionally marked as such, these two paragraphs seem to represent two different entries in the diary. In the first, Sophie, as Laura, is describing how she had hidden the turtle earlier in the day, protecting it from enemies. In the second, she is recording what happened later on that day, in the evening, as she returned to the bay, followed by Grannie May. Sophie has captured the gentle rhythm of this story. Her management of the dialogue here is particularly accomplished. The timing is gentle and reflective, with the utterances of the characters overlapping in a very natural and convincing way.

One more story provides us with a further example of Sophie writing in a particular style, this time that of a traditional West Indian folk tale. Anne had read the class many of the *Cric Crac* stories by Grace Hallworth and asked the children to invent some of their own. Sophie chose to write a story which contains many echoes of traditional creation stories.

In this story Sophie confidently uses several literary devices. She opens in a direct and lively style, going straight to the point of the story in the opening sentence.

Cric Crac: The Greedy Elephant

One Morning Greedy was sitting with a large pot of honey sucking and slurping getting every sweet juicy drop of the golden honey "mmmm" exclaimed the Greedy elephant as he digged down further to get more of his delicious honey. Suddenly the Greedy elephant started to pull his trunk out when he realized it was stuck!

His friends the snake and Crocodile asked to see if he wanted to play football in the field but "oh dear Greedy, it looks like you're stuck" hissed the snake.

"Well as a matter of fact I am, so would you mind helping me" said Greedy quickly.

"Well if I wrap myself around the pot and you pull Croc. I'm sure it will come off!" So the long snake wrapped himself around the large jar of honey and the Crocodile put the snakes, thick, scaly tail into her mouth and pulled and pulled and nearly bit the Snake's tail off. She tugged the scaly skin and hugged a bit more until her teeth nearly came out!.

She gave it one last pull and suddenly "Bang" the honey jar fell onto the floor and rolled down the ground. "Splash" it fell into the river, the snake and Crocodile turned around in laughter. "What is it" said Elephant.

"It's your trunk" said Crocodile "Its been stretched by the pot of honey" she said giggling. "Oh if only I weren't so greedy" said Elephant so from that day Elephants have long trunks and don't eat honey!

Sophie underlines the greedy elephant's enjoyment of the honey with an alliterative phrase. She seems to be trying to convey the tune of this traditional tale to the reader; it appears that she really cares how the story sounds.

When Sophie was interviewed about this story and the vocabulary she had used she said:

I just made it up, cos', like you have to think of words that will go with the story.....make it, like, cos'....interesting and exciting and add things.

She continued:

I just - you just have to think to make it how you could make it exciting and interesting, cos' you write it first into a draft sort of, and then you have to change it to make it exciting, so it's nicer to listen to.

This last comment is significant; it shows that Sophie is expecting the audience for her writing not to read it but to 'listen to' it.

Sophie manages the traditional story form well; her retelling is economical and there are no wasted words. She has appreciated that this kind of story is about plot – characters are not developed, every action must contribute to the denouement. Sophie integrates dialogue within the narrative skilfully:

His friends the snake and crocodile asked to see if he wanted to play football in the field but "Oh dear Greedy, it looks like you're stuck" hissed the snake.

The only part of the narrative that Sophie dwells on is the part where the elephant's trunk gets stretched. Sophie builds up the tension here through repetition, really trying to engage the listener/reader in the detail of the situation at this crucial part of the story:

So the long snake wrapped himself around the large jar of honey and the Crocodile put the snake's thick scaly tail into her mouth and pulled and pulled and nearly bit the snake's tail off. She tugged the scaly skin and tugged a bit more until her teeth nearly came out!

Sophie shows that she does really know now how to write a short story of this kind; the ending (a feature of story that was weaker in her earlier writing) is traditional and links perfectly with the beginning. Her paragraphing is careful, and she experiments with more complex sentence structures as she weaves dialogue into narrative.

Sophie has developed a real awareness of one of the most important elements in redrafting a text: making it 'nicer to listen to'. But how does she know whether her writing sounds better or not? It must be by reading it back to herself, and listening to it. This is an important discovery for a child to make, and one that can be greatly facilitated by being in a classroom where children are encouraged to read their own work aloud. Learning to listen to a text, which we know from her work on *The Midnight Fox* is something that Sophie takes to readily, further strengthens the relationship between being a reader and being a writer.

In his discussion of how to compose texts with the reader in mind, Donald Rubin (1998) highlights the importance of teaching his students to write whilst at the same time consciously reading their own texts, 'revisioning even their emerging meaning through the eyes of their audience.' Some more experienced young writers do this automatically as they rework their texts. But it is also something which can be explicitly taught, especially when children work with response partners. In this situation, the writer can become a reader, testing out their writing on an audience of one. Rubin suggests that:

> *Developing skill at reading one's own text should be as important to writing instruction as is skill in generating text.*

The Green Children: picking up a tune

Sophie took part in the drama work that her class did around *The Green Children,* and subsequently wrote a piece in role as the green boy. Once again in this short piece one can see how good Sophie is at picking up the detail of a story that she has listened to, and how readily she takes on the tune of an author's prose. But Sophie does add detail to her retelling, too; her first line, which is a striking one, is entirely her own contribution:

> ### *Writing in role as the Green boy*
> *As soon as I opened my eyes colours dazzled. I could not open my eyes properly.*
> *The colours started to fade. I could see strange creatures staring down at us. I dug my nails into my sister. "What are they" I asked. She told me she thought they were children. The oldest child sang us some soft words. I could see some berries in a leaf nest. Well I thought they were berries but they were not green. There were birds hanging. They had lost their song. They were not green. One of the creatures fell over a tree root. I looked harder, I realized that we must be lost. I started to cry. I could feel little bits of air wave over my face. It felt strange.*
> *My sister sat up. "Who are you? Why aren't you green? Where is this place?" she said. She looked scared. Little bit of water began to trickle down my nose. My sister told me to follow the creatures I didn't want to, all I wanted was to go home.*

Sophie's sentences, like Crossley-Holland's in this story, are brief and striking. *There were birds hanging. They had lost their song. They were not green.*

Her account of what the children first notice about the new world they have come to carries strong echoes of the Kevin Crossley-Holland story.

In this piece, Sophie has had to imagine herself into the role of the green boy, who is smaller and more fearful than his older sister. Her account is therefore very much seen from his point of view; Sophie's sense of significant detail here is acute and the green boy's story is written from fully inside the fictional world:

> *I looked harder. I realised that we must be lost. I started to cry. I could feel little bits of air wave crawl over my face. It felt strange.*

This is very well imagined; Sophie's writing is economical but fully conveys the sense of disorientation and loneliness that the green children feel in this unfamiliar world. In general, Sophie's writing in role here shows that she is aware of how writing sounds, and is quick to pick up on the characteristic tune of a particular text. This impression was later confirmed when we came to do a more detailed analysis of specific features of her writing.

Gaining maturity: writing from different viewpoints

Anne's reading aloud and the class discussion of literary texts enabled Sophie to try out a variety of styles and genres in the course of the year. Opportunities for writing in role, particularly, enabled her to find a stronger voice.

Early in the summer term, Anne read the class the story of Daedalus and Icarus as part of their study of myths and legends. After the reading she asked them to work in groups, exploring the relationship between Daedalus and his son. She invited them to picture in their mind the scene as father and son talked about their captivity in the labyrinth of King Minos, and what had led up to it. The children improvised a scene between Daedalus and Icarus in which they confronted their situation.

After the role play the class were asked to write as Icarus, telling the story from his point of view. Some children simply retold the story but Sophie's version was a more complex piece of writing. To begin with, she chose to update the story, setting it in a modern world of police cars and city streets. Secondly, she told the story in a sophisticated way, going into some of it in detail but simply alluding to other parts. The sequence of the narrative is not straightforward and right at the beginning Sophie looks forward to the tragedy of the ending:

> *While I was living with my father I'd never have thought that at one point of my life I'd be living with royalty and the next in a monsters cave, but you never know your future.*

Writing as Icarus

When I was living with my father I'd never have thought that at one point of my life I'd be living with royalty and the next in a monsters cave, but you never know your future.

It all started one late night my cousin was being invited for dinner, the strange thing was he wasn't very friendly with my cousin Talos and he'd already eaten with me.

Talos came not soon after I'd gone, my dad had raised his voice several times before they came upstairs they passed my room, I was still worried when I fell asleep but soon I'd forgotten Talos was even here. Suddenly my fathers shouting woke me with fright, I heard screaming, my fathers voice got louder a sudden scream then silence, pain, silence. I was too scared and too tired to think any more of it that night.

Early that morning dad had decided to take me out of school, but I didn't want to, so then we decided he'd drop me at school early and go out for a walk. We turned a corner you could see the school, my dad's eyes filled with water, his hand got tighter around my wrists, he started to say things. I couldn't quite hear them the wind blew in my ears making them go red like my face. Suddenly sirens took charge of all the noise around me. My dad ran, I ran, the police got faster. Suddenly they stopped, a big policeman jumped out and grabbed my father and then another one jumped out and took hold of me. We were pulled into separate cars I didn't struggle scream or shout. I just cried and sat with shame and disappointment whirling through my head my father had been exiled.

We were sent to Crete, my father was given a job from king Minos if he completed it me and him could stay in his palace. My father did as he was told. We were living in the palace. Until someone had broken their deal, and I ended up here, cold on the labyrinth floor. I'm scared and have sort of forgiven my father.

Sophie manages viewpoint very well in this piece of writing. The scene where her father and her cousin quarrel is done entirely from the viewpoint of the sleepy boy Icarus, with the quarrel half heard and half obscured by sleep. But it is the next episode which is particularly striking. This is the climax of this part of the story, the turning-point in their fortunes, where Daedalus and his son are snatched by police on their way to take Icarus to school. The whole account here is strongly imagined; everything happens at once and physical sensations, noises and visual impressions are all mixed up:

> …my dad's eyes filled with water, his hand got tighter around my wrists, he started to say things. I couldn't quite hear them, the wind blew in my ears making them go red like my face. Suddenly sirens took charge of all the noise around me. My dad ran, I ran, the police got faster. Suddenly they stopped, a big policeman jumped out and grabbed my father and then another one jumped out and got hold of me. We were pulled into separate cars…

It is a highly cinematic episode; there are strong similarities to the style of visual storytelling of dramas like *The Bill*. The speed and noise of the violent disruption are powerfully done. Sophie's teacher noticed that in her version she picked up on the extreme emotions in this situation more than other pupils did. She was also the only pupil to update the Daedalus myth and to tell the story in such a modern and visual way.

Three further pieces of narrative demonstrate Sophie's skill in writing from another viewpoint but more importantly show how she continues to develop her ability to write from *inside* the character, conveying emotions and responses to events.

These three pieces are all responses to the study of the same text – *Fire, Bed and Bone* by Henrietta Branford. This was one of the 'standard' texts chosen for the project teachers to introduce to their classes during the Summer term. These samples illustrate how Sophie is able to find three different voices within the same story, although the author only uses one, that of the female hunting dog through whose eyes the whole of the book is told.

After reading the powerful first chapter of the book and identifying the narrator of the story, Anne invited her class to vary the viewpoint of the narration and to write in role from the perspective of Humble the cat. Sophie begins her piece with a striking description, which echoes Branford's opening, but makes much more of the sound of the wolves:

> *I heard the wolves again last night, howling at the tops of their voices, long and loud, big and bold.*
> *I lay with shivers all over my body.*

'Long and loud, big and bold' is part of Sophie's addition, and is a striking demonstration of her confidence with this kind of literary patterning.

In this first chapter of *Fire, Bed and Bone*, the author gives just three pieces of information about Humble:

> '*Humble creeps in through the open window and curls beside me, soft as smoke.*
> *I can smell mouse on her. She has eaten, and come in to the fire for the warmth....*
> *Only she (Alice) hears, with me and Humble, the wild song of the wolves.*'

Sophie uses all of this material from the text:

> '*I heard the wolves again last night, howling at the tops of their voices....*
> *I went to my secret hunting field just now, I stayed out there for ages. I came in through the window....*
> *I've come in for warmth and comfort by the fire and up against the dog.*'

But she adds to it, describing her entrance through the window, for instance, like this:

> '*I came in through the window like the ghost of the cat next door, whose life was meant to end.*'

This mysterious line adds to the sense of foreboding begun by the description of the wolves, and emphasises the silence of the cat's movements.

Sophie skilfully retells the chapter through the cat's eyes, lifting some of the language directly from the text but also choosing her own. She sustains the viewpoint of Humble the cat throughout, again using material from the book but changing it, for example:

'I lie watching Alice lift her small red fist up to stroke the dog's soft furry ear.'

Branford, narrating as the dog had written:

'Alice reaches her small, red fist towards my ear and smiles.' (p.8)

Here we can see how Sophie has directly lifted language from the text, but elaborated the description.

Throughout this retelling of the chapter Sophie captures the same mood of quietness and stillness in the family home as in the original text. She manages to capture the author's tune, not only in her narrative style and use of language but also in the way in which the forthcoming birth of the dog's pups is hinted at:

'It shan't be long for the dog she can hardly move with her belly stopping her.'

Sophie has learnt this skill directly from the author, listening carefully to the way it is done. Her teacher, Anne, has helped her to learn from the author in this way by reading the text aloud and exploring its meanings through discussion. The force and emotion of this novel has moved Sophie and enabled her to rework its powerful material for her own readers. As Margaret Meek (1988) said of 'texts that teach':

If we want to see what lessons have been learned from the texts children read,
we have to look for them in what they write.

The second piece of writing which illustrates some of the lessons that Sophie has learned from the study of this text is written in role as the dog's puppy, Fleabane. In the story, Fleabane, now a fully grown dog, is separated from his mother, having been captured by the miller's son Lupus. His mother finds him roped up in a barrel with no straw for his bedding, ill-treated, beaten and fearful. Anne read her class this chapter and invited them to describe their experiences in captivity as Fleabane.

Sophie opens her story with a strong and moving image of the suffering Fleabane has endured, lifting the content from the original text:

'The hole at the top of the barrel lets in a howling draught, a draught that
sends frightening shivers down my back. Blood dribbles down the side of my
face....'

Branford's text refers to the pup's shivering in the barrel, and to the fact that the pup's ear is caked with blood. Sophie has remembered these details of the story to use in her own writing. But she gets right inside Fleabane's situation, contrasting the pain of his captivity with his thoughts of freedom:

'I don't want to move I only want to dream, dream of far, far away...'

In the second two paragraphs Sophie maintains this sense of a contrast between Fleabane's present life and his memories of his old life with his mother:

> 'My only happy times were with my mother, when we were out, anything could happen. Those enjoyable feelings of snuggling up against my mother and lying on the dirty but dry bed of straw. Then I found myself being dragged off to a new master...'

In the last paragraph, Sophie again recalls a specific detail and elaborates on it:

> 'I limp painfully to the other side of the barrel hardly moving with the large thorn, sticking and sharply stinging my left paw, it feels as if my body's being ripped apart by sticks....'

Branford's text reads:

> 'Something sharp was bedded under the skin of his pad – a thorn. I drew it with my teeth. His neck was chafed and there were the marks of a stick on his back.'

In this piece of writing, Sophie is able to write from *inside* the character, using her knowledge of the text to recreate the events from a different viewpoint.

Writing as Fleabane

The hole at the top of the barrel lets in a howling draught, a draught that sends frightening shivers down my back. Blood dribbles down the side of my face, I know I shouldn't try to escape, its just so tempting. I don't want to move I only want to dream, dream of far, far away where I could forget my terrible memories of being beaten with the metal whips leaving cuts long and large, sharp and sore.

The moment I found straw I was dragged, beaten, shouted at and thrown into a barrel, I'm surprised I've survived any of this world. My only happy times were with my mother, when we were out, anything could happen. Those enjoyable feelings of snuggling up against my mother and lying on the dirty, but dry bed of straw. Then I found myself being dragged off to a new master, a new life and a completely different style of living.

I am always being beaten, sometimes even when I catch the largest of animals, my mother was always pleased when she saw me hunting, and eating properly, but life has changed since then.

I limp painfully to the other side of the barrel hardly moving with the large thorn, sticking and sharply stinging my left paw. It feels as if my body's being ripped apart by sticks and long metal whips, my neck is held tightly by the rope making it hard to sleep, I don't know whether to carry on hoping or to just let the world overtake my life.

Sophie's third piece of writing drawn from *Fire, Bed and Bone* was written from the same point of view as Branford's own, as the hunting dog who narrates the whole story of the novel. Anne prepared for this writing by reading almost to the end of the book and then inviting her class to finish the story in their own way. She stopped at the point where the dog is out with her mate Serlo and their new offspring, Blackthorn, living wild in the woods.

Branford writes:

> *'I was the first to wake. I felt the weight of Serlo's great head resting on my flank. Curled at my back, Blackthorn snuffled. Something was coming through the wood. Something heavy, with four feet. The wind swung round a little, and a rich pig smell streamed down to my nose.'*

Right from the beginning of her piece Sophie captures the dramatic tension of this moment of a sleeping animal aroused by the scent of its prey. Her choice and variety of verbs signal sudden movement and the strength of animal instinct:

> *'...the lids of both eyes* shot *up, my hind legs* jumped *up...Serlo's head* hit *the ground with a thud, my long boney tail* swooped *right over Blackthorn's sleeping body, both dogs* jumped *up Serlo* growled *I* barked...'*

In this opening paragraph one can see how Sophie has used the detail in the novel as a starting point for her own writing. For example Sophie writes that 'Serlo's head hit the ground' because Branford had told her readers that his 'great head was resting on my flank'. Sophie also writes that the hunting dog's tail 'swooped right over Blackthorn's sleeping body' because Branford had described Blackthorn as being 'curled at my back.' It is clear that Sophie has a powerful physical sense of how the dogs are lying in this scene; she has literally been able put herself in their place.

In the second paragraph, Sophie imagines the return of the family, creating a mood of optimism and happiness as the dog is reunited with her mistress:

> *'...there was Comfort with a small ginger head popping up from behind her bony shoulder,...It really was one great day....I ran up to Comfort, I put my soft wet nose into Comfort's icy cold hand...'*

Remarkably, Sophie has worked into her version of the ending some details recalled from two chapters earlier in the book about Comfort's new baby and Comfort's own condition. In Chapter nineteen Branford had told her readers:

> *'There was a new red-haired, smudge-faced baby tied to her back....*
> *Comfort too had changed. She was thin, painfully thin....'*(p.112)

Sophie continues to draw on the details of this and previous chapters in her acknowledgement of the family's pain and suffering:

'I gave the children a warm friendly lick but I knew that inside all of them had been hurt in some particular way.'

In this sentence the word 'inside' is striking; Sophie is aware of the internal damage that has been done to the family, as well as of their physical deprivations.

In the last paragraph Sophie creates an atmosphere of nostalgia which echoes the mood of the end of the novel, as she recalls her master and their special relationship:

'I keep seeing things like Rufus and I and now I keep getting a special feeling Rufus is watching me and is proud of me for looking after his poor family.'

Recalling an earlier passage from the Branford text, she dwells on this remembered relationship between dog and master. She writes:

'Rufus must have been right I really am one brave Bitch.'

This final piece of writing clearly illustrates Sophie's growth and development as a writer and the confidence she has acquired in taking risks with the structure and composition of the narrative. The three pieces together, based on the study of one text, demonstrate Sophie's ability to enter worlds other than her own and write from a position of knowledge and empathy with characters and their situations.

Sophie began the year writing confidently in person as herself, but her writing showed significant advances when she began to write in role, in response to some of the texts studied in the class. She is a good listener and the reading aloud which was such a feature of this classroom helped her to experience the voices and styles of several different authors. From quite early on she showed a real ear for the characteristic tunes of a particular text, and a chameleon-like ability to imitate a style. For instance, she responded dramatically to the style of *The Green Children*, mirroring the length of Kevin Crossley-Holland's T-units exactly, as we found during the data analysis described in Chapter 7.

But her writing also shows a growth in feeling. There is a real inwardness in her exploration of fictional situations when she writes in role, as when she writes as Fleabane, the young dog in *Fire, Bed and Bone*. It is the emotional force of literary texts like *Fire, Bed and Bone*, and the opportunity to study and reflect on them in depth, which seems to have enabled Sophie to develop this affective strength in her writing.

Sophie did not seem to have reflected on herself as a writer much before this year but now sees herself as an author and has a real sense of control over her writing. Her good ear enables her to listen to her own texts, as well as those of others, and she consciously draws on this sense of the sound of a text in improving her writing.

Harry

Harry lives with his mother and his younger brother in Rotherhithe. He is a year 5 pupil in a mixed class of Years 5 and 6 at School E. His teacher, Justine, is also the school's IT Coordinator. Harry feels that his handwriting lets him down and so his teacher gives him the opportunity to use a word processor as much as possible; he is also able to take a pocketbook computer home to use for homework.

Harry is articulate and confident, with a clear idea of his strengths and weaknesses as a writer. In interview he said that he felt that he was good at creating unusual worlds and good at beginnings, but didn't always know at the beginning where his stories would go. They could, he said, 'just branch out anywhere'. He expressed a strong preference for reading action and plot-oriented books at home; this kind of text was in contrast to the literary texts he was studying in class.

Creating worlds

In the Autumn term, Harry wrote no stories, although he did write poems and dialogues. At the beginning of January, however, Harry wrote three stories in quick succession. In this picture of Harry's writing we begin with an analysis of his fictional writing from the Spring term, before going back to look at the poems that he wrote during the Autumn term.

In all of Harry's stories written in January, the influences of media texts, especially computer games and TV cartoons, are apparent. Two of these stories are 'rescue' stories, with the hero battling against multiple evils in order to save the day. They are also stories which demonstrate Harry's extraordinary ability to create virtual worlds, where almost anything can happen.

In the first story 'Rescue Long Face', Harry narrates the events as 'Abe, a spirit'. He had not written a story in role before this, but had decided that he wanted to be *in* this story (taking part in a story is, of course, a feature of computer games). As narrator, his tone is laid back, even laconic. He appears to be unfazed by the extraordinary chain of events that befall the central characters, of whom he is one.

Rescue Longface

Scarb lived in a place unknown to humans
called Oddworld, but anyway Scarb is a shy,
energetic inhabitant so you can imagine how
he felt when me, Abe, an ex-employee of the meat factory paid him a visit
asking him if he would go on a mission to see the spirit leader big Long face
and a mudkin and he would be turned into a god in return.

I could tell he didn't want to go but cautiously he
backed into the meat factory to start, so with me behind
he set off for the journey of a life time.

I knew Scarb was worried but he tried which shows how brave he was.
We both knew Paramite wasn't going to let him do it as we found out.

Scarb being the clumsy oaf he is tripped and fell but
luckily for him I caught him before he went head first
into a mine after he jumped over to safety.

We both knew that wasn't Paramite's last attack we found this
out when Scarb tripped a wire and released a bucket of acid that
just missed him and made a hole in the floor then Scarb's foot was
untangled and he fell in head first.

As I got down I noticed he had found the mudkin and released it from
Paramite's power. I was as good as my word and gave him half power.

His energy and power would come in handy now
because Paramite stormed in and it seems Scarb
had been playing with his power because Paramite
was getting smaller, (even I didn't know he could do
that) and he kept going until Paramite was the size
of a pencil then kicked him to god knows where.

At last Long face was out of Paramite's power
but what none of us knew Scarb was in, Paramite
returned and was about to turn Scarb into lunch
when Boom! Long face had blown Paramite sky
high and Scarb had full power.

But we all know evil geniuses
are harder to squash than cockroaches.

THE END...................?

In a strong opening paragraph, Harry introduces us to a completely unfamiliar world and immediately we know that we are in the genre of science fiction. This is a virtual world where things can happen without human consequences or emotions. From this point on we are in the writer's hands, we have to work hard to try to imagine what is going on and cannot use previous experience of more conventional fictions to establish the world of the story. The names of the characters 'Scarb', 'Long Face', 'Paramite' are strange – they are all aliens and all male and we are introduced to them all at once. In interview, Harry said that these names were influenced by names from computer games; he had strong visual images of what these characters looked like. He said he had taken most of the ideas for this story from a friend's computer game, and imagined the setting as being a spirit world, a place rather like heaven, except that it was inhabited by aliens.

Harry seems to be telling the story orally as he addresses the reader directly:
> ....but anyway Scarb is a shy, energetic inhabitant so you can imagine how he felt when me, Abe, an ex-employee of the meat factory paid him a visit....

As the reader we *do* have to imagine this as we are not told a great deal, either by the characters themselves or by the narrator. This kind of direct communication with the reader recurs in the penultimate paragraph:
> ....it seemed Scarb had been playing with his power because Paramite was getting smaller, (even I didn't know he could do that)....

Harry is writing in role, but he is a detached narrator. He sustains his stance very well; his tone is easy and nonchalant, despite the many crises encountered in the story. Harry structures the narrative clearly in paragraphs, marking transitions yet maintaining control as the omniscient narrator, for example:
> *I could tell he didn't want to go....* (par.2)
> *I knew Scarb was worried....*(par.3)
> *We both knew that wasn't Paramite's last attack....*(par.4)
> *As I got down I noticed he had found the mudkin....*(par.5)

It is this confident tone which drives the narrative.

An interesting feature of this story, and of others by Harry, is that there is no dialogue between the characters. Nor is there any evidence of an affective stance – no indication of how the narrator feels about either the events in the story or what happens to the characters. Although one of the main characters, Scarb, trips twice, the first time nearly landing 'headfirst into a mine' and the second time in a 'bucket of acid', and although Paramite, the enemy, is blown 'sky high', we are given no indication of how characters respond to these mishaps. This is the virtual world of the computer game where characters can be destroyed and very easily re-form – Harry deliberately leaves the ending open for a sequel:

> *But we all know that evil geniuses are harder to squash than cockroaches.*

Harry said that he had seen this kind of ending in books before and had thought that he could write another story: 'Paramite Returns'.

Futuristic fantasy

The second story written in January was called 'Farewell'. It is another example of Harry's ability to set a story in a futuristic world. This time the characters are human but, again, horrific things befall these strange invented beings, with no comment from Harry, the detached narrator.

THE FAREWELL

In the year 4816 a nuclear war broke out between U.S.A. and Russia.
Then in the year 4817 two twins the age of 8 won a holiday to U.S.A. not knowing what the consequences would be.

At the airport Stanley met a girl of the same age and introduced her to Kenny and immediately fell in love with her and she fell in love with him.

When they arrived in America they was shocked to find absolutely no sign of life and only one building was left standing but still bombs were dropping and they had to run like hell into a nuclear shelter but it was as cramped as a Sunday shopping bag.

In the end Kenny ran out into the building and it was their hotel but it was dirty and only had 2 rooms the kitchen and the bedroom They had a sleepless night and Kenny decided to go for a walk but god hated him and made a bomb drop bang on his head.

The next morning bits of Kenny were scattered all over America, by the time Stanley found Kenny's bits the bits were starting to rot so Stanley had to sew Kenny together then bury him but his spirit lived on for 2 years until an airplane crashed on top of him.

In the opening paragraph Harry sets the scene briefly and introduces the characters in a similarly terse style. We are told virtually nothing about them except their ages and that they are twins. The narration is bold and Harry sets up the possibility of horror in the second paragraph, when the twins are said to be going on holiday to America 'not knowing what the consequences would be.'

Although the story is set in the future, where fantastical things can happen, Harry injects a more familiar element into the story in the second paragraph. Uncharacteristically, he brings on a female character as love interest for one of the twins, although the reader is not entirely clear as to which one:

At the airport Stanley met a girl of the same age and introduced her to Kenny and immediately fell in love with her and she fell in love with him.

When Harry was asked about this female without a name, who neither says nor does anything, he explained that the only reason he had introduced her into the story was as a 'catalyst' (his own word) to propel Kenny into going for a walk. At the end of the story, she is not mentioned again, and the reader is left wondering whether she survives the ghastly fate which befalls Kenny.

The horror in this story is nuclear war. One of the twins, Kenny, meets with a ghastly death:

....Kenny decided to go for a walk but god hated him and made a bomb drop bang on his head.
The next morning bits of Kenny were scattered all over America, by the time Stanley found Kenny's bits, the bits were starting to rot ....

These events are horrific and the landscape is bleak but the cartoon treatment overlays the appalling events with a kind of sick humour. God is as capricious and unpredictable as any of the other characters, and more destructive. Harry takes no affective stance towards any of this. As narrator he uses language boldly as if translating the action from a screen onto paper, creating a virtual world where there is no respite in the violence.

In the last paragraph Harry moves seamlessly away from the plausible to the utterly implausible. In this fantasy or futuristic world, characters who have been destroyed can simply be reconstituted:

....so Stanley had to sew Kenny together then bury him....

But only a little later, we learn that there is no mercy at all in this world, as Harry writes Kenny out of the story once and for all:

...but his spirit lived on for 2 years until an aeroplane crashed on top of him.

The story ends as boldly as it began. Harry, as narrator, drives the narrative forward in an economical, concrete style, using language alone to create a world which again derives from media fictions. The reader inexperienced in these kinds of fictions has to work quite hard to follow this story and to understand the world that Harry has created.

Harry said that he was influenced in his ideas for this story by the TV programme *South Park,* a cartoon renowned for its bad taste and aimed at adult audiences. But the other source he cited were the stories in *Ali Baba and the Forty Thieves,* which he had recently seen in a theatre production with his class. It is easy to see both of these influences at work, and fascinating to realise that there are similarities between such different brands of fantastic narrative, which can blend together in Harry's story.

This story and 'Rescue Long Face' illustrate that, without any direct model offered for story writing from the literature being studied in class, Harry draws mostly on the world of media texts, both from the computer and the television screen. He is able to invent a style for himself, choosing fast-moving, sophisticated and casually violent narratives, where characters can be destroyed by others without any moral judgement being expressed. In this virtual world of death and destruction, characters do not feel, they only act.

In the same way that Harry plays with computer games, he now plays with language, creating fantastic situations through language alone. He is aware that words have the power to make worlds and that in these created worlds, as on the screen, absolutely anything can happen. Language here is, in Bruner's words 'constitutive of reality' (Bruner 1986). Harry has taught himself to translate the kinds of narratives that he enjoys into words, and in the process leaves out a good deal of what we have traditionally come to expect from written stories: description, a sense of the characters' motivations, any kind of inner life, any kind of evaluation of the action, plots which develop in comprehensible ways, any kind of explanation of why events happen.

A small-scale world

A third story, 'Down the Drain', was also written in January; this story was inspired by the story *Ruby* that his teacher, Justine was reading to the class. The class were studying a topic on the local environment and Justine had asked the children to write a story connected to that theme. She wanted them to write the story in forty-five minutes as a practice for the Year 5 SATs, and so provided little input. Here is Harry's story:

Down the drain

get me out --------------------------------HELP!

In an abandoned boat behind a house lived a family of small people, Kenny and Kevin are twin brothers and their mum and dad are called Louis and Rose.

One day Kenny and Kevin got bored and decided to go and explore the house, little did they know luck was not on their side. Kenny was daring and thought he would run around the fish tank but he slipped and sank.

Kevin saw everything and ran as fast as he could (which is not very fast because of the size of his legs) back to his mum and dad, told them every thing and darted back to the house.

By the time the news sunk in Kevin was already on the side of the tank, trying to calm down his brother.

When his mum and dad arrived the fish tank had been emptied and Kenny had gone down the drain, Kevin was about to jump down after him when Rose called him and told him not to be so stupid but nothing could stop this kid, his brother had gone down and he was going too.

Louis and Rose watched in disbelief but they decided they had to go down too. When they got to the bottom Kenny and Kevin had already made friends with a rat called Chip.

After a lot of discussion Chip agreed to give them a ride, but after a couple of hours Chip was too busy showing them every thing he didn't see the pipe and BANG! Chip was out cold.

Kevin noticed a pipe they could push Chip up and maybe even escape, after ages of pushing they came out of a shower and landed in a bath.

Almost straight away they were on the window sill and jumping out with Chip, they ran across a massive garden and they found an oak tree, which they all decided, would be a good place to rest and to see to Chip's injuries, and they have lived there ever since.

As narrator, Harry establishes the story world right from the beginning in his familiar economic style:

> In an abandoned boat behind a house lived a family of small people, Kenny and Kevin were twin brothers and their mum and dad are called Louis and Rose.

There is a marked contrast between the scale of *this* world and that of the two previous stories. Whereas in 'Rescue Long Face' and 'The Farewell' Harry demonstrated his skill in creating immense landscapes in which to set his stories, in this one he shows that he is also able to create a very small-scale world for these 'small people'.

The reader can more easily identify this kind of world; one obvious influence on the writing might be *The Borrowers*. However, Harry had never read this book, although he had seen clips from the film. He thought that most of his ideas came from the story Justine was reading to the class, *Ruby*, where the story is set in a tree.

In this story Harry uses twin brothers as the main characters again. Altogether there are five characters in this story, and Harry manages this cast skilfully. It is the male characters who have all the fun; the one female character, the mother, remains generally passive.

Harry once more demonstrates that he is able to write a strong flowing narrative and manipulate the characters to move the plot along. He does not tell us how characters are feeling, nor does he write dialogue. He manages to avoid dialogue throughout the story – for example in the fifth paragraph, when Kevin wants to follow his twin brother down the drain and his mother intervenes, Harry uses indirect speech:

> *Kevin was about to jump down after him when Rose called him and told him not to be so stupid…*

Harry confessed that he found it difficult to integrate dialogue with his narration. He said:

> *Not many people speak in my stories because when you go into speech it's hard to get out of.*

This shows that he was making a conscious choice in avoiding dialogue. It is a decision made for reasons of craft: Harry is not yet sure of his skill in managing dialogue. The movement between narration and dialogue does seem to be a problem for some young writers. We sometimes see stories written by children which are almost all dialogue, with little or no narration. Harry's stories were the opposite, showing his ability to develop a situation through action and demonstrating his considerable skill in managing narrative structure, controlling plot events and maintaining consistency of style. His stories had a real onward momentum and drive and this was reflected in the fact his T-units (see chapter 7) were exceptionally long – Harry was able to remain in syntactic control in narrating long chains of events.

Managing dialogue

But Harry *was* able to write dialogue, although in a different genre. One of the writing tasks that Justine set for the children following a reading of *The Wind in the Willows* was to write a playscript. The first scene of this was to be a monologue spoken by Mole, followed by a further two scenes where other characters could be invented. The dialogue between them would be written as a playscript.

In the following extract from this script we see that Harry *can* write speech; in fact he can write it extremely well, adopting the same style and humorous tone as Kenneth Grahame.

> *Ratty: Would you like to come over*
> *Mole: How am I going to get over there*
> *RATTY POINTS OUT A BOAT*
> *Ratty: I will swim over then take you over in the boat*
> *Mole: You mean I, I….can go in that*
> *RATTY SWIMS OVER, STEPS INTO THE BOAT*
> *Ratty: Step lively, haven't got all day*
> *MOLE JUMPS INTO THE BOAT*
> *RATTY STARTS ROWING*
> *Mole: Can I row?*
> *Ratty: No it's too hard*
> *Mole: Please*
> *Ratty: For the last time, no*
> *MOLE PUSHES RATTY OVER AND TAKES THE OAR,*
> *STARTS ROWING*
> *RATTY: No stop you're going to tip the boat you silly ass*
> *THE BOAT FALLS*
> *MOLE LOSES CONSCIOUSNESS*
> *Ratty: Mole where are you, where are you mole oh there you are.*
> *RATTY PULLS MOLE TO LAND THEN SHAKES HIM*
> *MOLE WAKES UP*
> *Mole: Ahhh I'm on firm ground again, sorry*

The combination of a good literary text and a quality reading of it by the teacher has enabled Harry to parody the author's style but, more importantly, it has given him the confidence to experiment in writing dialogue. In this piece he draws characters completely through their speech, without having to worry about integrating dialogue with narration. He does, however, include helpful stage directions. It is apparent that he has thoroughly understood how to set out a playscript.

Harry had tried to read *The Wind in the Willows* a couple of years before but said that he had found the language too difficult. He was now reading it by himself, as well as listening to Justine read it aloud in assembly. Hearing texts read aloud is not only an important part of children's development as readers, but also their development as writers. Having listened to the tune and the rhythm of the text, young writers like Harry are able to have a go at retelling, reworking, and even parodying an original. The text acts as a kind of scaffold around which the apprentice writer can work, exploring the genre and taking on the style.

For example, Harry has really picked up the upper-class tones of Ratty and Mole in creating his playscript. In freeing himself from the role of narrator and becoming a script writer, he is actually revealed to be a very accomplished writer of dialogue. It may have been this experience of managing dialogue in playscript form which gave Harry the confidence to use direct speech in a story, 'No Time to Lose', which he wrote at the very beginning of the Summer term.

> **No time to lose.**
>
> *"Its mine" "No its mine" Phil and Lil were off on another argument about one of their toys but this time it was serious they didn't know that in a couple of seconds their life would change forever.*
>
> *"Uh oh"! the Reptar doll flew across the air and smashed against the wall with the head rolling along the floor.*
>
> *They were just about to argue about whose fault it was but thank god for us evil Reptar was released with Reptar the Great not far behind. Immediately Phil, Lil and Reptar the Great knew there was big trouble, "I will destroy all" roared evil Reptar but Reptar the Great knew that if they could find the idol of Reptars all would be saved.*
>
> *As quick as anything they were somehow transported to the Temples of Doom in Zorgan.*
>
> *"We must find the idol" said Reptar " but beware we will face many dangers". They found this out almost straight away because only ten paces in was a raging fire pit, "We have no choice but to jump" said Phil but quickly adding "do we?"*
>
> *But Reptar and Lil were already over and with no hesitation Phil joined them.*
>
> *Later they faced many more dangers including spike pits, raging volcanoes, falling rocks and maybe one of the most savage, deadly, torturous things you could imagine tickle boxes after many more treacherous, annihilating dangers like these they found the wondrous, amazing, sparkling, golden, marvellous, magnificent idol of Reptars, but celebration was cut short as soon as they removed the idol. "Guys" shouted Phil "there's a bloody boulder that looks like it could squash us any second, RUN"!*
>
> *So they ran like maniacs back to the teleporter where they were taken back to the house and placed the idol back in the toy box where the two Reptars were kept forever.*

Such is Harry's confidence that he now actually opens the story with dialogue:

'It's mine'
'No it's mine.'
Phil and Lil were off on another argument about one of their toys but this time it was serious.

As the story about these terrible siblings progresses, Harry experiments with different ways of integrating the dialogue into the narrative. In the second paragraph, we have:

'I will destroy all!' roared evil Reptar.

And in the fourth:

'We must find the idol' said Reptar 'but beware we will face many dangers.'
They found this out almost straight away.....

Here we can see that Harry as narrator is in total control, linking the last sentence with the previous dialogue in a very skilful and easy way. Not only has he found a way to cut between dialogue and narration, but he manages this skilfully without interrupting the flow of the narrative.

'We have no choice but to jump' said Phil but quickly adding 'do we?' But Reptar and Lil were already over and with no hesitation Phil joined them.

This story demonstrates Harry's growing confidence and willingness to take risks and try out a kind of writing that he was wary of attempting at the beginning of the year. His management of dialogue here demonstrates quite a conscious approach to the work of integrating dialogue with narration; Harry has been observing how this is done. The cohesive structure of his story does not suffer, as he uses the dialogue to help drive the events forward, whilst also sustaining his role as narrator.

Poetry writing

At the beginning of the school year, during the Autumn term, Harry's class wrote several poems, using an approach to poetry writing which laid heavy emphasis on simile and metaphor. Some of the poems were about the Second World War. The children studied a range of texts before writing themselves. Justine read them extracts from Michelle Magorian's *Goodnight Mr. Tom*, Shirley Hughes' *The Lion and the Unicorn*, and some war poetry. She showed the class newsreel footage of children leaving their families and travelling to the countryside as evacuees. They were then asked to write a poem entitled 'I am an Evacuee'.

In this poem we see Harry trying out a range of literary devices, some more successfully than others. For example he makes good use of the repetition at the beginning of each verse:

I am an Evacuee

I am an evacuee,
In this great big house,
The man that took me is a towering giant
Clutching my possessions so so tight.

I am an evacuee,
and if I was an animal,
I would be
As scared as a mouse running From a cat,
As cold blooded as a snake
As angry as a beaver with it's home
Knocked down
Or as lonely as a dog locked in a pound.

I am an evacuee,
Wandering about,
Looking blank
Then standing still
As if I have no control,

Bang boom crash in London
But here silence nothing happens.
I am an evacuee,
Standing all alone,
It might be a big adventure
Or a massive **NIGHTMARE** from which
You don't wake up from.

I am an evacuee,
Wondering what will happen,
The tag that holds information
Is tied round my neck,
I am as puzzled as a crossword
Or as stunned as a bear in a trap.

I am an evacuee,
Nothings going right,
I am as blue as the sea.

In the first verse we can see that Harry has remembered some of the details about the character of Lenny in *The Lion and the Unicorn*, where Lenny arrives at the mansion house clutching onto the badge that his father had given him. Also, in the penultimate verse, Harry shows his ability to empathise with the character's situation and to use historical information he has learnt about the plight of the evacuees in a literary context:

The tag that holds information
 Is tied around my neck

Harry had seen pictures of evacuees wearing such tags in the old newsreels and had heard about this again in Shirley Hughes' story.

In the second verse Harry moves away from the subject matter strangely, using a range of similes which seem intended to convey the evacuee's loneliness. He has been encouraged by his teacher to list possible similes to use as a way of making his writing more interesting. But this list of comparisons with different kinds of animals has the opposite effect from that intended; instead of the similes focusing attention on the experience that Harry means to highlight, the reader feels distracted by the images and diverted from the subject.

Ironically, it is verse 3, where Harry omits all similes, that most powerfully conveys the feelings of the evacuee:

I am an evacuee,
Wandering about,
Looking blank,
Then standing still
As if I have no control,
Bang boom crash in London
But here, silence, nothing happens.

Here Harry simply imagines the evacuee stranded in a non-place, in a state of blank, almost traumatised inaction. He uses onomatopoeia effectively to create the sounds of the Blitz, and to contrast the dropping of the bombs in London with the empty quiet of the countryside. The shorter lines at the beginning of the verse contrast with the longer dragged-out line at the end, with 'silence' as its middle word. This line changes the rhythm, underlining his sense of loneliness and emptiness and of having 'no control'.

Listening to texts read aloud

Carol Fox (1993), in her study of pre-school children's oral storytelling abilities, found that children were able to internalise patterns and structures of language from listening to stories and media texts (such as news reports and weather forecasts) read aloud. She found that their responses to stories depended not only on what happened in the story, but also on the way in which the stories were told. Discussing the importance of reading aloud in the early years, she says:

....listening to highly meaningful and elaborated stories....can generate extraordinarily complex linguistic and narrative structures.

The same could well be said of KS2 children who are successful writers. By hearing texts read aloud, and exploring their meanings through talk, young writers are often able to take on the whole feeling and rhythm of a text, not just a few new words to add to their vocabulary. But encounters with texts can also lead young writers to observe how situations can be explored from different viewpoints, and how characters can be fleshed out. For Harry, whose preferred texts come from the worlds of computer games and cartoons where inner life is hardly important, it is particularly valuable to explore texts which are more than a sequence of arbitrary events.

In the Spring term, Harry's class studied the narrative poem, *The Lady of Shalott*. Here is Harry's writing in role as the Lady of Shalott. He is imagining his life under a curse, condemned by an 'old hag' to be confined to his room, or die:

After a year went by I started to get lonely and bored sometimes I had urges to go out but I remembered what the hag said so to pass time I distracted myself by singing or gazing at the flowers or people on their way to Camelot. The reapers heard me sing a lot but when they looked up they could not see me as I only see what happens in my magic mirror. Sometimes in my mirror there are no people so I gaze at flowers. I see lilies, daffodils, bright red roses all dancing in the wind.

There is no real action here, only a thoughtful description of the character's predicament, which conveys her pain and sadness. Harry is widening his range as a writer through writing in response to literary texts. He has already shown that he is a noticing writer, who picks up easily on the features of different genres. Now he is learning to explore fictional situations in more depth, and to take on different kinds of personae.

A story in chapters

In the Summer term, Justine's class planned and wrote several chapters of a short novel about the Marie Celeste. In preparation for this writing they were introduced to the story of the Marie Celeste and involved in drama work about the mysterious ship. They also read some extracts from Berlie Doherty's *Street Child* which became the model for an introductory piece of work, and from her book *Daughter of the Sea*.

Like all other children in the class, Harry began work on this extended writing project with a piece of writing in role as an old sailor. The name of his chosen character is Tom Hawk and the title of the piece is 'What is Your Story?' This was intended as a preparatory piece of writing, introducing a character who has some kind of direct knowledge of the story of the Marie Celeste. Harry begins his writing in role in a way that attempts to capture the voice of a garrulous old sailor, and which has very strong echoes of the Berlie Doherty text the class was given as a model. His chosen character is a kind of ghostly survivor from the tragedy.

Tom Hawk. That's me, that's my name. I used to be a man of the sea but now I am staying on firm land after what happened that time when I was out in the deep blue.... That's Billy I used to haunt him but I gave in and now we are best mates, but he has asked me that question a thousand times and I just can't tell him, in my anecdote I lost everything even my life.

But in the narrative that follows, Harry reverts to a narrating style familiar from his previous fictions, but more melodramatic and ambitious:

My tale is of the sea and a boat in the far west Atlantic ocean where jagged rocks become hazards and deadly, where sea monsters wait for victims. It's where my fellow men still haunt the lees and some wait for a boat to give a fright, while some stay where no living thing has been before....My tale is well guarded but not by my fellow men, something far more deformed and noxious than them. So noxious it would make your blood freeze like ice so noxious it makes Satan an angel.

Harry's next piece of work on this project was a 'link-box' plan for the Marie Celeste story. The plan begins simply ('The Marie Celeste sets sail') but becomes far more complicated as Harry has to pack his later 'link boxes' with incidents in order to fit in all the events he has thought of. ('He summoned a range of monsters each with a different purpose, a god of fire to destroy the ship, Shiva goddess of ice, Ruhana god of lightning to destroy the crew and Bahnaunt O to guard the remains of the ship'). It is likely to be difficult for him to manage and sequence such a long and complex fiction.

Harry then does a formal plan for Chapter 1, first detailing the characters and the setting and then answering a series of questions from his teacher (eg 'What part of the story are you going to tell?'). One of these questions asks: 'What is your hook at the end of the chapter?'. Harry's class was used to thinking about how authors keep their readers' interest by ending chapters in a way which makes them want to read on.

Harry's first chapter starts by briskly establishing a number of facts about the basic situation at the start of the story:

Chapter 1: The great voyage

The old crumbling dock could barely hold the colossal ship known as the Marie Celeste the greatest ship on earth with a crew of 32 all of them were in pub but the Captain, Benjamin Briggs soon commanded them to get to work.

Tom Hawk was a Navigator on the great ship he and the rest were working like ants to prepare for the voyage to Genoa in Italy with a cargo of beer to trade. Tom held the silver sword tight, although it was only three inches and could not protect him from any real danger as the sun shone "REFLECTED A SIGN OF HOPE INTO HIS HEART".

His brother James was a bit apprehensive as his best mates had lost their lives on a voyage and he didn't want to join them at least not yet so Tom knew telling him that the sword would bring them good luck.

"Get back to work," said Briggs he was their boss everyone hated him he was the complete opposite but they had to obey his orders.

The boards of the docks began to creak and everyone spun to see who it was and a mysterious figure as black as the night advanced towards the ship and said "I wish to remain anonymous as my name and identity does not of convenience to you, I have come to ask may I be a member of your crew?" but with a hasty reply he had the answer no " then your ship will be cursed in a great storm" and with that he left.

"Never mind 'im" said Briggs "the sea is as calm as a kitten lets set sail" Tom didn't like the sound of what the wizard had said but there was no turning back the ship was already a mile from port and the sky was as grey as unpainted metal.

Harry shows narrative confidence in this chapter, but seems to be somewhat hampered by the requirement that he should make frequent use of similes in his writing in this story. Some of those he chooses are inappropriate to the situation.

'Never mind 'im' said Briggs 'the sea is as calm as a kitten let's set sail.'

He has made a list of similes on the facing page in his draft book, under the rough headings of : *Descriptions/Sounds* and *Feeling*. They include:

The waves were as angry as a bull

The waves charged at the ship like a soldier at war

The ocean's sounds penetrate your mind like a thousand daggers

As vulnerable as a new born baby

The sea is a deep porthole wanting people to see its depths but only the dead may see

Throughout this story his accustomed narrative style, which is direct, laconic, and marked by a swift succession of events with little description or explanation, is replaced by a much more elaborate style, where the emphasis is on heaping up descriptions and similes. These follow one another so thickly that the effect is often overdone. Chapter 2 begins:

There was no storm yet but grey clouds still hovered like a vulture waiting to awaken a great tempest maybe the worst on Earth where waves are like a tiger hunting for prey and where the peaceful goddess of blue becomes a raging demon of blue and the crashing, roaring, gushing and whistling can still be heard after even by the dead.

Harry seems to be attempting something very difficult: managing a long story with chapters and writing in a style which does not come naturally to him. This story is therefore less successful than his stories written in January, where the narrative drive is maintained throughout, and where the world of the story is created economically, without much in the way of colourful language. He is trying to meet the requirements made of him in this assignment, doing detailed planning, and inventing figurative expressions to embellish his story. But in some important ways he seems to have lost control of his writing. Some of his similes are tired or forced, and the writing is uncertain in its tone.

Nevertheless, Harry can still, in places, write with enormous verve and flair:

The tempest was a great blue demon unable to control the desire to kill and they were isolated and vulnerable, easy prey for an assiduous enemy. Tom shouted to the helmsman: 'Change course head for France!' but the tempest did not like the fact that they was trying to escape him so he grew more powerful and with one hard blow a bolt tore the sail through the middle.

Here we are back in the world of the Arabian Nights or the computer game, strange fantastical worlds where malevolent demons and dire events are common. It should be remembered that this is first draft writing; Harry is an exceptionally fluent writer.

Harry did not finish this story in chapters, and it is difficult to see how he would have resolved such an apocalyptic narrative and brought it to a conclusion. He has to manage a complex plot, to establish characters, and to imagine and describe a vast context for the story. It seems to be harder for him to do this in a story with a realistic basis than when he is dealing with one of his own invented worlds.

Harry was an individual and original writer, drawing on sources from media and computer games as well as books, in his narratives. This did not mean that his style of writing was unliterary, it was sometimes indeed highly literary in the particular 'high style' which is sometimes characteristic of science fiction or graphic novels. His stories were characterised by a strong sense of narrative control and narrative drive (the length of his T-units reflected this). In his invented worlds events were often arbitrary or surreal, but plots had considerable momentum as well as humour. During the year he extended his range, learning to incorporate dialogue into his narratives, and attempting different kinds of genres.

Harry also had a genuine ability to imitate style and to take on different voices. But although he attempted everything that he was asked to do in class, and worked on the planning of his writing and on his descriptive passages, his later work was markedly less assured than some of his more idiosyncratic early pieces and lacked their verve and energy.

During the year, unlike many of the other case study children, Harry never really seemed at ease as a writer when he was writing in response to a literary text. (Of all the case study children he was the only one who did not write in role in response to either *The Green Children* or *Fire, Bed and Bone*.) He appeared more confident when he was firmly in control of the subject matter of his writing; he was much more at home with his invented worlds. In these pieces, it was apparent that he had a real sense of a reader, and real confidence and ease as a writer. But despite these limitations in his range, the inherent strengths of Harry's writing were impressive. If he could find more influences to which he could respond positively, he was likely to develop strongly as a writer.

Emily

Emily lives with her parents and her two siblings, an older sister and a younger brother, in Rotherhithe. She attends School E and is a year 5 pupil in a mixed Year 5/6 class. Her teacher described her as a good reader who enjoyed discussing books but said that she was less confident in writing, needing a lot of individual support. She placed her at level 3 for reading and level 2/3 for writing on the CLPE scales. Emily was eager to please and very happy to talk about her work. During the year her confidence as a writer grew; she needed less reassurance and ventured to use her own ideas more.

The first sample of Emily's writing was written near the beginning of the school year. This story was not based on a literary text but its genre – a murder mystery – was one that Emily's teacher had chosen to explore with the class. Before writing, the class brainstormed lots of ideas together to build up a possible plot line. Together they chose the title – 'Strange but True'. Here is Emily's story:

> **Strange but true**
>
> *Bang,*
> *Kevin's car had just broke down......*
> *In the middle of nowhere*
> *in the middle of the night.....*
>
> *He turned on the radio, wanting to listen to some music to calm his nerves,*
> *"NEWSFLASH there is a murderer in the city woods"*
> *"That's silly" replied Kevin.*
>
> *Kevin stepped out of the car and a little shiver went down the back of his spine, he trembled as he walked slowly to the woods, pulling his collar up to cover his neck. He shivered with fear. The trees came down on him like hands reaching to get him, as he walked through the woods, his heart was beating faster than the West wind he carried on slowly until he heard a scream, just then in the tinkle of his eye he saw a wallet lying on the floor it had loads of money in it he saw a man lying on the floor Kevin went over to him he said he has broke his leg and that there is a murderer in his house, now Kevin is getting braver because he has someone with him as they made their way back to the house they heard the hooting of an owl, they get back to the house they walked slowly up stairs they heard some footsteps in his bedroom they tried to make no noise so they went in the bedroom and it was, who is the murderer nobody knows. Why did they come nobody knows.*

Exploring a genre

The opening paragraph of this story is striking. Emily has presented the barest of details about the setting, the time and the character in three short phrases, each punctuated by an ellipsis, so that the layout on the page looks more like a poem than a story.

> *Bang,*
> *Kevin's car had just broke down....*
> *In the middle of nowhere*
> *in the middle of the night....*

If we read the opening aloud, we can hear what Emily is trying to do. Right from the start she sets out to draw readers into her writing by building up the tension and atmosphere, to alert them to the fact that this is a 'spooky' or mystery story. The unconventional opening, with its half sentences and deliberate repetition of 'In the middle of', indicates that Emily is experimenting and is very aware of how her text might sound to an audience.

It also tells us that Emily knows that a writer of a mystery tale has to *leave out* certain parts of the story in order to create a mystery for the reader to solve. Emily consistently attempts to do this throughout the story. For example in the second paragraph, she begins:

> *He turned on the radio.... "NEWSFLASH there is a murderer in the city woods"*

She does not tell us anything about the rest of the news bulletin, assuming that the reader is familiar with this kind of radio announcement and will be able to fill in the possible details. She also assumes that the reader will guess that the character, Kevin, has broken down in the area of the murder – although she has not hinted at this. In her redrafting, Emily corrected this omission with an extra sentence:

> *He had just passed a sign saying city woods.*

The third paragraph begins with a long atmospheric sentence as Emily moves her character out of the car and into the woods:

> *Kevin stepped out of the car and a little shiver ran down the back of his spine, he trembled as he walked slowly to the woods, pulling his collar up to cover his neck.*

Here Emily's use of description, to build suspense and to convey Kevin's fear, is powerful; what is remarkable about this sentence is its length and its construction. It is her skilful management of the verbs in this sentence, her imagination of the character's small, fearful actions, and her slow pacing of the narrative which lead the reader to anticipate that something untoward is about to happen. Suddenly, outside the car, Kevin feels vulnerable. Emily reinforces this notion in the next, much shorter, sentence:

    'He shivered with fear.'

From here on, however, it becomes much harder for the reader to anticipate what is going to happen next; the threads of the story simply do not tie up. The reader has difficulty in making sense of the situation, and the writer may have experienced similar difficulties in making clear what happens. There is no further paragraphing and no full stops from 'The trees came down on him ....' right up to the end of the story, suggesting that the writer is not fully in control of the material.

Emily moves into a rapid, almost breathless, sequence of events. Her earlier sense of control of atmosphere and management of suspense have disappeared; caught up in the chain of events, she is no longer in control of the narration. The overall effect of the final paragraph is somewhat confusing. There is a lack of cohesion in the story, and the reader, left without a trail of clues to follow, cannot draw any satisfactory conclusions about the events in the wood and their meaning. Emily has yet to master an indispensable feature of this genre, which is the importance of the plot, and of the clues the reader needs to follow the mystery.

It is interesting to look at Emily's redrafting of this long paragraph, where she attempts to link the events together in a more cohesive way. For example, the reader may question how Kevin could possibly have seen a wallet lying on the ground 'in the middle of the night'. In the redraft Emily explains this by first telling us that there was a full moon:

    "He gazed up at the full moon in the dark, gloomy sky....'

and then by describing how Kevin:

    'kept his head down and carried on walking slowly afraid to look up'

– so that he was bound to see anything lying on the ground. This is effective redrafting, as it enables Emily to account for plot events by linking them to the character's state of mind. It shows what she is able to do with intervention from her teacher. In the redraft she recovers her awareness of audience, whilst maintaining her efforts to create tension.

Emily did not write a final draft of the story and so we do not know whether she would have incorporated her new ideas in a finished version. The redrafting she did is an example of normal practice in her class. She is encouraged by her teacher to reread her writing and to redraft and edit it as part of the classroom routine. The teacher, as the first reader of a child's text, can help young writers like Emily to focus on particular features of the writing, in this case the linking of plot events.

In the last sentence of the story Emily deliberately chooses to maintain a sense of mystery in the form of a teasing question-and-answer:
 '*Who is the murderer nobody knows. Why did they come nobody knows.*'

This abrupt and mystifying ending again demonstrates, as did the unusual beginning, Emily's awareness of audience and her willingness to experiment with narrative. But she appears to be exploring a genre that she has not had much experience of from her reading. One indication of this is that, although she is trying to create an atmosphere of mystery, she has not yet worked out how to construct a mystery.

But Emily tries out particular generic features, such as deliberate withholding of information, a spooky beginning and ending, and the rapid building of suspense. Her concern about how the story will *sound* suggests that she is writing for an audience to *hear* rather than for a reader (who would have more time to register the gaps in the plot that Emily is glossing over) to read. Emily made stories to be read aloud, once saying: "I really hope that Lizzy reads my work out".

Understanding and anticipating the events of a story is part of being an experienced reader. A writer has to construct narratives in a way that allows the reader to anticipate and to guess. Whereas an audience can ask questions of a storyteller to fill in these gaps, readers have to work out the clues using only what the writer tells them. But mystery stories cannot be completely explicit; they need to leave things unsaid – and these gaps need to be of the right kind. The gaps that Emily has left are not always of the right kind – although the reader is alerted to the nature of the genre, s/he cannot quite follow the thread of the story. In this kind of narrative, Emily's sense of style is not enough to carry her through.

Gaining control of a genre

However, a story written by Emily at the beginning of the Spring term in Year 5 shows her developing her story writing skills and constructing a narrative which obviously reflects stories read and heard. At this stage in the year Lizzy was giving her Year 5/6 class some practice at writing timed stories for the SATs. Because this was essentially a practice session for a test, only the title was given. Right from the beginning of Emily's story it is possible to detect the literary influences of a text that Lizzy had read to the children in class.

The Curse
Characters: Lizzy, Ally and John, Cruella, Stuart.
Setting: Southend.

Long, long ago there lived a young girl named Lizzy She lived with her mother and father in a little cottage in the woods.

That fine afternoon a person knocked on the door and said to Lizzy's father "Give me your only child" said the old lady in a spooky voice "for what" replied her father. "richness" she said so her dad talked it over with Lizzy and they decided she would go with her, when she got there she got treated very badly and got chucked into a cellar and found a man sitting in the cellar next to her, she asked him what his name was but he wouldn't reply so she asked him why he was there and he replied to that question "I'm here because the old woman is not any old woman she's a witch and she said that I have to stay in this cellar until I have fallen in love with a woman for a year, Lizzy was astonished and said "please show your face to me" "no" he shouted and turned away. That night Lizzy decided to light a candle and shine it on him so she did, as soon as she saw the face of the man she fell deeply in love, just then some wax fell on his bare chest and woke him up "what are you doing I told you not to look at my face" "I can't resist the love of your beautiful charmed voice" Lizzy replied with a twinkle in her eye "I have fallen deeply in love with you" said Lizzy holding the candle over his face "I have to go now to a different castle with all the rats and the witches and black green gloomy eyed cat" "can I come with you" "I'm sorry you never obeyed my rules" "will you tell what castle it is, so I can make my way to you" "all I can tell you is, it is east of the sun and west of the moon" that night she could not sleep without the man next to her. She asked the witch if she could go to see her mother and father. The witch said yes but only to see them and not to go anywhere else, Lizzy also did not obey the witch's rules but she took the man's clues to the castle and was off like the fastest tornado that has ever spun. She came across an elderly lady and said "do you know where the castle is that lies beyond east of the sun and west of the moon no but if you go to my sister just at the next stop she might be able to tell you, thank-you and she went off to try and find the elderly lady's sister, until she came to the next stop until she asked the lady do you know the castle that lies beyond east of the sun and west of the moon and said yes it lays right over there just follow the path until you come to the front castle doors until she did, did come to the castle doors she knocked 3 times and the doors flew open she walked in and there was a staircase she walked up slowly until she came to another door she walked through and found the man sitting on the floor.

Right from the traditional opening, Emily establishes a strong storytelling voice in the manner of tales which derive from the oral tradition. We can hear the familiar narrative style of the fairytale and detect clear influences from *Hansel and Gretel* and *Beauty and the Beast*. We can also clearly identify some of the traditional narrative features of this genre – witches and castles, rats and cats, three sisters, three knocks on the door and the 'little cottage in the woods'.

Emily is helped in her management of the narrative structure this time by a very strong literary model, *East o' the Sun* and *West o' the Moon,* which Lizzy had read to the whole class and of which this is a partial retelling. Emily's memory of the shape of this tale is reflected in the language she chooses to move the story on, taking the main character, 'Lizzy', on her journey to find her love. Although she does not consistently use paragraphs to mark transitions, apart from the introduction, the reader can hear where they should be. Emily knows how this story goes and her writing signals the stages of the story clearly:

That fine afternoon....when she got there....that night....that night....she came across....

It is as though Emily has absorbed the *tune* of the fairy tale genre and confidently uses this knowledge to write her own version. We hear this tune not only in her narration of events but also in the dialogue she writes for the characters (shown here with regularised punctuation):

"Give me your only child," said the old lady in a spooky voice.
"For what?" replied her father .
"Richness," she said.

The inversion ('for what?') is an indication of Emily's sense of what is appropriate to this genre. Her choice of words, for example 'spooky voice' and 'richness', also indicates a desire to introduce colourful and appropriate language, although the wording she arrives at is immature. The overall sense of a carefully constructed narrative is much stronger here than in her first story.

Another feature of the dialogue which shows how Emily has internalised the rhythm and structure of the original, is the repetition of the formulaic question which accompanies the patterning of the events:

"Do you know where the castle is that lies beyond east of the sun and west of the moon?"

and the various answers which propel the main character, Lizzy, onward in her quest for love.

In this version of *East o' the Sun, West o' the Moon,* many of the elaborate details in the story are lifted from the original, for example:

> *That night Lizzy decided to light a candle and shine it on him, so she did. As soon as she saw the face of the man she fell deeply in love. Just then some wax fell on his bare chest and woke him up.*
> *"What are you doing? I told you not to look at my face."*
> *"I can't resist the love of your beautiful charmed voice," Lizzy replied, with a twinkle in her eye."*

Emily's text is close in many details to the original read to the class, and she is able to weave the dialogue into the story. With well-known models for her story in her head, Emily is able to write with a clear direction and focus.

Even though the narrative structure of this story is stronger, the barely punctuated second half progresses at an over-rapid pace, and Emily loses control of the prose. The reader finds it increasingly difficult to follow the text as Emily races towards the conclusion. This loss of control is, of course, a reflection of the timed conditions that the text was written under, but also indicates what is likely to 'give' when Emily begins to rush. She is more concerned to finish the story than to make its shape clear to the reader. Perhaps this is because she knows that if she is asked to read her work aloud, she will be able to 'correct' it in her oral performance.

East o' the Sun, West o' the Moon, which is a version of the story of Cupid and Psyche, has served for Emily as a powerful model of a particular genre, in this case fairytale. The content here is much more satisfying than that of her earlier murder mystery story, and is inextricably bound up with a characteristic narrative style. Young writers like Emily need the influence of this kind of strong literary text, which provides them not only with structural ideas for their writing but also with ideas for the content.

Writing in role

In February of Year 5, Emily was introduced to Kevin Crossley-Holland's version of the traditional tale, *The Green Children.* After the drama session and discussions in class about the ending of the story, Lizzy asked her children to imagine what it might be like if the green girl, Airha, decided to return to the 'green world' with her new companion, Guy. Their discussion led to the notion of a curse having been put upon the green land. Lizzy gave the children the title 'The Return' and asked them to write in role as one of the green children, telling the story of how this curse might be broken.

THE RETURN

This is what happened....

Guy and I had been searching for days which seemed like years for the tunnel which led me here, to this multi-coloured world. Eventually Guy and I gave up and decided to go home, well my foster home, when I thought I heard the voice of my lost brother telling me the way home, he said to follow the sunlight, I thought my mind was playing games with me, but I was wrong, I asked Guy if he would come with me "It might be the way to the tunnel" "Why" he replied " I feel it in my heart" he smiled, I took his hand as we walked through the sunlight, we started to spin around and something made us shut our eyes, then all of a sudden we stopped we opened our eyes and found ourselves in front of the tunnel. Guy and I looked at each other and jumped with joy until we lost our energy. I whispered " thank-you brother" Guy clung his arm around me as we walked into our worst nightmare.

As we walked through the tunnel we heard the dead souls telling a story of 2 worlds changing colour I was listening very carefully when there was a big clang between the 2 worlds, at that moment I was feeling very scared because there was water dripping like the howling of wolves and it was dark, damp and very cold, Guy felt like an ice cube with his arm around me, and I took another step when all of a sudden I felt the warm breeze slicing through my skin and the green sunlight swooping over me. Guy and I stepped into the green world, for some strange reason one half of me felt happy and the other sad because I wished my brother was here so he could have made home as well.

The land owner Rose, came over and told me about my brother dying and how he was the most precious gift to our people. "This is what happened", began Rose, " when your brother died, Airha, a curse was put on our green land and the only thing that can cure it is your love with Guy, you must prove your love to each other."

Guy and I gazed into each others eyes and saw our future together, he bent down and picked a Rose-bud and he swept it into my hands. I felt the petals and smelt the greenness. As I smelt it, the petals unfurled and a bright light shone in my face from the stigma. The rose which was once green turned ruby red, "THE LAND IS SAVED" exclaimed Rose....

Emily chooses to begin her tale in the same way as Kevin Crossley-Holland. Writing in the first person, as the character, Airha, she is well inside the story. There are indirect references to the original text here – the dead brother, the 'sunlight' and the 'tunnel' – as well as direct references to the drama that was created by her class. For instance the 'dead souls' are a reference to their treatment of the episode of the green children walking through the tunnel.

Emily manages the beginning well, economically introducing the characters, the setting and their situation all within the first sentence. The reader can hear the familiar tune of the original story, especially in the dialogue between the two characters. But the tone suddenly changes at the end of the first paragraph as Emily slips out of the author's style into her own voice.

In the second paragraph, it appears that Emily has forgotten that she is writing in role as Airha. She begins to use images which do not fit with the tone of the piece:

"there was water dripping like the howling of wolves"

The simile here does not work; Emily is focusing on imagery at the expense of sense.

Part of the process of redrafting in Lizzy's class is an emphasis on extending children's knowledge and use of vocabulary with the help of thesauruses which are made available during the writing sessions. In the second paragraph we see Emily taking on this challenge of experimenting with language, as in:

"the warm breeze slicing through my skin and the green breeze swooping over me"

One can trace this idea back to the original text:

"Around me, the air was so warm, warm as my own skin, and then it moved. I felt it move! It slipped across my face."

But Emily's choice of verbs is forced and causes the reader to question the words' appropriateness to the context. She seems to be more concerned to find unusual language than to convey meaning. Her writing shows that she has the confidence to experiment; she knows that words can create worlds and engage an audience. But she sometimes plays to this audience in an exaggerated way so that attempted 'poetic moments' sometimes result in obscurity.

Empathy with characters – the power of drama

In Emily's last paragraph, we can detect influences from the end of the original tale as the two characters from the two different worlds form a union. Here is the original Kevin Crossley-Holland ending:

"Guy hunted for me and he found me in the greenwood.
He put a blue flower in my hair; he took my fingers and wrists
inside his warm, large hands.
'They don't want me,' I whispered. 'They never will.'
'I love you,' he said, and that is what he said.
'You love me?'
'And here can be home,' he said.
'How can that be?'
'Home is your friends in your own green country. Home is your
friends here....'
'Both?' I asked.
'Here and there, home is your heart,' cried Guy, and his face was
pink and shining. 'Will you stay here with me?'

Emily captures the warmth of the relationship between these two
characters, in her own story, particularly in the dialogue she writes in her
opening paragraph:

"I asked Guy if he would come with me.
'It might be the way to the tunnel.'
'Why?' he replied
'I feel it in my heart.'
He smiled, I took his hand as we walked through the sunlight
to the tunnel..."

One of the most interesting outcomes of the Writing at KS2 research
project was the variety of writing activities that the teachers planned for
their classes as a result of studying this one text. All of the teachers asked the
children to undertake some first person narrative, writing in role, as one of
the characters in the story. In most cases, the children were asked to write
about what had actually happened in the story, either from the same
narrative viewpoint or a different viewpoint. Lizzy was the only teacher to
ask the children to imagine what might happen if the story continued. It is
clear that this idea arose from close study of the last part of the text, which
ends like this:

"'My country and your country, they can both be my home.'
'They can,' said Guy, and all the leaves in the greenwood trembled.
'And when I find my way back...' I began.
'I will come with you,' Guy said."

In her story sequel 'The Return' Emily shows she is gaining confidence and
extending her writing through exploring this kind of first person narrative.
This enables her to get inside the character and her situation, reporting not
only on events but on the character's complex response to events:

'Guy and I stepped into the green world, for some strange reason one half of me felt happy and the other sad because I wished my brother was here so he could have made home as well.'

However, one of the strongest influences which has enabled Emily to write so confidently from the viewpoint of the main character was almost certainly her participation in drama workshops around this text. Talking about the value of drama in enabling children to write with a voice other than their own, Susanna Steele (1999) says:

'It is the reframing of children's viewpoints of events within the context of the imagined world that is important.'

Writing in role is powerful because it enables children to come at material they know well from a new viewpoint, and also to imagine an area of language appropriate to the character they are taking on. Writing in the first person has enabled Emily to get inside her characters and begin to imagine their inner states of mind more fully.

In her discussion of *First Person Reading and Writing in the Primary Years,* Margaret Mallett (1997) highlights the potential value of drama work before writing. She says that involving children in some kind of improvisation, discussion and close text reading is a way to enrich the characterisation in stories. 'One way to help children gather imaginative insight into a character's feelings and situation is to provide drama work before inviting the writing.' Mallett sees this as an important preparation for writing in role.

Many teachers use these methods in the classroom in quite an informal way, for example using 'hot-seating' to enable children to experience the feelings and emotions of characters in stories before going on to do their own writing. Activities such as these enable young writers like Emily to enter into the fictional world. Working in role, they are able to reflect on situations and events in language which is different from their everyday speech. By taking on the voices of their characters, children can go on to write more confidently in the language which they have tried out in the drama.

In the work on *The Green Children,* one factor which appeared to be important was returning to the language of the actual text during discussions of how the writing might take shape. Where teachers focus discussion on the text, and on the choices that authors make when they write, they help to draw attention to style and structure, feeling and content. This double support from both the experience of the drama and the language of the text, created a powerful way into writing, and enabled Emily to combine the emotions explored in the drama with the rhythms and language of the text.

Poetry: issues of structure and feeling

Emily's stories reflected her growing familiarity with certain genres and her growing ability to take on a persona and write from a different viewpoint. Much of the improvement in her work could be ascribed to the reading and writing experiences that she was given, and her ability to draw on the influences she was exposed to. But in poetry she had fewer models at her disposal, and her poetic writing did not progress in the same way.

In the Autumn term, Lizzy had been working with her class on the topic 'Britain Since the 1930s'. One aspect of the work was to look at the plight of evacuees. To illustrate this Lizzy chose to read two literary texts – *Goodnight Mr. Tom* by Michelle Magorian and *The Lion and the Unicorn* by Shirley Hughes. She also read them the poem 'Evacuee' by Edith Pickthall and showed them some old newsreel footage of evacuees leaving their homes during the Second World War. Together, the class reflected on the events and experiences of evacuees in the stories and brainstormed some ideas for a poem. Lizzy provided the children with the structure for the poem and asked them to plan some ideas before writing their draft. Here is Emily's draft:

I am an Evacuee.

If I were a colour
I would be the colour
blue

If I were an animal
I would be a rabbit
scurrying down my burrow
hiding away from the
Poacher's powerful pistol.

I am an
evacuee.

If I were a person
I would be Little Red
Riding Hood with her
red shiny cape escaping
from the flesh eating wolf.

Emily uses the repetitive structure with which she had been provided to introduce each new image. Her finished poem contains lots of comparisons, drawing on her knowledge of science and the environment, but many of these images are not really appropriate to the subject matter. Only one is actually drawn from the world that Emily is trying to evoke:

I am an owl hooting in the darkness of the blackout curtains

If it were not for this line and the refrain 'I am an evacuee', the reader would not know that this was a poem about evacuees in wartime. Emily seems to have completely forgotten about the topic, as none of the reflections from the class discussion on the texts that have been studied feature in her poem.

This poem demonstrates Emily's immaturity as a writer and her inexperience in reading a wide variety of poetry. Her approach, which is to focus on the effect of each image in isolation, prevents her from taking a broader view of the meaning of the whole text. Here, form has overcome content, the emphasis on imagery has taken over, and what was intended to be a helpful structure has actually drawn the writer away from a closer consideration of the material.

A romantic story

In the Summer term Emily wrote two stories: an Arthurian story about a Queen who falls under an enchantment, and a long story in chapters about the Marie Celeste. The first story ('Into the Forest') contains some striking images: Queen Lizzie is led by Merlin to 'kind of a frosty lake what had a lily laying on it' and a hand emerges from the lily to give Lizzy a silver necklace. The story is confidently but breathlessly told:

Into the Forest
The Tale Begins . . . .

Queen Lizzy was bored so she decided to go for a little walk in the forest, she was admiring the forest so much she (had) got lost and for some reason she felt someone breathing down her neck, so she turned around and there in front of her stood Merlin the mystical magical magician man he is a wizard he foretells the future, "come with me I have a surprise for you" so she followed him he led her to some so kind of a frosty lake what had a lily laying on it opened and out came a hand with a silver necklace" she gave it to queen Lizzy she tied it around her neck and asked "why have you gave me this necklace" " because it holds a magical forest inside it and because you are our queen we wouldn't be able to trust anyone else with it" "thank you". Merlin transported her back to the forest she sat down and looked at it. hanging on the necklace was a crystal ball, she rubbed the crystal ball 3 times she didn't know why she had a funny feeling, then with a puff of smoke she was trapped, trapped inside the ball with no escape the necklace fell to the ground she screamed "help, HELP" but there was no answer day turned into night and night turned into day when she heard galloping of a horse then it stopped it was no luck, she looked outside was heaven, but inside here was hell all the trees had fallen and the wind howls like the clashing, clanging of swords. A knight noticed the necklace and he picked it up the queens mouth opened wide as she fell in love the knight saw the queen in the crystal ball and his heart stopped beating, she appeared in her lovers arms you have freed me you will be my king . . . . I am sorry but I have a curse on me because I saved your life. I cannot fall in love with anyone anymore for I do love you . . . . The knight Sir Lancelot has been turned into a spider that weaves a web of Camelot.
The tree connected and made arches as they galloped on their horse together into dream land.

Emily seems to have written this story rapidly. It is unfinished and there is no evidence that she redrafted or proofread it. But the narrative has a strong onward movement and some confident literary turns of phrase ('day turned into night and night turned into day'). Later in the story there is the romantic climax:

> ...the queen's mouth opened wide as she fell in love the knight saw the queen in the crystal ball and his heart stopped beating, she appeared in her lover's arms you have freed me you will be my king.....

Emily is having some difficulty in managing this story, but she seems to have clear pictures of the action in her head. She enjoys writing romance.

The group poem which follows this piece of work in Emily's file is one that has been worked on by the class in shared writing. It is also based on Arthurian legend. It gives a very clear indication of what counts as 'good writing' in this class, with its emphasis on imagery, especially similes and metaphors and animal imagery, and on unusual and highly literary language:

> *Arthur's cloak was billowing as he charged towards his foe.*
> *Brandishing his sword high above his head he approached the dark*
> *Shadow in the distance.*
> *The sun darkened as the clouds overcame the light.*
> *Pellinore's evil eyes glowed like a vicious cat.*
> *Arthur meandered like a snake, that led him to the gruesome*
> *Silhouette....*

Here the imagery is appropriate to the encounter, but the writing is melodramatic and thick with imagery. The models that Emily is receiving for her writing are of this kind of intensely embroidered language.

A class story-writing project

Later in the term, Emily undertook the writing of a long story based on the Marie Celeste, work that the whole class was involved in. Like her peers, she first did a piece of writing in role as a sailor who had taken part in the tragedy, and then attempted a story in chapters written in the third person. This story began with a scene of boarding the ship, and continued with a chapter about the storm that caused the shipwreck; all the children's work followed the same pattern.

Emily's writing suggests that she experienced considerable difficulty with this work. Her writing in role as 'Jack' is unfocused; she tries to create an ominous atmosphere but only succeeds in being obscure:

> *Jack that's my name, I live with my 19 year old daughter. I visit the park*
> *everyday because it brings back memories of when I was younger. Every night*
> *before I go to bed, I pray to a person who is always in my memories, night*
> *and day. I picked up my paintbrush and dipped it in water and started to*
> *paint when a flash back appeared in my mind I couldn't find myself so I ran*
> *to the park and finally found myself and I wondered why I was in the park*
> *I sat down and a shiver shuddered up my spine it was that same bench in*
> *the same place, then a storm appeared like the one that ruined my life,*
> *THIS IS MY STORY!*

Emily's liking for melodramatic turns of phrase is apparent in this writing, but there is not much sense that she knows where her story is likely to go. In the two chapters that follow, she describes Jack going on board the ship and the ship setting sail. Then the storm arrives and Emily has the job of describing a major shipwreck, without much to help her except, perhaps, her experience of the film *Titanic*.

> *Big bang, everybody screamed then a flash of lightning struck the boat big waves drowned people on deck the captain shouted "all board the deck there are life boats waiting for women and children first and then men".*

Emily tries to use colourful language and imagery, in the way her teacher expects, but the images are not always particularly apt or helpful to the meaning, and are sometimes odd and inappropriate:

> *….suddenly he saw water sliding through the bottom of the door like a lift shooting down floors and floors of a building.*

This long story in chapters is a very ambitious piece of writing for Emily to attempt, yet if we look back and compare this piece of work with her writing at the beginning of the year, she does not seem to have made marked progress. In striving to impress her teacher and the reader, she has not always succeeded in keeping a focus on the meaning and structure of her writing.

Emily always has an eye on her audience, and especially on her teacher as audience. She is eager for her work to be read aloud to the class. Generally Emily is anxious to please the teacher and carries out her assignments conscientiously, following suggestions that are given. She tends to hurry through her writing, and this shows; some of her pieces of writing leave an impression of being breathless and rushed. The erratic use that she makes of paragraphing and punctuation is significant: she has not yet learnt to stand back and structure her writing or to mark that structure accurately for a reader.

In her class Emma is expected to be extending her vocabulary and making plentiful use of similes to enrich her writing, but this constant emphasis on style and language is not always helpful to her – she is already over-inclined to adopt an exaggerated and melodramatic style, and needs no encourage-ment to embroider her writing.

Emily seems to write best when she writes in role, in an extension of drama, as in her work on *The Green Children* where she becomes part of the story and writes convincingly from inside the story world. She is also responsive to stylistic influences, and under the influence of strong literary models can write with some assurance, making extensive use of literary language and turns of phrase. But where good influences are lacking she is less confident, often striving after melodramatic effects without a clear sense of the overall direction of her text.

Emily is a dramatic writer with a liking for melodrama, mystery and romance. These are natural inclinations in a young writer of her age. In time she will need to become a more critical reader of her own writing and to focus more closely on meaning and on the development of her stories. If she succeeds in doing so she will lose some of her dependency on the teacher and be able to achieve a stronger individual voice.

Yossif

Yossif is Spanish and lives with his parents in South London. Yossif's mother is Spanish and speaks Catalan and English; his father is from Sierra Leone and also speaks Catalan and English. Yossif attends School D, which he joined in Year 4. Prior to coming to London, he had been educated in Barcelona, attending nursery school from the age of three and then primary school from the age of six until he came to England. Yossif's knowledge of stories has mostly been gained from school rather than home. At school he was educated in Catalan, but would also have learned some Spanish.

Yossif had little spoken English when he first arrived at the school a year previously; although both parents were able to speak English, they had always spoken to him in Catalan. At home, they still speak Catalan for about eighty per cent of the time. Yossif's parents are very supportive of his learning. His father takes a special interest in the presentation of his work (Yossif's handwriting is extremely neat) and encourages his reading with CD-ROMs. At the beginning of the year Yossif was assessed as being at stage 2 as a learner of English.

Yossif was an experienced reader and writer in his own language; his mother described him as working above the average level of his peers in Spain. However he was not yet fully literate in English. Early in the year, Yossif's teacher, Carol Kirwan, placed him at Level 2/3 for reading and at Level 2 for writing on the CLPE scales, although she also judged him to be a fast learner. She felt that Yossif would be likely to make rapid progress in the technical aspects of writing but might need some encouragement to express personal feelings and responses. During the year we were able to observe the effects of reading literary texts on this bilingual child's writing.

An early story
Yossif's baseline samples of writing from the beginning of the year help to make clear what he knows about writing. An early story by Yossif, written towards the end of September 1998, was based on *Pinocchio.* Carol had read a version of this story to the class and asked them to write a retelling of the beginning. Here is Yossif's (unfinished) story:

Pinocchio

Once upon a time there was a old man that wanted to have a child, he then a wood boy and after painted the wood boy the man went to sleep. In the night a angel appeared and give the boy that called Pinocchio life, and Pinocchio went to wake up his dad, "said who are you", I'm Pinocchio how you can be a real boy no you are wood boy but a angel give me life.
The old man had one cat and one fish then the old man went to sleep, the fish went too, the cat as well the old man said to Pinocchio to tomorrow you will go to school like all

Yossif begins the story in the traditional way, introducing the character and his situation economically, with the barest of details :
Once upon a time there was a old man that wanted to have a child, he then a wood boy and after painted the wood boy the man went to sleep.

Even though it is clear that Yossif is not yet completely at home in English, this is a confident opening, and one which bears the marks of traditional storytelling style. Apart from one omission (after 'then') the introduction is clear and takes the reader straight into the story. Right away we can see all the elements that Yossif is trying to cope with at the same time as he learns to write in English – in terms of both transcription and composition.

Judith Graham points out that this retelling of the beginning of *Pinocchio* owes as much to Disney as it does to Collodi. In the original story, the 'blue fairy' does not appear until later in the book but in the Disney film she is indeed present in the first scene. Similarly, the cat and the fish are both members of Gepetto's household in the film.

Yossif's first sample demonstrates his narrative competence and his ability to sequence events and maintain a consistent style. It also demonstrates his willingness to have a go at the unfamiliar linguistic conventions of written English. At this stage Yossif does not seem to have a strong sense of a reader, he seems to be merely reporting the events as they happened in the story he heard.

Building confidence: journal writing

At the beginning of the year, on taking over the class, Carol found that many of her children were disaffected and did not have a positive view of themselves as readers and writers. Several had social and emotional problems and found it difficult to build positive relationships. Their experiences of language and story seemed to be very limited – although they could tell stories about themselves.

Determined to address these issues, and knowing that the children had to feel better about themselves before they could begin to learn, Carol decided to do some journal writing with her class. Her purpose was to give the children daily writing practice, to enable them to express personal thoughts and feelings in written language, and to give them written feedback, possibly leading to a written dialogue, which might help to forge and foster relationships.

As the children began to write in their journals every day, they also began to read Carol's responses and listen to her reading some pieces from her own journal. Gradually some children began to want to share their writing with individual friends or occasionally with the whole class. In this way Carol was able to make the reading-writing connection explicit to the class; they were given an immediate audience and helped to see the purpose of writing.

One piece of personal narrative written by Yossif as a journal entry in the Autumn term illustrates how many different linguistic features he has to cope with, as a bilingual writer, at the same time. His story is a simple piece of personal writing about going to stay with his grandma, waking up before everybody else and watching TV, and having a good time, with lots of good things to eat.

Swimming

A long time ago, when I was about 8, I was in my grandma's house when I woke up I went to see the T.V.
Then my mum and my sister woke up then my mum then my milk with Kato, then two minutes later my grandma came from the shop, she bought all of fruits, meat, milk, melon. . . .
Then my mum's friend call if we want to go with them to the swimming pool, after my mum asked me "Do want to go the swimming pool" and I said yes. I was so happy to go to swim, I went to ask my friend if can come, his mum said yes. We went to the bus stop to go to the swimming pool we met at the bus stop. We went to the swimming pool with a bus. When we was in the swimming pool (unfinished)

Like many children, especially those relatively new to English, Yossif over-uses the same connective ('then') to carry the narrative on

> *'Then my mum and my sister woke up then my mum then my milk with Kato, then two minutes later my grandma came back from the shop.'*

His story is a straightforward record of what happened until the third paragraph when the really exciting invitation to the swimming pool arrives and Yossif records his own response: 'I was so happy to go to swim.' Everything about going swimming is interesting, even the bus journey, and Yossif records it all:

> *'We went to the bus stop to go swimming we met at the bus stop. We went to the swimming pool in a bus'.*

In fact he spends so much time on this build-up that he has no time to write anything about the actual swimming.

Throughout the year Yossif always has a go at writing and tries to get his meanings across. He uses the English that he has got, much as he would have to do in speech. This kind of straightforward speech-based writing enables him to make full use of the language of everyday conversation, but on the other hand it does not really move him into other areas of language. The great advantage, however, of the diary writing for Yossif (and for all the children in Carol's class) was that it got them writing every day, and after a while this began to show in what they were able to do.

Playing with time sequences
A second story, 'King and Queen', written by Yossif at the beginning of the Spring term, shows that he has moved on from these earlier pieces.

King and Queen

The story began in a beautiful palace in a village and it was in the Kings castle. The Kings name was John II. He had a baby boy that was named Eric I. The King and Queen were going to die.
The King and Queen were happy to have a baby, the king said to the servants to buy the best clothes in their village. 17 years later he was a man he was generous, handsome and kind. Then he had to be King but he never wanted to be a king. He never knew that his dad was kidnapped Eric's mother told Eric I the truth that his dad was dead Eric said the people like truth he was kidnapped.

In this story we can see definite development in Yossif's retelling. There is a strong hint of an oral storytelling voice in the purposeful opening:

The story began in a beautiful palace and it was the King's castle.

But after introducing the characters, Yossif as narrator unexpectedly tells the reader that:

The King and Queen were going to die.

He seems to be experimenting with the time sequence of the story, referring ahead to a future event so that the reader is warned about a forthcoming tragedy. In her analysis of pre-school children's oral stories, Carol Fox (1993) found the beginnings of this particular competence in two of her case study children. As she says:

Warning or hinting of future events is ....a long-established literary convention.....

and she points out that devices such as this – moving beyond the story time or 'prolepsis' (Genette 1980) – occurs in children's stories 'when the stories are strongly influenced by books.'

In the next paragraph, Yossif successfully reorients the story back to the chronological time sequence but moves events on rapidly, in a sentence that sums up the passage of time. Once more we hear the familiar tune of the traditional tale in the description of the character, Eric I:

Seventeen years later he was a man he was generous, handsome and kind.

But from here on the narration becomes much less clear and the reader has great difficulty in making any meaning. Yossif has a complicated story to retell here and he does not quite succeed in establishing why Eric had to be King or whether his father was dead or had been kidnapped. His language in the remaining fragment of the story loses connection with book language.

However, Yossif is attempting a lot more here than just a continuous straight narrative. He is not afraid to take risks in narration, he attempts a complicated time sequence, and he has picked up the tune of the original tale in his confident beginning.

Choosing the right text for retelling

Carol, Yossif's teacher, was concerned that many members of her class seemed to have very little experience of hearing stories. They were often struggling with the basic elements of composition and their stories used a very limited vocabulary. At the beginning of the Spring term she set about reading several short stories to the children, asking them to retell the stories. She chose mostly folk stories and traditional stories, with strong narrative structures. Carol hoped that this would enable the children to shape narratives more confidently and to use a wider vocabulary, experiences which they could then take into their own story writing.

At the beginning of February Yossif composed another story which was a retelling of a traditional story:

Roasted Peanuts Don't Grow!

Once there was a nephew, and his uncle Guro was the uncle and Tsuro was the nephew. A long time ago they had an argument They were arguing about when Tsuro was shooting rocks at the bee's nest. Tsuro told the bees that his uncle throw the rocks.
The bees came out to sting Tsuro then they bit Guro until he collapsed. That was two harvests ago.
They each planted peanuts for harvest, harvest arrived Guro had 2 bags of peanuts as well as Tsuro.
Guro roasted the two bag of peanuts. Tsuro only roasted one bag and left one bag.
Now came the sowing time winter the rain came and went this is time to plant peanuts on the soil. Guro never knew much he decided to sell all the roasted peanut.
Tsuro's peanuts were growing.
They were growing through the soil growing healthy green peanuts. 'Tsuro will you expect to the roasted peanuts to grow?'
His uncle was disappointed that his nephew's peanuts grew and his don't grow.
His nephew walked him back and in sympathy he said, "uncle roasted peanuts don't grow."

In this story Yossif demonstrates that he is able to extend his vocabulary and experiment with some literary devices, although he has some difficulty in pacing the narrative and managing the dialogue. He opens his retelling in the traditional way, anticipating the reader's possible difficulty in distinguishing between the identities of the two main characters:

Once there was a nephew and his uncle, Guro was the uncle and Tsuro was the nephew.

In this retelling, Yossif is able to complete the story and sequence the events with a clear beginning, middle and an ending, one that links back to the title. He includes many details, especially of an argument which had taken place between the two characters in the past and which sets the pattern for the rivalry between uncle and nephew.

Yossif uses some book language to move events on, for example:
That was two harvests ago.
and
Now came the sowing time....the rain came and went....

His sentence structures are much more varied in this story and there are signs that he is beginning to experiment with them, for example:
About peanuts Guro never knew much.....

He is also beginning to try out other literary devices, such as repetition. For example towards the end of this story, Yossif uses repetition very deliberately to emphasise the main theme of the story:
Tsuro's peanuts were growing. They were growing through the soil growing healthy green peanuts.

This combination of the short sentence and the longer sentence is obviously deliberate and intended to make sure that the reader picks up on this essential point in the story.

Just as the reader begins to anticipate the likely ending of the story there is a curious line:
Tsuro will you expect the roasted peanuts to grow?

This is an interesting narrative moment: the question seems to come from the narrator and to be directed to the character, although we might expect it to be directed to the reader. It seems to look forward to the ending; we understand from it that we should *not* expect roasted peanuts to grow. Although Yossif has not made his viewpoint quite clear here, he is obviously attempting more than straightforward narration of events.
The joke at the end of the story is the moral of this tale and Yossif appropriately writes it as dialogue.
'His uncle was disappointed that his nephew's peanuts grew and his don't grow. His nephew walked him back and in sympathy he said, "uncle roasted peanuts don't grow."'

Although he has retold this story faithfully, he is not able to develop it much. In this kind of fable, the point of the story can be stated in the moral; events are merely played out to illustrate the moral. The world of the story is actually very small which makes it hard to do more with it than attempt a faithful retelling.

Writing in role: an early attempt

In March Yossif wrote two pieces of first person narrative in response to the work on *The Green Children*. Fiona Collins, the drama consultant, asked the children to write a letter home to their parents in role as one of the green children. The first draft was written immediately after the drama session and the second almost three weeks later.

London

Dear parents!

This world is different from our world in this world not everything is green some of the other things are different colours and the animals are not green there all kinds of different colours. The birds are not green.
This world is totally different from our own world.
I like more this world because where we live everything is green and not more colours. In this world you can see different colours. This world is
better than my world and they have green beans that's what I eat in that world.
When it was getting night time the moon nearly took my eyes.
I communicate with them by sounds or with singing.
They don't speak like the same because when they are speaking like they're singing and when they're singing it's like they're talking.

Yossif

Dear mum and dad!

In the morning when I woke up, the sun blinded us because of the sun's light.
The people from this world are not green, and the fruits and birds are not green either.
What they eat is not green only some of the things.
They have green things like plants, beans, peas and green colour pencil.
At night time the moon nearly took my eyes, the sky changed it's colour the sky became dark blue and black like it was going to rain.
I always eat the same food, beans and peas.
I'm having a good time here.

XXXXXXXXXXXXXXXXX mum dad

It seems to be difficult for Yossif to write in role at this stage, especially in terms of maintaining an authentic viewpoint. For example, in the first letter, Yossif writes:

I like more this world.... This world is better than my world....

and in the second he writes:
I'm having a good time here.

One has the sense that Yossif is writing as himself rather than as the green child, for at no time during the Crossley-Holland tale is the reader ever given the impression that the character prefers the new country and nor was this a feeling that arose out of the drama.

In these descriptions we can hear influences of the text in the language Yossif chooses, for example in the beginning of the second letter:
In the morning when I woke up, the sun blinded us because of the sun's light.

In the text, Crossley-Holland writes:
....the sunlight blinded us.

And in both pieces, Yossif chooses the same unusual phrase to describe night falling. In the first he writes:
When it was getting night time the moon nearly took my eyes.

And in the second, he remembers more of the text and extends the metaphor:
At night time the moon nearly took my eyes, the sky changed its colour the sky became dark blue and black, like it was going to rain

The original text reads:
Above our heads, the sky began to change colour! It was so strange: the dark light almost took our eyes from us.

In these letters in role, Yossif shows that he can recall details and use some of the literary language of the text but is not yet able to sustain a convincing role; the green boy's viewpoint does not figure much in Yossif's letters. Rather, they seem like the kinds of letters that Yossif himself might have written on coming to England. It may be that Yossif is writing out of this experience of coming to another country, and losing his sense of the original story. Generally it is the task of retelling a story which powerfully supports Yossif as a bilingual learner, as we have seen in the stories previously examined.

Adopting a style
A poem written by Yossif early in the Summer term illustrates a shift from the personal narratives in his journal to a more literary way of using personal experience. At the beginning of this term, we introduced a second standard text, *Fire, Bed and Bone* by Henrietta Branford, to the project

teachers. Yossif's teacher, Carol, began to read this story to her class and they spent quite a long time studying the first chapter. They discussed the fact that the whole story is told through the eyes of the hunting dog and looked in particular at how the author uses repetition to reinforce this viewpoint for the reader. They examined the following three paragraphs of the text:

I know the world beyond the house. I know Rufus's byre. I know Joan's house which stands beside the village field. I know all the village. I know the Great House barn and sheep pens; I know the Great House fields. I know every small place where oats and beans and barley grow.

I know where the rabbits creep out from their burrows. I know where the wicked wildcat leaves her stink on the grass as she passes. I know where foxes hunt, where deer step out on fragile legs to graze. I know where the wild boar roots and where the great bear nurses. I know where the little grey bear with the striped face digs for bluebell bulbs in springtime, when the woods are full of hatchlings that fall into your mouth, dusted with down, and the rabbits on the bank are slow and sleek and foolish.

I am a creature of several worlds. I know the house and the village and have my place in both. I know the pasture land beyond the great field. I know the wildwood. I know the wetlands all along the river, where every great green leaf that you step on has a different smell. I know the high, dry heath.

Carol then invited her class to write a poem about their own home surroundings, using this device of repetition.

Here is Yossif's poem:

I know my hostel, behind my door where I sleep, all cosy and warm in the winter dreaming.

I know the market, at the beginning of the street — it's busy, with strong smells of different foods.

I know the street of old Kent road they are busy all the time,

I know the cab drivers which are always busy.

I know the car park of Tesco which there's a lot of cars.

I know the coach park near my hostel.

I know the sweet shop where every thing is cheap behind my house.

I know the Royal Mail car park behind the football pitch.

I know the Royal Mail post Office where you can send packages to Africa, Europe and the wildworld, the office is in the park.

I know the old dirty laundry.

I know the school in Peckham queens road.

I know the clean and neat mosque which you can pray to god.

I know the telephone boxes

In this piece we can see how readily Yossif has taken to this shape and how a supportive but not limiting structure has enabled him to focus on gathering images, so that the reader builds up a clear picture of Yossif's world. The device acts as a scaffold for Yossif's ideas but allows him to vary the length of the lines when he wants to extend a description. For example, the opening line:

> 'I know my hostel, behind my door where I sleep, all cosy and warm in the winter dreaming.'

is contrasted with some of the shorter lines:

> 'I know the old dirty laundry'

in a way that creates a strong, rhythmic chant. Yossif is able to use Branford's structure, revealing what is important to him about his world in much the same way as the author did, in role as the hunting dog. The reader can picture the geographical features of his world: his school, the busy road, the market and the park – but also learn something more about him, for example:

> 'I know the clean and neat mosque which you can pray to god,'

which tells us something about his faith; we know that Yossif is Muslim.

The other place which is especially significant for him is the post office, so important that he mentions it twice:

> 'I know the Royal Mail car park behind the football pitch.
> I know the Royal Mail post office where you can send packages to Africa, Europe and the wild world, the office is in the park.'

This line tells us that Yossif knows about sending packages. He has family in other parts of the world (he has lived in Spain and his father is from Sierra Leone) and the post office has a special meaning as a link with them. He seems to have lifted the 'wild world' from Branford's text, where, narrating as the dog, she tells her readers:

> 'I know the wildwood.'

This poem seems to have been significant for Yossif not just in terms of his development in literacy but also in terms of establishing his sense of belonging to his relatively new home in England.

Writing in role

As the term progressed and Carol continued the study of *Fire, Bed and Bone* with her class, they embarked on further pieces of writing. One of these was a letter which Carol invited her class to write in role as Rufus, the dog's master. In Branford's story, the peasants want an end to serfdom. Rufus and his wife are captured for talking of rebellion and are held in captivity by soldiers in the stable of the Great House before being moved on to

Maidstone Prison. They are separated from their children who are taken care of by a neighbour – Ede. Carol asked the children to write a letter to Ede in role as Rufus, describing their experiences in captivity.

Yossif's letter in role opens with a strong sense of time and place and loss:
> *'We have been in this prison three months, Ede. We can't wait to see our children.'*

Throughout the rest of the letter he draws on the events he has heard in the story as a source of ideas for his content. In the novel, Branford, narrating as the dog, tells us:
> *...Four figures slumped against the walls, facing inwards. They sat on filthy straw, wet with their excrement. Chains held them to the walls.*

Yossif recalls this detail to create his own meaning:
> *'Where we are there is a stench of human excrement. We have no freedom. We have to stay in a small cell like a box. There's me, Comfort, and two more men.'*

We can see that Yossif has not only taken the events from the text but also lifted some of the language to describe the appalling conditions in the prison. The events in this story have moved Yossif and enabled him to empathise with the character's condition; his writing here is strong, plain and confident.

Earlier in the letter Yossif describes the dog bringing baby Alice's hat and recalls it as a source of comfort and relief:
> *'One dog came with Alice hat and we were very happy to know that Alice was still alive.'*

This refers to an incident in Branford's text where the dog takes Alice's hat right up to the prison wall and Comfort is able to hook it through a chink:
> *I looked through then and saw her, rocking, holding the small hat to her cheek, smelling her daughter's smell upon it, kissing it.*

Throughout this piece of writing Yossif demonstrates that he is able to write in role, drawing on the text more as a source of ideas than a source of language. This time, the form of a letter has been much more successful in providing Yossif with an audience for his writing. The audience was not only imagined, it was also simulated, as Carol invited her class to swap their letters and write a reply to Rufus in role as Ede.

Writing in role – a story revisited

Three months after the work on *The Green Children* something rather extraordinary happened in Carol's classroom. Yossif asked Carol if he could write a story on the computer. He chose to retell the story of *The Green Children*. By now Yossif knew this story very well but he worked without a copy of the text. He was very eager to show his story to the Project Coordinator when she visited the classroom. This is what he had written:

The Green Children

This is what happened. One of our lambs skipped into a cave and we went to rescue it. It was scary and dark and we saw eyes and hands looking and trying to grab us. We heard bright bells.

When we came out of the cave the ringing was sunlight. We saw faces but they were not green, there was a tall girl and another girl dangling two birds which had lost their songs. There was a boy who buckled and bumped his brains and his bottom.

And a little boy who was holding berries. My little brother pinched me and I said, "they are children I think!" and then they fore fingered us. The tallest girl came out and I asked her "who are you! And then she turned her back to us. She beckoned us to follow her through the woods, when we came to a house then a woman came out of the house.

The mum looked and circled us after that she brought us some pigeon pie… rabbit mince…peacock-in-a-roll I have never seen or heard those things words before, and the food smelt and tasted wrong. I said we will wait until we go back home.

Then one young man passed through the door with some beanstalks. The young man split open one for me to see what was in side there was a froth in the bean I ate them anyway they tasted all right.

After we ate was ready to go back home. The cave disappeared we couldn't find our way back home it brought sorrow to our faces. Then my brother began to cry and he threw what he had in his hand. The children soon began to us some words. After seven weeks my brother wasn't eating or speaking to me. The mum sang some words to my brother.

My brother soon lost his song, I was lonely then and I soon learnt their language. They brought me to a festival everyone wanted to buy me but Guy said no.

They asked how much these she cost.

They said; 'she's not for buy or sell' just because she's green and you are white.

They asked how much does she cost.

They said she's rotten that's why she's green.

I ran away because I was scared of the people Guy found me and put a flower in my hand.

He made me warm, comfortable and confident.

We went back home and we danced altogether.

This retelling is remarkable in two ways: not only are there direct and indirect liftings of the language from the original text, but all the events of the story are there, correctly sequenced, and they make perfect sense to the reader. And yet, Yossif is working from memory. He has internalised so much of this text, and has yet been able – so steeped is he in its rhythms and language – to change it too, condensing the story at times and at other times supplying new material.

Right from the opening of the story we can hear the remembered language of Kevin Crossley-Holland's text:

> *'This is what happened. One of our lambs skipped, into a cave and we went to rescue it. It was scary and dark we saw eyes and hands looking and trying to grab us. We heard bright bells.'*

Crossley-Holland's opening goes:

> *This is what happened. One of our lambs skipped into a dark cave, and we ran in to rescue it. We heard bells in the cave, bright bells, and we stumbled towards them.*

One can see how close Yossif is to the original text but also how he has interpreted the meaning, and engaged with the events in role as the character. For example, he says of being in the cave that 'it was scary' – an appropriate response, even though at no time during this text does Kevin Crossley-Holland tell his readers how the character feels.

Yossif interprets the character's feelings in this way on two further occasions. The second is after the green boy, Airha's brother dies, when he tells us:

> *'I was lonely then and I soon learnt their language.'*

This is beautifully condensed from the original. Again it shows Yossif's focus on meaning, his awareness, in role as the green girl, that he would have to learn this language or have no-one to communicate with.

At the end of the story, again with great economy of style, Yossif describes the character's emotions. After the incident at the market fair, he writes:

> *'I ran away because I was scared of the people, Guy found me and put a flower in my hand.*
> *He made me feel warm, comfortable and confident.'*

In the text, Kevin Crossley-Holland had written:

> *'I ran away then. I ran out of the town and did not stop running for a long time.*

*Even then, on my own, the voices of the fair people jeered and hooted
and screamed inside my head.
They don't want me here, I thought. I don't belong. I never will.
Guy hunted for me and found me in the greenwood.
He put a blue flower in my hair; he took my fingers and wrists inside
his large warm hands.'*

Yossif's version of this episode shows how well he has maintained his focus
on meaning. His last sentence is strongly phrased, he can imagine how supported and comforted Airha feels by Guy's love.

Yossif's story contains many words and phrases remembered directly from
the text, for example – 'then they forefingered us', 'she
beckoned', 'the young man split open' and 'the cave had disappeared'. But
what is more interesting is how Yossif has chosen his own words and
phrases throughout the story to recreate the meaning of the story. For
example, near the beginning he writes:
'My little brother pinched me...'
recalling Crossley-Holland's:
'My little brother pressed his nails into my left arm.'

Yossif's story language is close to the original text but he often confidently chooses his own words, which are appropriate to the context. Carol had
read the story to her class several times and they had read it by themselves
and together in groups. Multiple readings, and especially reading aloud,
have enabled Yossif to remember the language of the story and store it up
for future writing.

Throughout the story, Yossif demonstrates that he is able to sustain his voice
as narrator but this time a narrator in role as a character, the green girl. This
appears to be a significant development for Yossif, as the device of writing
in role is something that he had not used in story writing before. It seems
not only to have enabled him to develop a stronger voice but also to have
made him imagine the story from the inside. Yossif's choice of language is
tightly woven into the narrative. The most interesting aspect of the piece is
the amount of detail that Yossif has remembered from the text long after the
class had finished studying it. Perhaps the sheer force of this text, with its
themes of otherness, love and separation and the lyrical quality of its language, has enabled Yossif to confidently retell it in a voice which is so close
to the voice of the original text. In doing so he has taken a leap along the
oral-literate continuum.

Yossif began the year as a very inexperienced writer in English. He was, however, always willing to use the language that he had, and to attempt whatever he was asked to do. Early pieces which were written in language close to speech did not greatly extend Yossif's writing ability in English. It was when his teacher began to put more emphasis on the study of traditional tales that Yossif began to develop more visibly as a writer. He embarked confidently on retelling a range of stories, helped by his good ear and his ability to remember and echo whole passages, sometimes long after they were first told. These texts were an excellent support to his learning of written English.

By the end of the year, Yossif was attempting far more and had developed a more conscious literary style and a much stronger sense of a reader. He wrote in role, and drew on his ability to retell a story, continuing the style of a particular text in a way which showed he had really picked up on its language and rhythms. But he also responded strongly to the themes of particular texts. The opportunity to rework them in various ways enabled him to explore them in more depth, and to make them his own in a way that was reflected in his later writing.

Joe

Joe is a Y5 pupil in the same mixed Y5/6 class as Emily. He lives with his parents and his older sister in Rotherhithe. His class teacher, Lizzy, described Joe as mature and articulate in his relationships with adults but said that he worried about criticism of his writing. It is possible that he suffered an initial lapse of confidence at the beginning of the year, when he had been seated with children who were all in Year 6. Joe's mother had expressed concern about his written work: his teacher was trying to build up his confidence by setting him personal targets. Although she thought he needed to attend to redrafting, she had placed him at level 4 for writing and at level 3/4 for reading on CLPE reading scale 2.

Joe was an articulate, mature and friendly pupil who was keen to talk about himself and his writing. He enjoyed discussing the books he had read; his favourites included *Tom's Midnight Garden*, *Nightmare Stairs* and *Blabbermouth*. He was prepared to be reflective about his reading and writing.

Three poems

In the Autumn term, Joe wrote two poems which illustrate his use of the standard format for poetry writing in use in his year group. The class were studying 'Britain since the 1930s' and his teacher had read some literary texts related to this theme with her class. These included the novel *Goodnight Mr. Tom* and some war poetry. She focused the children's attention on images of war and together they brainstormed possible starting points for writing. Then she invited the children to write a poem, providing them with a framework to use. Here is Joe's poem:

Your Nightmare

I am war
I am your Nightmare,

I am war, your total destruction
I am Mike Tyson's enormous blubber fist
ripping out your heart,
I'll be around the corner waiting to pounce on you,
Like a leopard scratching your back

I am war
I am your Nightmare,

I am a plane crashing against your house on purpose
When you go to walk your dog
I'll be waiting upon the fog.

I am death itself
I am a crocodile taking you down and twisting you
around till you have lost all your breath

I am war
I am your Nightmare

I am a rollercoaster dragging you to death,
I'll be watching you upon your bed at midnight
And you would have the worst nightmare and then wake
Up and see your fate ....ME

I am war
I am your Nightmare.

The first device that stands out in this poem is the repetition of the refrain after every verse. 'I am' is also repeated at the beginning of most verses. This use of repetition is effective in building up a menacing feeling, but the images that Joe creates of war are a strange assortment. Several are metaphors of different kinds of violence, not specifically related to, or evocative of, war itself. For example in the first verse we have:

> *I am Mike Tyson's enormous blubber fist ripping out your heart,*
> *I'll be around the corner waiting to pounce on you,*
> *Like a leopard scratching your back.*

Joe seems to be listing horrifying scenes rather than choosing images which might make a reader think about war.

Three days later Joe wrote a poem entitled 'Poem about Peace'. In this poem Joe again uses the same basic format provided by the teacher, with a similar double line refrain after each verse and the same use of personification of the subject. Once more – following the practice in this class – he makes extensive use of animal imagery, introducing a goldfish, a dolphin, an eagle *and* a panda in the second verse. These similes, rather than contributing to a picture of peace, only serve to confuse. Joe is concentrating on the generation of similes and metaphors rather than on the overall meaning that they are there to support.

In these two poems Joe tries out literary devices, especially similes and metaphors, within a given format or writing frame. But this attention to form rather than content leads him to neglect his central themes. The kind of poem structure that he is using seems to have led him away from a focus on meaning and away from the texts which have been read in the classroom; there are few obvious literary influences in his writing.

A story from early in the year

A story written by Joe in September did not arise from the reading of any literary text, but was based on a class 'brainstorm' session. Lizzy wanted to introduce the use of 'plot boxes' for planning stories and she set the scene for writing a murder mystery. The children worked on a whole class example, before writing individual stories.

The mystery man with a cricket bat

It was a frosty, snowy night passing by to midnight, the cold flakes were up to John's ankles. John Silver old wrecked car had broken down at the side of the road next to a path through a wood.

John sat in his car thinking how he was going to get back to his girlfriend's house so he could get some sleep before morning. Slowly he fell to sleep, he slept longer than he thought He put the radio on "Someone has been murdered in Anfield woods in Shropshire the murderer has not been found and neither has the man that was murdered." John looked at the sign next to the path it said, Anfield woods Shropshire. He looked around perturbed anxious to get out of his car. He was terrified he looked at the watch it was exactly midnight aaarrrrrrrrrhhh, some one screamed from in the woods. He got out of his car stepping slowly in the snow and walked towards the sign (that said Anfield woods, Shropshire) he looked at a sign on a tree it had a picture and said murder beware (there at that moment he took his first steps into the woods) onto some flaky leaves that made a crackle noise when he crunch them. He began to feel worried and pushed the branches out of his way and got caught on a prickle bush that ripped his trousers, There in the distance he saw a wallet and a coat just sticking out from around a bend. It was his lucky night he thought to himself John walked in and out of the creepy bushes to the wallet and coat. He finally got there, John began to pick up the wallet and was just about to put it in his inside coat pocket when he looked beside the path, the snow was red and a hand and a leg was sticking out of it John picked most of the snow feeling horrified. He looked at what was under the snow, he was petrified. It was a dead man that had been stabbed by someone. He stepped one or two steps back and dropped the wallet. He ran like mad jumping over bushes and over logs winding himself around the bends till the end of the path. At the end there was a row of houses. John knocked on one a few times no one was there He knocked on the next someone answered the door. He came out and stood on the dirty mat in front of the door and asked John in a deep crusty voice 'why have you come here at this hour?' "Come with me with a coat or a blanket." He came with a coat and something under it. John didn't ask him what they were running too fast to talk. John went ahead and couldn't see the man behind him. He got to the stabbed man and waited for the man idling behind him, he came and threw the coat to John. He wrapped the blanket around him, suddenly the man that brought the coat had a cricket bat in his hand. He brought the bat up ready to hit John. John got up with his hands in front of his head and started to run, Lucky for John the man was slow he was too slow to follow and turned back. John got two ten pence pieces and phoned the AA and his girlfriend from a telephone booth that he found up the road he broke down on.

In Joe's story, the narrative has a clear direction, although there is no paragraphing. In the opening two sentences Joe gives us a description of the setting and introduces the character and his situation:

> It was a frosty, snowy night passing by to midnight, the cold flakes were up to John's ankles.

Joe seems to be aware of a reader and sets the scene carefully, trying out unusual phrases and a consciously literary vocabulary (for example, 'passing by to midnight' and, later, 'slowly he fell to sleep').

As narrator, Joe controls events well, all the time moving the character, John, from the car to the woods, to the sinister house and finally to safety. He describes the emotions that John feels as events unfold; we are told that he is 'terrified....worried....horrified....petrified'. There is, however, some doubt in the reader's mind as to whether Joe knows *why* his main character went into the woods, apart from the needs of the plot.

Joe manages to sustain the right sort of tension for this genre, building up the atmosphere in a way that suggests he is strongly aware of the reader. There is also evidence to show that he is rereading his writing as he works; every now and then he seems to realise that he may not have made his meaning totally clear to the reader and attempts to rectify this, sometimes over-making a point in the process.

For example, as the character John finds himself alone in his broken down car at the beginning of the story, he switches on the radio and learns that:

> Someone has been murdered in Anfield Woods in Shropshire.

Immediately afterwards, John:

> ....looked at the sign next to the path it said Anfield Woods Shropshire.

After John hears a scream from the woods, Joe tells us that:

> He got out of his car stepping slowly in the snow and walked towards the sign (that said Anfield Woods Shropshire).

It is as though Joe is trying a bit too hard to make the setting for the action absolutely clear, and is not sure what details it is essential to include and what can be left out. He has perhaps been too intent on carefully specifying the context, with the result that the events lose some dramatic impact.

A story with a message

A second story, 'The Dump', was written by Joe at the beginning of the Spring term. The class were studying a topic on the Environment and Lizzy invited her pupils to write a story connected to this theme.

The Dump

Jimmy was sitting in front of the TV feeling about his illness, he had caught it from the dirty river the Thames. He was desperate to tell the council and hopefully make the river less polluted.

Days passed and it had nearly been a week and Jimmy was feeling a lot better from his sickness. People living all by the river were catching this disease and he was determined to do something about it.

Jimmy sat and wrote a letter to the council to ask for some kind of help. And then went out to post it.

Later as the days were hot the council wrote back with no sympathy at all, so Jimmy thought that he would go and find people to help, some people didn't care but lots did.

Jimmy had got together a good big variety of people that wanted to do something about it. They all went to the council. As the council had seen what they wanted they started to help.

They planned that the next Sunday they would all go down to the river with any tools or things that they thought would come in handy to make the river tidy.

The next clean out was Friday and then Sunday. Time passed quickly and it came to Friday, (the river was looking amazing, the council had been during the week and had done something to the water, he didn't dare ask as he thought they would think he didn't like it).

Their last day planned came and we were all bringing out old rusty trolleys and planks of wood and all sorts of things. The river was looking and smelling really great and birds were swimming all over it

After they finished they all went and celebrated down at the nearest pub.

Jimmy went back after they had celebrated and sat gazing at the setting sun upon the river thinking about what he had done.

In the opening paragraph of this story Joe looks forward to what is going to happen. But instead of foreshadowing the events, he hints at the whole of the plot, including the resolution. This does not entice the reader to read on; we already know what is going to happen.

Throughout this story we can see a real development in Joe's ability to use paragraphs, which he mostly does to mark the transitions of time:

Days passed....Later....They planned that the next Sunday....The next clean out was Friday....Their last day planned came....

Paragraphing has enabled Joe to structure his narrative with a clear beginning, middle and end, as he relates events in a workmanlike manner. He maintains control of the narration, only losing control momentarily towards the end when he forgets that *he* is not the central character:

The last day came and we *were all bringing out old rusty trolleys.........*

Although technically competent, this story is emotionally sparse. There is little sense of a created story world; in a story about the environment we needed to be given a fuller picture of the river and its surroundings. The hero of the piece, Jimmy ends up sitting 'gazing at the setting sun upon the river thinking about what he had done', just as he had begun 'sitting in front of the TV thinking about his illness''. But there is little in the story which allows the reader any insight into the character and his motivation, despite his heroic deeds.

A story with a traditional structure

These two stories were followed by a third – 'The Curse' – written a couple of weeks later. Lizzy had given the class the title only, as practice in writing timed stories for the SATs.

The curse

Now, my friends, listen while I tell you a story that
happened a long time ago (more than 200 hundred years ago in fact)
it all happened when Lark (a young boy) was strolling along
on his way to the farm to go and see his dog. Then appearing
out behind an oak tree came an old crooked man with
an ugly face like a painted pig came walking over to Lark.
Lark wasn't afraid as the animal looked like it was a man
but when the creature spoke, his voice matched his ugly face
Lark looked up at the old man, then, the man struck his
hand and made a noise and then spoke, "if you don't milk
the cows for a whole month then you will become a
cow yourself!"
Lark listened to the old stranger but didn't feel
anything would happen.
He kept going for about 2.5 weeks going every morning
and milking the cows then went to do things.
That next day he had planned to go out and have
a jam-packed great fun day out with his friend.
It was a stormy day with lightning forking the sky
Lark and his friend weren't going any where and were just
staying in playing monopoly. The day passed quickly and Lark
had to go home. He thought this was strange because he was still
Lark and not the cow.
He didn't milk the cows for the rest of the month
but still he was no cow.
Lark went and told his father what had happened
and they explained.
They said that it was them and they had played a
trick on him to make him milk the cows. He felt useless
and stupid because he had not noticed for a whole 2 weeks
and a half and Lark and his family lived to be
an old age, I should know because I am that young boy
(Lark).

Right from the beginning Joe establishes a close relationship with the reader, adopting a strong oral storytelling voice:

Now my friends, listen while I tell you a story that happened a long time ago. (More than two hundred years ago, in fact.)

In this story, there is a more literary style and a more traditional narrative structure. The whole story plays a more familiar tune to the reader, with echoes of literary language, eg:

Then appearing from behind an oak tree....

and

He didn't milk the cows for the rest of the month but still he was no cow.

Joe skilfully structures the narrative, using appropriate paragraphing and including some detailed description, eg:

....an old crooked man with an ugly face like a painted pig

and

It was a stormy day with lightning forking the sky....

He also uses dialogue effectively to highlight the moment of the curse:

....the man struck his hand and made a noise and then spoke,

'If you don't milk the cows for a whole month then you will become a cow yourself!'

Although the end of the story feels slightly rushed (and probably was if Joe had to complete it in forty-five minutes), it is again framed as a direct communication with the reader. It feels as if Joe is telling the story to an imagined audience:

....but Lark and his family lived to be an old age, I should know because I am that young boy (Lark).

This story shows a marked development in the quality of Joe's writing. Perhaps this is because he has not had to think of all the content himself but is basing his ideas on a story that he knows. At one level Joe is a fairly skilled writer, he can construct and control a narrative and use paragraphing and punctuation effectively. But on another level, Joe needs help with developing his ideas and one of the ways he can sometimes get ideas for content is by listening to good literary texts.

Writing in role

Later in the Spring term, Joe wrote a story –'The Return' – as part of the work inspired by *The Green Children*. After the drama session, Lizzy read the Kevin Crossley-Holland story to her class several times. During their discussion they talked about whether the green girl, Airha, would be really happy in her new world with Guy, and whether she would ever try to find her way back to the green country. Lizzy invited her children to imagine how this might happen and to write the story of the green girl's return.

The Return

This is what happened .....The last brick was placed, a strike of lightning forked the sky and roaring thunder followed, snow started falling heavily as I ran back to Guy. I told him "Its happened, its happened I must go back and you have to come too" Guy and I ran fastly to the middle of the woods where the statue stood "Its here" I cried "Whats here" guy replied. I didn't answer, I just ran in the cave dragging Guy with me. The snow, thunder and lightning suddenly stopped we were in the cave and the door closed.

The cave suddenly shook and made a huge sound like a yawn, it was moving . . . . . Then it bashed against the green world, the door re-opened, It was my world, but, there was something not right, not right at all. This is what happened . . .

A curse had appeared and it is all my fault, I had left the land. It was winter although it was June. Snow fell everyday. Sunrise and sunsets had past .... But still it was covered in snow. Half a year had passed, I still haven't found my relatives. Guy and I were becoming too cold to live as was too much of a contrast. Freezing cold ice hanged from mine and Guys wrinkly bodies. That night we both slept but Guy didn't wake up. The lush green grass and Olive green weeds were appearing and our land was coming back. The trees stood still and I went back, back to my family and I left Guy still in a wood to breathe the fresh air. The curse was ended.

Joe begins the story in the same kind of oral storytelling voice as the Kevin Crossley-Holland text. In the opening sentence we can see that Joe is experimenting with a much more complex sentence structure, revealing his identity at the end:

> *The last brick was placed, a strike of lightning forked the sky and roaring thunder followed, snow started falling heavily as I ran back to Guy.*

In this first paragraph, Joe manages to create an impression of panic and tension in the dialogue between the two characters as they run from the snow storm into the cave:

> *"It's here" I cried*
> *"What's here" Guy replied.*
> *I didn't answer, I just ran into the cave dragging Guy with me.*

Throughout this first person narrative Joe demonstrates that he is able to move between reporting the speech between the green girl and Guy, and narrating events as the green girl.

The second paragraph attempts to build up the tension inside the cave by describing the transformation from Guy's world to the green country. One can see the relative immaturity of Joe's writing in his choice of vocabulary, for example he writes that the cave 'made a huge sound' and 'it bashed against the green world.'

At the end of the paragraph Joe uses repetition effectively to alert the reader to the possibility of something unexpected:

It was my world, but, there was something not right, not right at all.

In the last paragraph of the story Joe again lifts some language from the Kevin Crossley-Holland text:

'This is what happened…

He is consciously imitating the narrative style of the story. He describes the scene and the passing of long periods of time using a variety of short and long sentences, which echo the rhythms of the original text:

It was winter although it was June. Snow fell everyday. Sunrise and sunsets had passed but still it was covered in snow.

Joe tries to give the reader or the listener an explanation of what had been going on since the green girl left her home land. His struggle to manage the time shifts involved is reflected in changes in the verb tenses, for example:

A curse had appeared and it is all my fault, I had left the land….Half a year had passed, I still haven't found my relatives.

Writing in role, Joe manages to sustain a viewpoint and develop a sense of audience. There are indirect influences of the text read in the tone and style of his narration, although the reader's understanding of events is of course dependent upon prior knowledge of the original story. Although unfinished, this story illustrates Joe's increased willingness to take risks and experiment with narrative structure and language.

Summer Term 1999

In the summer term, like other children in his year group, Joe worked on a long story in chapters, based on the mystery of the Marie Celeste. The way of approaching the writing was common to Justine and Lizzie's classes, as the teachers planned this unit of work together. Drama work and the study of certain texts formed part of the preparation for the writing, and the first piece of writing that the children attempted was written 'in role' as the main character in the story, a sailor, introducing himself. There was a direct model for this writing in the first chapter of Berlie Doherty's *Street Child*.

Joe's first piece of writing in role for this unit is extremely accomplished. He has really thought himself into the persona of a man who is down on his luck and on the streets. His tone is assertive and chatty, with speech rhythms which echo the Berlie Doherty text:

Ryan, Tommy Ryan, that's my name and I'm sticking with it. Nothing I've got better than my name, not that I've got much anyway. Only got my guitar and cap, special. They're the only things I need see, I mean I'm living under a bridge – what else would I need?

Joe sustains this voice throughout the writing and makes the character come alive. There is a sense of direction and control in the writing, and Joe succeeds in giving the reader a sense of anticipation at the end of the piece:

One of the questions was "When you want to do things do you go ahead and do it?", there was something about that question that got me, just going ahead and doing things and I thought to myself, I'm going to do something. And this is what I did….

In the next piece of writing Joe embarks upon the story proper, which is written as a straightforward third person narrative with Tommy Ryan as the main character. In Chapter 1, 'The Ship', Tommy is on the dock about to board a ship. Throughout the chapter, Joe hints at mysterious things to come:

Each step Tommy took, he got an extra feeling to go back.

and

The boat looked curious, guilty and like a crime. Tommy was near the innocent boat, his mind told him to go back but he knew to go on.

'Innocent' is an inappropriate adjective here, but the general sense of foreboding is clear, as it is in other parts of the writing:

He was at the great ship standing, staring at the stair that were leading onto the story.

The boat was called the Enigma and if you read on you will see why.

Joe manages this first chapter very competently. Although the atmospheric hinting is a little overdone, it does demonstrate Joe's awareness of a reader. There is a strong sense of confident control of the narration. But as the story advances Joe seems to lose this control and his writing becomes increasingly weak. One of the weaknesses lies in Joe's use of imagery. He has embroidered his writing with similes, and often these have little relevance or power to illuminate. Chapter 2, about life on board ship, begins:

Onboard the Enigma.

Time spirited past and every one was onboard and was around the edge like teeth in a dog's mouth. They were waving like friends greeting others and crying like babies in distress. Tommy was nearly wetting himself seeing all this water from people's eyes.

The orange sun set and music approached, of course he only begged but then he found a friend, he means girl to dance with we were tangoing. tightly together talking. Dark turned to light and morning approached.

He slept till midday because of all the booze he had last night and got up in his underwear and said

" Oh, toff over there what's for breakfast" and the man replied, "Don't you mean lunch and I'm no toff I'm just richer than others".

Tommy dived back on his bed like a bungee jumper. The day reached an end all Tommy did was beg and ate.

The next day was more or less the same until 3 o'clock arrived; the dolphins fought the waves like cornets reaching the ocean and stars came early and gleamed like diamonds.

The next day was magical; the day Tommy made love. There was nothing better than this day for Tommy, the young woman (48) was called Peggy Mitchell, she was a dish, full of curiosity and kindness. Nothing better than her voice, all squeaky like a mouse. Only got a few grey hairs here and there but still his beauty.

The next day something deadly happened....

Joe seems to have been encouraged to search for similes, and he is applying them willy nilly. He often uses similes that are either quite inappropriate or tired, eg:

Tommy dived back on his bed like a bungee jumper.

or

Stars came early and gleamed like diamonds.

These similes are distracting to the reader, and probably also to the writer, who seems to lose direction at this point.

The next chapter, 'The erupting tempest', continues this trend. Similes abound, sometimes two to a sentence, and the pile-up of images and adjectives that results is often unintentionally humorous in its effect, eg:

Tommy still as a tiger hunting down its prey in the rich thin grass lay on his bunk, clutching the side like a terrified spaceman flying into orbit.

and

Now his heart was beating like ten drums from rock bands. He got up from his bunk trembling like jelly.

Joe is attempting to describe the chaos on the ship as the storm overtakes it, (which is reminiscent of the film *Titanic*). But the sense of a reader, and of a strong narrative voice, which so marked the earlier pieces in this unit of work, have now disappeared as Joe struggles to make his writing sufficiently 'descriptive' by overloading it with images. The final chapter is a letter written in role as Tommy:

> *If you find this ship it will probably be rusty as an old fireplace. I call my friends guitar and cap but they will be wrecked as well....Not much do I have, not much do I do. I go around like a boomerang, going place to place but never do I get out of this.*

This is a weak piece of writing compared with the introductory piece written in this same role. Putting these pieces side by side, we can see how Joe's writing has deteriorated in the course of this unit. He seems to have lost control of his writing.

Joe has had to manage an extended piece of writing in chapters, about a subject of which he has very little experience, either from life or from literature. He seems to have structured this extended text, with an introductory piece of writing in role and a first chapter which hints at the tragic climax of the story, according to a class plan. While he is working within this plan he writes confidently and manages the task well. But in what follows he has to draw on his own resources, and he does not seem to have a sufficiently strong imaginative grasp of his story to take it forward.

During the year Joe has written confidently in a number of different narrative styles. He has a strong sense of a reader, as we see from the assured storytelling voice that he adopts in several pieces of writing, such as 'The Curse' and 'The Return'. But Joe also organises his writing with a reader in mind, and is aware of the information that he needs to provide the reader with. He has a good overall sense of the direction of a text and can control the development of a narrative.

Some of the problems that Joe faces stem from the heavy emphasis that is placed in his class on the use of similes and figures of speech to enrich writing. Instead of improving his writing, this kind of focus on stylistic embellishment weakens it, as we can see from his long Summer term story, and takes away from his focus on narrative development. In a long story like this Joe's focus needs to be firmly on the development of plot and character, and he seems to be constantly detracked by having to hunt for similes and metaphors.

Joe is potentially a strong writer with a particularly clear sense of the structure of a text. He fulfils his assignments conscientiously throughout the year but the tasks he is given are often over-determined, with too few opportunities for Joe to develop an individual voice. However, certain aspects of his style are already apparent: he has a dramatic instinct as a writer, and is learning to manage suspense well – he begins and ends the year with a mystery story and obviously has a feeling for this kind of narrative. With more opportunities to use his own ideas and develop his emergent personal style he could improve rapidly as a writer.

Grace

Grace lives with her mother and her younger brother in Croydon. She attends School A which she joined in Year 3. Her family is from Uganda. At home English and Lugandan are spoken.

Grace's teacher, Noreen Mannion, described her as an independent, confident and expressive reader, one who preferred to read stories rather than non-fiction, but who needed to be presented with more challenging fiction and encouraged to reflect on what she read. Grace was considered a competent writer; she wrote stories by choice and enjoyed reading them aloud to the class.

The voice of the narrator

In Grace's baseline sample of writing we looked for what she knew about writing: her competence in constructing narrative, her use of literary conventions, and any connections between her writing and her reading. Her story, 'Look Who's Talking!', written early in September 1998, gives a good picture of her independent writing at the beginning of the year. Noreen had asked the class to write a story by themselves in response to a SAT question. There was very little in the way of discussion or preparation for writing; only the title was given.

Look who's talking

My names Niome I'm going to tell you a very weird story. I was sitting down in class I had finished all my work I was reading a very boring book so instead I looked out of the window like most children in the class do. Any way I was chewing my pencil at the same time. Then suddenly a little voice came from my pencil saying, "Hey how would you like it if someone was writing with your feet and chewing your hair off." "Who said that", I shouted look down. Then I saw my pencil talking. I screamed the whole class looked at me. The teacher sent me to the corner. That day was so embarrassing I even wanted to cry. But I couldn't . Everybody was asking me why I was screaming. Denise just kept on bullying me as usual. I only told my best friend Jake do you know what he did he just laughed at me my best friend I didn't dare tell anyone else. The next day I put my school pencil away and used a different pencil. The same voice came from my pencil-case. But this time it said "Get me out of here I'm suffocating in this thing". Me and my mum Joe had a talk that day she just thought I was crazy, and took me to the doctors. My pencil talked again this time everyone heard it. I told them I said that me and the pencil were friends forever. Sometimes people thought I was crazy because I always talked to myself Well that's what they thought anyway. I didn't always use the pencil in case it broke. I didn't want that to happen. I wonder how he can talk well I bet I'll never find out. Hey I wonder if he can do my homework. It will save me time.

About 2 years later my pencil case fell and someone stepped on it the talking pencil snapped in half that was the worst day of my life. (well I think so anyway.) In my bedroom I had a picture of him on it, it said
IN MEMORY OF
PENCIL, MY BEST
PENCIL.
I'll never forget him.

Grace opens her first person narrative by talking directly to the reader:
My name's Niome I'm going to tell you a very weird story.
There is a strong sense of "the way a story is orally told" (Labov, 1972) throughout Grace's story. There is also a desire to entertain, to capture the reader's or the listener's attention with a direct storytelling voice.

Grace sets out to establish the ordinariness of the day when the events took place, so as later to introduce the reader or the listener to a set of contrasting magical events which propel the story into action. She establishes how the narrator, Niome, is feeling:

> *I was sitting down in class I had finished all my work I was reading a very boring book so instead I looked out of the window like most children in the class do.*

We hear the voice of the narrator reporting events in a conversational style:

> *Anyway I was chewing my pencil......*

The pencil is the magic talking pencil which is going to disrupt this normality that Grace has established. Because of it, the narrator, Niome, is to be punished by her teacher, bullied by her friend Denise, taken to the doctor by her mother, and viewed as 'crazy' by most of the children in the class.

The possibilities of the talking pencil are not fully developed in the story, although they are hinted at ('I wonder if he can do my homework. It will save me time'). Instead, the story is brought to an end rapidly with a time shift. Grace moves back from fantasy to reality by killing off the problem pencil rather summarily:

> *About two years later my pencil case fell and someone stepped on it the talking pencil snapped in half....*

The final words of the story are a memorial to the pencil, decorated as a plaque:

> *In memory of my pencil, my best pencil. I'll never forget him.*

This story clearly illustrates Grace's competence as a writer of narrative. She knows how to structure a story clearly with a beginning, middle and end, and how to develop a narrative idea. She is able to fictionalise herself, taking a role within the story as a storyteller and commentator, and she has a sense of how the story will sound to a reader.

If we compare this first story with a later story, 'The Lucky Mascot', written at the beginning of January 1999, we find striking parallels between them. Once again Grace stresses the dull ordinariness of the opening situation:

> *Darren was a normal boy, who lived on a normal neighbourhood, with normal friends.*

Whilst establishing the story in a familiar setting, the opening prepares the reader for something extraordinary to happen. The story is again told in a colloquial first person style, with the narrator, Frank, speaking directly to the reader.

This story too deals with the theme of friendship or popularity, with the consequences of *not* being popular, and with the disruptive effects of a 'magic' or 'lucky' object on friendships. But the problems of the talking pencil and the magic mascot are resolved in very different ways. In the second story, the magic mascot exerts a positive influence on events, helping Frank to score a winning goal in a confidently described football match and reconciling the two friends. Claiming a share of the victory for it, Darren says:

I guess it was my lucky mascot after all.

and 'tucks it back under his shirt' in a way that suggests that there may be more adventures to come.

Grace seems to have a strong internal model of how to construct a narrative. She uses a first-person narrator, establishes a setting, introduces magical objects, and explores their consequences. She carries the story along confidently, creating a clear structure, building up suspense, and marking the conclusion. The language she uses is often strongly patterned ('I screamed. The whole class looked at me. The teacher sent me to the corner'. 'After I said all those horrible things to Darren he wouldn't sit with me, talk to me, or look at me any more'). Where has she learned to do these things?

It is difficult to source exact literary influences on the two stories written by Grace. Grace herself could only say that she got the ideas 'from her head'. And yet there are, undoubtedly, links between what Grace has heard and read and what she has written. In examining the influence of reading on writers, Myra Barrs (1992) suggests that 'written language is stored in the ear'; when children hear stories, they do not simply listen to what happens, but store up the rhythms and cadence of the language, which they draw on in their own stories.

Part of learning to write is therefore a question of learning how to write the tune, and of learning what resources there are at our disposal to enable us to create tunes for our readers.

Bartlett, in his study of memory (1932), considering what children recalled from hearing and reading stories, found that they remembered parts which were especially interesting to them personally. From this he developed his theory of 'schematas' or 'actively developing patterns' which brought 'remembering into line with imagining'. In her stories Grace successfully combines what she recalls from stories she has read with elements from her imagination. This, combined with details from her personal experience, results in two stories which are quite typical of her age, with a magic episode firmly framed in a realistic story of school friendships.

Retelling a fairy tale – the influence of media texts

Another story written by Grace came from a source which was much easier to identify. Noreen had read some versions of the fairy tale *Cinderella* to her class and invited them to retell or create their own versions of the story. Grace's retelling draws heavily on the Disney video of the story as well as on other versions heard and read. During discussion, Grace confirmed that although she had read the story of Cinderella many times, and remembered her mother reading it to her when she was very young, the strongest reference point for her retelling was the Disney video, which she knew extremely well.

CINDERELLA

Long, long ago in a little cottage, Cinderella was washing, polishing, scrubbing, and all the work she usually does. When her two sisters were shouting calling her name. "Cinderella!" Poor Cinderella, all day she had to work. (non stop.) Cinderella was fed up. Then one day an invitation was delivered at the cottage. Peaches read it out loudly. "It says that the Prince is having a ball on Saturday, and he would like us to come." "oh dearest sister we have to get some new clothes," said Flowers excitedly. Cinderella watched them laughing, and practising to dance. But she didn't think they stood a chance. Peaches has long blond plaited hair, she always wore her ridiculous make-up. But Flowers is even worse. She had black and green dyed hair. She looked like a clown.

They always wore ugly dresses. Well Cinderella thought it suited them. Ugly girls with ugly dresses. The day of the ball came. So Cinderella got all her courage and said "Can I go to the ball?" Her sisters laughed and laughed. "Of course not, you can't go to a ball dressed in rags. And you don't know how to dance. And you have lots of chores to do", they said. "All I have to do is wash the dishes. Please let me go" begged Cinderella. Well if you wash, the dishes, scrub the bath. And clean our bedrooms up. Then you can go.

"Bring bring. The door bell rung. "Well Cinderella looks like you can't go" laughed the sisters. As soon as the coach man saw the sisters he fainted. "Look sis, we look so beautiful he fainted." Showing off they walked off to the coach. Poor Cinderella sat there crying. "Don't cry." Cinderella wiped her ashy face. "Who is that?" asked Cinderella sobbing. "I'm your fairy godmother." "What. The one that keeps me safe?" "Yes."

"Where have you been all this time when I've needed you!?"

"Feeling guilty she said." Please don't shout at me. I'm getting old and my spells are going wrong."

"How come I can't see you?"

"I forgot to tell you, I'm invisible"

"Oh no!" sighed the fairy godmother

"What? why are you shouting" "You're meant to have some horses and a carriage to get to the ball." panicked the fairy godmother.

"Mother goose has the carriage and Aladdin has the horses."

"What am I going to do?" panicked Cinderella.

"Ask someone to give you a piggy back."

"Very funny." moaned Cinderella

The fairy godmother and Cinderella sat there thinking. "Cinderella, I have it." Said the fairy godmother. "What?" asked Cinderella.

"Get a pumpkin, lizards and mice."

"You are very odd, what do you need them for?" said Cinderella confused.

"Please just do it." pleaded F.G.Mother

Cinderella ran quickly into the house. When she had everything she said the magic words. "Bibedy, Bibedy bob. Stick and curbs, Bibedy Bibedy bob" "Oh no. I said the wrong words."

"I'll have to make you fly there." Sighed F.G.Mother

"Don't be silly. Try again." suggested Cinderella.

At the very beginning of this story Grace economically establishes the scene and the main characters, with herself as a strong narrating voice:

> *Long, long ago in a little cottage, Cinderella was washing, polishing, scrubbing, and all the work she usually did when her two sisters were calling her name.*

Grace includes significant details such as the list of chores that evoke the 'usual' drudgery of Cinderella's life. The two sisters' unequal relationship with her is also strongly signalled – and all this is told to the reader within the opening sentence. In her original draft, this opening consisted of two sentences:.

> *....and all the work she normally does. Then her two sisters were shouting....*

Her teacher, in conferencing about this story with Grace, had suggested that she list other connectives which she could use to combine these sentences. After this intervention Grace had changed 'then' to 'when', much improving the structure.

Interventions of this kind help to improve young writers' texts by drawing attention to the need to keep the reader in mind. In her study of teachers' reponses to students' writing, Sperling (1998) stresses the importance of the teacher responding to pupils' writing at all stages of the process, before and during work in progress as well as after writing has been completed, in order to help them shape their compositions. On many visits to her classroom we observed the way that Noreen orchestrates the different elements in discussion about texts, including children's texts. She always set out both to explore meaning and to focus on the language of the text. This kind of discussion can take place with the whole class, with small groups or with individuals – both orally and, sometimes, in writing, as when Noreen responds to individual pieces of writing. As Sperling suggests:

> *This conversational process helps to make visible the implicit writer-reader negotiation that is believed to occur when writers write and readers read.*

Grace does not arrange her text into paragraphs. And yet, if one reads her story aloud, it is possible to *hear* the first transition in her narration:

> *Then one day an invitation was delivered at the cottage.*

Her retelling continues with an elaborate description of the two ugly sisters, drawing on visual images from the video text. Grace moves events on with dialogue between the sisters and introduces some humour when the coachman faints at the sight of the two ugly sisters. She includes a piece of dialogue to make the reader laugh at the ugly sisters' interpretation of this:

> *"Look, sis, we look so beautiful he fainted."*

Up until this point in the narrative Grace has maintained control of the plot, and woven her own version of the visual narrative, recalled from the video, in with the dialogue of the characters, sometimes using the words of the video. From this moment on, however, she is unable to sustain this balance between narration and dialogue, and the rest of the narrative is all carried on through dialogue, with all the problems this entails. Grace does not resume her role as narrator and loses her way. The influence of the video here is too strong; dialogue has been allowed to get out of hand and becomes the dominant element in the story.

Grace did not finish this story but she did have ideas about how she could have finished it, which she explained in an interview:

I was thinking of making the prince who's very clumsy and everything, and Cinderella hasn't even seen him before so she doesn't know.….And Cinderella doesn't want to go over to the Prince. And when he comes over, she's like telling the godmother, change the size of my foot or something.

Grace said that she dismissed this idea for an ending although she did not know why. Perhaps she was divided between the need to have a conventional ending and her desire to play with the story and send it up, as the video does.

In her discussion of texts that teach children how to be readers, Margaret Meek (1988) acknowledges the importance of media texts in children's development as readers:

Evidence from research emphasises the importance of images. It's schooling, and the teaching of reading as a concern with words alone, that puts into our heads the notion that books with pictures are a preliterate form of storytelling, while all the time the very force of television shows us that this is not the case.

The power of texts, whether visual or literary, leads to our emotional involvement with stories. When we ask children to retell stories, we see something of the quality of their engagement and their interpretation of the original text.

Speech-based narratives

Grace was very aware of dialogue and often chose to write in first person as a narrator. She was interested in speech-based narrative and had a knack of writing in a conversational style. With this in mind, it is particularly interesting to examine a mini-play written by Grace during the Autumn term, when Noreen and her class were writing playscripts. As part of this work Noreen invited the class to be 'dialogue detectives' and create a piece of dialogue from something overheard. This piece of writing illustrates Grace's ability to structure scenes, construct dialogue and pace action.

Scene 1: Stage shows inside Marks and Spencer's, when lady came up to me.

GRACE:	Mum can I have this skirt, please please. (pleading)
MUM:	Ok, but don't get too excited (not very happy)
GRACE:	Thank you! (hugs her)
LADY:	Hello are you buying that skirt as well.
GRACE:	Yes I am (shyly)
LADY:	Well. Can you help decide which one to buy for my daughter. (asking)
GRACE:	Yes sure I can (pleased to help) I think you should buy that silky one, over there. (pointing)
LADY:	Thank you very much dear.
MUM:	Thank you for being so nice. (thanking)
LADY:	Don't mention it.
MUM:	Do you have to walk home by yourself?
LADY:	Yes I do.
MUM:	An old lady like you. (surprised) We can drop you off, where ever you're going.
LADY:	I couldn't, you're probably rushing somewhere. I don't want to slow you down.
MUM:	Don't be silly, I insist. (happy to do it)
LADY:	Well if you insist. Are you sure about this?
MUM:	Yes I am, come on let's go. When I say something I mean it.

Scene 2: stage shows inside car.

MUM:	Now where do you live?
LADY:	I live at Tavistock Road, near those flats. And it's on St. James Road
MUM:	Ok. But when we get near the flats you have to direct me.
LADY:	Ok I will.
MUM:	We're here, is it that house Number . . . (not able to see properly) 36?
LADY:	Yes. Thank-you for dropping me off. I don't know to thank-you.
MUM:	The way you can is by not making a fuss. It was nothing. (pleased) (Lady gets out, and they wave at her.)

The dialogue is based on an experience that Grace had had during a shopping expedition to Marks and Spencers with her mother. Grace reproduces the language and style of an everyday encounter in a store. She underlines the somewhat excessive politeness of the adults to each other in this scene. She also manages to convey the slight impatience and irritation of the mother, who is doing a good deed by giving an old lady a lift:

Mum: ...come on let's go. When I say something I mean it.
and at the end of the script:
Mum: The way you can (thank me) is by not making a fuss.
The reader can see the humour in this characterisation.

Grace makes consistent use of stage directions, a feature of dramatic writing which enables her to convey more about the feelings of the characters and how they speak the lines. She paces the action well, indicating clearly to the reader a shift from one scene to another.

In a second dramatic piece, 'Forbidden Forest', Grace shows that she can easily manage a dialogue between three characters. She confidently uses the dialogue to mark out differences between the personalities of these characters, so that the reader can hear what they are like: Lucy, the brave and plucky one, Amanda, the scared and rather reluctant explorer, and Fiona, the sensible peace-maker. She develops an argument between Lucy and Amanda that holds up the plot and creates suspense. Again, she consistently uses stage directions to add to the characterisation.

These speech-based narratives demonstrate Grace's confidence in managing a number of writing conventions and her ability to try on a new and unfamiliar genre, which she had very little experience of reading.

The Green Children

Half way through the Spring term, following drama and storytelling work on *The Green Children*, Noreen invited her class to write a poem in role as one of the green children, describing their experiences of arriving in the strange land. In preparation for this work, Noreen read the text to her class a number of times. She focused attention on that part of the text where the green children emerge from the cave to find a sea of faces staring down at them. Then she moved into a discussion of how this experience would have seemed from the viewpoint of the green children:

Noreen: What was so amazing about the faces that the green children saw?
Child: They weren't green.
Lee: They were wearing different coloured clothes.
Ashling: Their hair wasn't green.
Noreen: Imagine seeing people for the first time with red hair, blonde hair, black hair. At that time the children didn't have the words to name those colours but later on we know they learnt the language. I want you to imagine the colours that the green children saw when they emerged from the darkness for the first time. Close your eyes....

After much brainstorming, the children began work in pairs to give precise names to the colours the green children saw. At first the children simply gave the colour names they knew, but Noreen pushed their thinking to invent their own names, such as poppy red, sunshine yellow, bluebell blue and bark brown. The children moved from this word-level work to creating phrases that they might want to use in their poems. Later Noreen took the children back to part of the text, as a possible starting point for a poem. She wrote two sentences from the first paragraph of the story ('In and on and up! Up and out of the cave!') on a large sheet of paper and invited the children to help her compose a shared poem. They offered lines for the poem, with Noreen scribing their ideas. From here, the children moved on to independent writing, working from a process of initial drafting to revision, with peer support, and then completing a final draft.

Here is the final draft of Grace's poem:

The Green Children

In and on and up,
Up and out of the cave!
Stumbling over all the different confusing colours.
I looked up and saw the ocean blue glittering sky,
Silent and calm as ever,
I was shocked.

I saw silky petals from a purple velvet flower,
The flower swaying in the flowing cold breeze.
I felt my emerald green hair, dancing away with the breeze.
In the Green Country there is no breeze,
Only the still warm green air.

The bark of the tree, pine brown,
Rough and hard, I felt it with my hands.
I saw the green jade leaves, soft and silky.
I felt comforted, I nearly felt at home.

Grace chooses to use the model offered by Noreen for the first two lines of her poem. Writing in role as the green girl, she captures the tune of Kevin Crossley-Holland's language, not just in the opening verse, but also in the second, with its strong ending:

'In the Green Country there is no breeze,
Only the still warm green air.'

She uses the text as a starting point to develop her own ideas from the class discussion. There are indirect liftings from the text, such as 'hair dancing away with the breeze' ('my hair danced'). But above all Grace elaborates on the work on colours, building up vivid images. Grace uses adjectives sensitively, without overdoing them, and draws on alliteration and balance to pattern the verse:

'*The flower swaying in the flowing cold breeze*'

One can see from the layout and length of the verses that Grace is experimenting with the form of poetry, varying line lengths and creating brief, striking statements:

'*Silent and calm as ever,*
I was shocked.'

In role as Airha the green girl, Grace focuses mainly on describing what she sees in this new land. She moves from feeling 'shocked' by the strange and unusual colours in the first verse to recognising familiar shades of green by the last verse. Grace's use of 'nearly' in the last line is very well judged:

'*I felt comforted. I nearly felt at home.*'

Writing in role

During their discussions of *The Green Children*, Noreen talked with her class about point of view and the fact that the whole story is told by one character, the green girl Airha. Together they looked at the text and the illustrations closely to identify other characters in the story, and considered how telling the story from these characters' points of view might shift the version of events. Noreen built upon the children's previous experience of thinking and behaving in role as villagers during the drama session. Finally she invited the children to tell part of the story, writing in role as one of these characters.

The Green Children

My name is Joseph and I have a story to tell. You might not believe me, but I didn't believe it myself when I first saw it. Even though I'm old, this story has never come out of my head. I remember it as if it was yesterday. I was very young when it all happened. It was a normal day when everybody would go to the fair, buy something, or go on terrifying rides. Bargains going on and children breaking things and messing about. I owned a stall back then, at the fair, the fair was visiting the village Woolpit. I even remember what kind of day it was. The blazing sun shone down on us. The ground was hot like fire, it burnt my feet, until everything went quiet, there was a big crowd of people all staring at one thing. I struggled to get through the tremendous crowd. A normal boy was approaching us with a strange green creature standing right next to him? Everyone was shouting things out, and pointing their fingers. What was it? Nobody knew. I had come with my Grandma, and she had already fainted. The green creature came closer, and closer, I noticed it was a child. But before I could say anything else, the green child ran away. I couldn't see her anymore, she was camouflaged with the olive green grass, and the silky green leaves, that was the last time I saw her. I was confused. Most people thought it was their imagination, but I knew it was real. I saw her, I will never forget that moment, and I'll always wonder what she was and where she was from.

Grace chose to describe the scene where Airha, the green girl arrives at the market town, writing from the point of view of one of the market traders. Her narrative opens with a direct storytelling voice and hints at things to come:

> *'My name is Joseph and I have a story to tell. You might not believe me but I didn't believe it myself when I first saw it. Even though I am old, this story has never came out of my head.'*

Grace prepares the reader for a fantastic tale. She uses the original text as a source of ideas for the events, but greatly expands on the incident that she chooses to recount. The Kevin Crossley-Holland original contains virtually no descriptions of the fair, whereas Grace, probably drawing on the experience of the drama, gives the reader a strong sense of time and place, with an opening that economically establishes Joseph's role: 'I owned a stall back then at the fair.' She sustains her chosen viewpoint throughout the narrative. The narration captures the atmosphere of a market fair with all its bustle, bringing it alive for the reader. Grace uses her imagination to create a strong sensory memory of the fair day:

> *'I even remember what kind of day it was. The blazing sun shone down on us. The ground was hot like fire, it burnt my feet until everything went quiet.'*

There are some indirect liftings from Kevin Crossley-Holland's text in the language of Grace's narrative, as in:

> *'Everyone was shouting things out, and pointing their fingers.'*

(Kevin Crossley-Holland's text reads *'the fair people started to forefinger and shout'*.) But in general what is remarkable in this piece is the way in which Grace creates new strongly imagined material around her memories of the original text. This is exemplified by the culminating episode in the narrative:

> *'The green creature came closer and closer. I noticed it was a child. But before I could say anything else, the green child ran away. I couldn't see her any more, she was camouflaged with the olive green grass and the silky green leaves, that was the last time I saw her.'*

There are no sources for this passage in the Crossley-Holland text at all, although the economy of the telling suggests that Grace has picked up on his style. She is obviously also building on the language work that the class did on naming colours. The use of repetition and the variety of sentence length here indicate that Grace is aware of how her writing will sound. The reader and the writer are working in perfect harmony in Grace as she 'listens to herself write'. Phrases such as 'What was it? Nobody knew' show that Grace is gaining control of the narrative form by finding a voice just as strong as her own voice.

One of the notable aspects of this piece of work is that it carries strong echoes of Grace's earlier stories, 'Look Who's Talking' and 'The Lucky Mascot'. As in those stories, Grace begins by establishing a strong first person narrator, describes a 'normal' scene which is going to be broken into by a magical, lucky or uncanny event, and returns the story to normality at the end. In fact Grace rounds the story off in a way strongly reminiscent of the ending of 'Look Who's Talking':

> *'I'll never forget that moment and I'll always wonder what she was and where she came from.'*

Grace's preferred narrative model is very much in harmony with the material she is writing about, resulting in a piece of work which, although brief, is shapely and satisfying.

Fire, Bed and Bone

In the Summer term, Noreen introduced Henrietta Branford's *Fire, Bed and Bone* to her class. She read and discussed the first eight chapters of the story with the class and then invited them to write their version of a section of the story in role, as in the book.

Fire, Bed And Bone

I gave Fleabane a bath. I could see he was still tired, so I let him sleep. I had a feeling that we had a long day ahead of us. While Fleabane was sleeping I crept out of the den, and looked over to the old Farmhouse. I remembered my fire, bed and bone. Fleabane has lived life as a wild dog. I taught him how to hunt for food and sense well with his nose. I'm very proud of him.

The next day, I went to visit Rufus and Comfort in the stable. I saw their faces. Dirt mounted on them. They want to go home as much as I do. I could tell. They looked terrible. I hate the Miller. He did this. He told on Rufus and Comfort. He doesn't care. One of these days he'll get something he deserves.

I wish we could be a family again. We will be a family again.

I'm worried about Fleabane. I am worried he might join a pack. I don't want him to join a pack. I want my fire, bed and bone back. I want Fleabane to join me. I want him to leave the wild. But what if he doesn't want to? What if he wants to stay here in the wild where he has been bought up? I guess he

would call this his home. I won't let it happen. I have lost both my other two puppies, I shall not lose Fleabane. He's all I've got now. What shall I do?

I went to see the children yesterday morning. They were safe and sound. I was really worried about Alice, (the baby) the most. They were amazed at how big Fleabane had grown. After we had seen them, we went back home. I though of how we used to be safe, and happy. Now we had lost all of that.

Fleabane wanted to sleep. I lay down. I watched him fall asleep, but I couldn't stay awake and I fell asleep myself.

He was growing every day, Sooner or later he would live his own life. I loved Fleabane and I don't want to lose him. I'll make sure of it.

That night I couldn't sleep. I could sense danger. I looked around suspiciously. I saw nothing. I looked again. I knew there was something wrong. I walked out of the den, leaving Fleabane asleep. I looked over to the old Farmhouse. I saw a lady and a man entering. Rufus and Comfort? I thought. Or wasn't it.

In the first paragraph Grace economically establishes a sense of time and place, looking forward to the day to come, and harking backwards to her life in the old farmhouse.

> 'I had a feeling that we had a long day ahead of us....I crept out of the den, and looked over to the old farmhouse. I remembered my fire, bed and bone.'

Grace writes confidently in role – which we know is her preferred style of narration. She establishes the mother dog's sense of pride in her pup ('I told him how to hunt for food and sense well with his nose') and of protectiveness towards her master and family, now imprisoned:

> 'The next day I went to visit Rufus and Comfort in the stable. I saw their faces. Dirt mounted in them. They wanted to go home as much as I do. I could tell. They looked terrible. I hate the miller. He did this.'

Grace's style with its short sentences echoes that of Branford's text.

Grace develops the emotional situation, dwelling on the anxieties of the mother dog for her pup and his future in the wild:

> 'I'm worried about Fleabane. I am worried that he might join a pack. I don't want him to join a pack. I want my fire, bed and bone back. I want Fleabane to join me....But what if he doesn't want to? What if he wants to stay here in the wild where he has been brought up?.....What shall I do?'

As in Branford's story, the mother dog is the emotional centre of Grace's narrative, striving as hard as she can to hold her extended 'family' together. Her anxious self-questioning captures the feeling of being pulled in many directions.

Grace's narration shuttles between the investigation of states of mind and the development of the plot:

> 'I went to see the children yesterday morning. They were safe and sound. I was really worried about Alice most. They were amazed at how big Fleabane had grown.'

There are direct references to the book here, but significant additions, as in the reference to baby Alice, always the mother dog's favourite. Throughout the story Grace sustains her viewpoint, developing a version of the events of the book in a style which very much reflects that of the original text.

In this piece of writing, Grace demonstrates her development as a writer of first person narrative. It is as if writing in role as the mother dog allows her to write from an 'adult' perspective. She explores the emotional state of the character at length, conveying a real sense of trying to cope with a mass of responsibilities. But she does not lose sight of the events of the story, or of the double plot (Fleabane's adventures and the plight of Rufus and Comfort). She keeps all the threads together.

The final piece of writing by Grace from this term is a poem also based on *Fire, Bed and Bone*. Noreen had reread the first chapter of the novel to the class and invited them to rework the scene as a poem, again from a particular viewpoint. Here is Grace's poem:

FIRE, BED AND BONE

Glancing at the dark stagnant heavens
 Watching a gazing star,
  pass by.

Watching the swishing tree,
 swaying in the night like a
  Hand reaching out for me.

The wind howling,
  It was
   Talking.

Hearing rain hitting the rocky path way,
 hitting it like a
 ball bouncing off the ground.

I lifted my ears,
  I could hear every drop.

Lying on the soft hay.
 Listening to the glowing sparkling fire,
  ticking away.

I feel the night breeze,
  the window is open.

Mumble climbs through the open window,
 she curls up beside me,
  soft as smoke.

She has come for the
  warmth.

The children fidget in their sleep.
 Only Alice the baby is awake,
  Listening to me.

Rufus snores in his sleep,
  Grindecobbe grunts.

All is still, I can no longer,
 Keep my eyes open.
  I need to rest.

Tomorrow,
 Is the day.

In an earlier poem on *The Green Children*, Grace had experimented with line layout. But here she has patterned the layout carefully so that each three-line verse is followed by one which is made up of a single line. The poem shows a developing awareness of form, but the form has a function, with the single lines providing an arresting pause between episodes.

Unlike the Branford text, which does not move outside the house, Grace starts her poem outdoors in a stormy night where everything is in motion. The first three verses deal in turn with the 'dark stagnant heavens' in which a star rushes by, a tree swishing in the wind, and rain falling on rock. Grace uses similes and metaphors to make the scene more vivid.

But it is when the poem goes indoors (with a transition that is truly well managed, as the dog by the fire listens to the rain: 'I lifted my ears. I could hear every drop') that the poem really gathers strength. Grace really captures the atmosphere of a house asleep, with only the dog wakeful and alive to every sound. Her much plainer language here sometimes echoes that of the text, but the arrangement of the material is entirely her own, and the poem is beautifully controlled. Grace chooses to end the poem with a line from the book, but she gives it new prominence and significance by placing it as the closing single line:

> *'Tomorrow,*
>> *is the day.'*

Comparing Grace's remarkable maturity of tone in these last pieces with the chatty style of her early pieces one can see how much she has learnt about writing in the course of the year. She began the year as a girl who could 'read and write' competently. Her initial strength was in writing humorous pieces, often containing dialogue. But the study of literary texts has moved her on to consider more serious themes; by the end of the year her writing has a new thoughtfulness and focus.

In her classroom, shared writing and the discussion of the choices available to writers have encouraged her to think more consciously about her writing and about how she can structure her work. The focus in this class on the whole process of writing, through the modelling, discussion and conferencing that have gone on, has helped her to see about how she can control the power of words. But without the contact with powerful literary texts Grace might not have moved on from 'writing to entertain'. The books she has been introduced to have opened up new possibilities of thinking and feeling for her and there is a sense in the later pieces that she is now learning something more about herself as well as about writing.

CHAPTER

7

Data Analysis

In addition to the case studies set out in the previous chapters, which describe and track individual case study children's progress during the research year in considerable detail, we wanted to be able to look at some data from the project more intensively. We therefore made a selection of three pieces from the case study children's writing:

a) one was an early piece of narrative writing, generally from early in the Autumn term;

b) the second was a piece from the Spring term (in most cases done as part of the class work around Kevin Crossley-Holland's telling of *The Green Children*);

c) the third piece of writing was from the Summer term (in some cases this was part of class work on *Fire Bed and Bone*).

These pieces of writing are printed in Appendix 3. In order to assess the progress that individual children made during the year we needed measures which would enable us to analyse the growing strengths of their writing in more detail. We therefore analysed the three sample pieces of writing against a group of eight indicators, which were selected in the course of the project.

The eight indicators selected are described below. The first four are indicators which are relatively straightforward to pin down and which are therefore easily 'countable'. These indicators in children's samples were initially counted by the research director and then checked by another member of the research committee. The last four indicators are not so easily countable and were therefore impression scored; they were scored on a scale of 1 to 6 (6 high) by eight teachers and members of the research committee.

Countable indicators:

1. Breaks in the time sequence
This indicator is taken from Genette, who also refers to breaks in the time sequence as 'descriptive pauses'. In general, this indicator refers to places where the narrative pauses, or where the flow of the action is halted, usually because of either a descriptive or a reflective passage. This feature seems to be a particularly reliable indicator of a writer's growing ability to imagine a narrative world more fully, to pace the action in a more varied and skilful way, and to build up an atmosphere. It can occur, for instance, when the writer is trying to create suspense, and is delaying the action. It is therefore a measure of the control the writer is gaining over narration.

2. Mental state verbs

This indicator is adapted from Torrance and Olson (1992) who drew attention to the importance of what they originally termed 'cognitive verbs' as an indicator of growing maturity in writing. It is relatively easy to count mental state verbs (such verbs as 'wonder', 'realise'). When authors describe characters' states of mind in this way, or when a first person narrator reports on her/his own thoughts and feelings, the reader is given more insight into the inner lives of the characters. The fictional world seems more fully imagined. The evidence from our sample suggests that when children's writing begins to explore characters' feelings and thoughts it gains in interest and gives an impression of greater maturity.

To some extent the increase in mental state verbs in the writing of children in our sample might be attributed to the nature of the texts which were introduced through the project, both of which were narrated in first person. On the other hand, we collected several examples of early texts by the same children which are narrated in first person and which contain no mental state verbs.

3. T-Units

T-unit length is a measure of syntactic complexity (O'Donnell et al 1967) and is a well established measure in analysing prose writing. A T-unit is defined as 'one main clause with all the subordinate clauses attaching to it' (Hunt, 1964, 1965). T-unit length has been found to increase with age and there is therefore the possibility of comparing children's average T-unit length with the scores of language users of the same age in other studies. T-unit length has been shown to vary according to discourse mode and also according to individual author's styles (some famous authors write in very short T-units) so it is at best a partial measure. Nevertheless it is a helpful indicator, among others, of children's growing control of written language.

We were encouraged to use T-units as a measure by Carol Fox's successful use of them in her study of young children's oral narratives, which informed our data analysis at many points. At the same time we would echo Fox's warning that 'it is pointless to value syntactic complexity for its own sake'. During the project year, we found children's T-units were shorter in some pieces of later writing than in their 'baseline' samples. This was probably a response to the texts that we had introduced; by this time it was clear that both the texts chosen contained relatively short T-units. The children's results on this measure have to be read in the context of these facts.

4. Non-right-branching sentences

We have found this generally recognised indicator to be a useful reflection of increasing sophistication in writing. It is based on the fact that most sentences branch to the right, grammatically speaking. Where a non-right-branching sentence (like this one) is introduced, this is generally done for emphasis, which derives from the delaying of the main verb. Non-right-branching sentences are far more likely to be found in writing than in speech. We found that (with one notable exception) case study children did begin to use more non-right-branching sentences as their writing became more carefully crafted and took on influences from their reading of literature.

Scorable indicators
The following indicators were impression scored, rather than counted.

5. Narrative voice
We took this indicator from Genette, basing it on his question: 'Is the narrative voice maintained and does it include other voices?'. In Genette, this is of course a measure of mature writing. However, it is also an excellent means of assessing how far young writers have confidently taken on a narrator's role and are sufficiently in control of their text to maintain this role. The point of view from which a story is told influences everything about the selection of the material. Although many of the children's texts were told by a 'hidden, all-knowing, third-person narrator' (Fox 1993), several of their later texts, because of the literary texts which we introduced as models, were written from a particular viewpoint in first person. We believe that the adoption of a role of this kind, which involved them in writing in first person but not as themselves, was helpful to the children's development as writers; it obliged them to become much more conscious narrators, and more aware of the narrative voice they were adopting.

There was a clear development in children's later writing on this measure, but it was not an easy measure to score because of its three-part emphasis on a) the voice in which the narrative is told b) the maintaining of that voice and c) the way in which other voices are included in the narrator's voice. We asked our scorers to impression-mark, taking into account all three factors, on a scale of 1 to 6 (6 high).

6. Sense of a reader
Writers may indicate their awareness of readers in many ways, from a direct address to the reader on the one hand, to the way in which material is sequenced and introduced, in such a way as to take account of the reader's viewpoint, on the other. Sometimes the way in which writers omit information or leave 'gaps in the text' can also indicate their awareness of a reader, in that they are challenging the reader to fill in what is left out. We did not expect to find examples of this sophisticated kind of playing with

the reader in our case study children's texts, although we sometimes did see them beginning to do this. Our question to the scorers was modelled on Genette's question above, and was as follows: 'Does the writing indicate that the writer is aware of a reader and is catering for a reader's needs, and is this sense of a reader sustained throughout the piece?' We could of course have omitted the second half of this question, but the ability of a writer to keep a reader in mind throughout seemed a good indicator of the kind of growing control of a text that we were hoping to track through our study.

We asked the scorers to score on an impression scale of 1 to 6 where 1 indicated writing with little apparent awareness of a reader, and 6 indicated writing where the writer was evidently highly conscious of a reader and a reader's needs. We found most of our writers did develop a heightened sense of a reader in the course of the project. The reasons for this may partly be found in their reading, but must also derive from the ways in which their teachers helped them to work on their writing and to listen to their writing, as well as from the audience that was created for their writing in the classroom.

7. Literary turns of phrase

This indicator refers to literary conventions (of the 'once upon a time' variety) but also to phrases and parts of sentences which have a literary ring, in the most obvious sense. Children often experiment with literary sounding language, as part of taking on the role of writers. In the children's stories which she studied, Carol Fox noted examples of grammatical complexity which clearly derived from the writers striving after poetic and literary effects. Similarly, in our sample, we noted phrases such as 'The blazing sun shone down on us'; 'cold on the labyrinth floor'; 'the trees came down on him like hands reaching to get him'; 'we walked through the sunlight to the tunnel what seemed like heaven'. Although some of these examples are clearly experimental in character, we wanted to track how far children began to use more language of this consciously literary kind in their writing in the course of the project. Literary turns of phrase do not necessarily improve the writing, but they show children becoming more aware of language, using it more deliberately, and beginning to focus on style as well as content in their stories. We therefore again asked our scorers to score on an impression scale of 1 to 6 where 1 indicated writing with no obvious examples of literary turns of phrase, and 6 indicated writing where literary turns of phrase are to be found throughout.

8. Echoes

Although much of what the children wrote could be said to echo, directly or indirectly, writing that they had read and were familiar with, we did not use this indicator in every case. This might have led to speculation about the sources of the echoes that scorers thought they perceived in the writing, and what we wanted to track were echoes of texts that we knew they had read. We therefore only used this measure in relation to the standard texts which were introduced during the course of the project – which were Kevin Crossley-Holland's *The Green Children* and Henrietta Branford's *Fire, Bed and Bone*. This enabled us to look closely at how far children were drawing in their writing on these two models. We counted as echoes both what could be termed direct 'liftings' from the model, or phrases which were stylistically very close to the model. We asked the scorers to mark on a six point scale where 1 indicated writing with no very obvious echoes, and 6 indicated writing where echoes permeated the whole piece.

The results of assessing the work on these eight indicators are shown in the three tables below, which show both the countable and the scorable indicators. The tables refer to three sample pieces of work, one from the Autumn term (except in the case of Harry, for whom no narrative samples exist from the Autumn term); one from March or April in the Spring term, and one from the Summer term.

EARLY	No. 1 Breaks in time sequence	No. 2 Mental state verbs	No. 3 T-unit length (as range)	No. 4 NRB sentences	No. 5 Narrative voice	No.6 Sense of a reader	No. 7 Literary turns of phrase	No. 8 Echoes
EMILY	3	1	9/17	3	3	3	3	—
GRACE	3	8	8/28	0	4	3/4	2	—
SOPHIE	1	0	11/24	0	3	2	1/2	—
HARRY	1	6	14/37	4	3/4	3/4	2	—
JOE	3	3	11/30	1	4	4	2/3	—
YOSSIF	0	1	8/15	0	1/2	1/2	2	—

MIDDLE	No. 1 Breaks in time sequence	No. 2 Mental state verbs	No. 3 T-unit length (as range)	No. 4 NRB sentences	No. 5 Narrative voice	No.6 Sense of a reader	No. 7 Literary turns of phrase	No. 8 Echoes
EMILY	5	7	11/31	3	4/5	4/5	5	3/4
GRACE	5	11	8/18	2	5	5	4	4
SOPHIE	4	6	7/10	1	4/5	4	3	4/5
HARRY (not Green children)	0	3	12/31	3	4	3/4	3/4	—
JOE	2	0	7/16	0	4/5	4	4	3/4
YOSSIF (not Green children)	6	2	7/13	0	3/4	3/4	3	—

LATE	No. 1 Breaks in time sequence	No. 2 Mental state verbs	No. 3 T-unit length (as range)	No. 4 NRB sentences	No. 5 Narrative voice	No.6 Sense of a reader	No. 7 Literary turns of phrase	No. 8 Echoes
EMILY	2	2	11/30	2	4	4	4	—
GRACE	8	18	7/17	2	5/6	5/6	4	5/6
SOPHIE	4	2	10/22	0	6	6	5	6
HARRY	2	2	10/31	0	4	4	4	—
JOE	3	2	10/19	1	4	4/5	4	—
YOSSIF	0	2	8/16	3	5	4/5	5	5/6

Commentary

The tables show some general trends but also quite clearly indicate striking differences between individual writers in relation to certain indicators. In general they reveal a growing command of narrative, especially in relation to the way in which these young writers are learning to explore fictional worlds and the inner lives of characters. We will take each indicator one by one, and then discuss what they reveal as a whole.

1. Breaks in the time sequence

This proved to be a very helpful indicator, especially in the contrast that it highlighted between the children's writing in the earliest sample, and the writing that followed work on *The Green Children*. In the earliest samples few of the case study children included any descriptive or reflective pauses in their narratives. The main exceptions were Emily and Joe, who were writing the same type of mystery/suspense stories; in these cases the pauses clearly derived from the mystery genre that was informing their writing and were designed to build suspense. But in the middle piece, most children who wrote about *The Green Children* included more breaks in the time sequence in their writing. This seemed to indicate that children were writing about a much more fully imagined fictional world, very probably as a result of their involvement in the drama work around the book as well as because of their repeated readings of this powerful text. When Grace writes:

> *'I even remember what kind of day it was. The blazing sun shone down on us. The ground was hot like fire, it burnt my feet, until everything went quiet...'*

she is obviously really inhabiting the world of the story. She has a much fuller view of what is going on *around* the action, and can move about the fictional world more easily in imagination.

It is noteable in this middle piece that there is marked increase in breaks in the time sequence in the writing of all three girls, but not in that of the boys. In Emily's piece of writing 'The Return', the breaks in the time sequence occur when the narrator, the green girl, recounts what she was feeling as she returned to the green world:

> *'at that moment I was feeling very scared because there was water dripping like the howling of wolves and it was dark, damp and very cold.'*

and

> *'for some strange reason one half of me felt happy and the other sad because I wished my brother was here so he could have made home as well.'*

Here, the breaks in the time sequence occur as Emily explores the character's feelings more fully, again imagining from the inside how it feels to be in this situation, and registering complex emotions.

In the final piece of writing there are, in general, more breaks in the time sequence than in the first piece in both the boys' writing and that of the girls. Sophie, writing in the role of the cat in *Fire, Bed and Bone*, draws on the original source text in order to create her own new version. The first chapter of *Fire, Bed and Bone* sets the scene for what is to come, and so is full of reflection and description, as is Sophie's narrative. Sophie's writing is full of echoes of Branford's text, but her invented passages are all in the spirit of the original, and fill out the quiet scene of a house asleep:

> *'The strange howls echo through my ears. I snuggle up to my tail hoping the dog will come and lie against me.'*

Both Harry (for almost the first time) and Joe include breaks in the time sequence in their Marie Celeste stories, again as part of building atmosphere and creating the world of the story more fully. Joe even signals that he is aware of one of these descriptive pauses:

> *'Men were stealing from people, one tried to steal Tommy's, but he just smacked them and clipped them around the ear and said get lost! and they ran a mile and a half away from him. But that's going off the point.'*

In the case of Joe, Harry and Emily, who are writing the first chapter of a longer mystery story, breaks in the time sequence naturally occur as a build-up to what is to come:

> *'Joe felt lonely, as his friends had disturbed him, so he decided to write in his diary. He felt a bit tired so he lay on his bunk with a glass of water next to him...'*

Breaks in the time sequence were a good indicator of a growing maturity in the case study children's writing, because they so clearly showed when children had begun to 'live through' the narrative and inhabit their own fictions more fully. They also demonstrated these young writers' growing awareness of the need to build a fictional world for a reader, and to fill in the *background* of the action as well as simply telling the story.

2. Mental state verbs
The number of mental state verbs in the children's texts increased, although not uniformly, across the three samples. Again, this increase was more

striking in the girls' writing than in that of the boys, and there was a bigger jump between the early and the middle piece than between the middle piece and the late piece of writing. The striking increase in mental state verbs in the middle piece of writing seems most likely to derive from the fact that the children had all been involved in drama work around *The Green Children*, and had therefore literally been 'putting themselves in the place' of characters in the story. When Emily writes:

> 'I thought I heard the voice of my lost brother telling me the way home, he said to follow the sunlight, I thought my mind was playing games with me, but I was wrong'

she is recounting an actual episode from the drama that her class created.

The incidence of mental state verbs might also, of course, partly be a consequence of the fact that, both in the work on *The Green Children* and in the work that related to *Fire, Bed and Bone*, children were often writing in role as first person narrators, and thus reporting on their own thoughts and responses. However, we can demonstrate that this is not necessarily so by looking at the case of Sophie, who wrote as a first person narrator in her first piece of writing and included no mental state verbs at all, whereas she included 6 and 2 in the later pieces of writing. In general, mental state verbs seem to indicate that writers are paying more attention to characters' responses, thoughts and feelings; they are a good indicator of a writer who is strongly imagining the inner lives of characters.

One writer who appeared to have a marked sense of the inner worlds of her characters was Grace, in whose work the number of mental state verbs rose steadily from 8 in her first piece, to 11 and 18 in her second and third pieces of writing. Grace is quite explicitly concerned with what goes on inside her characters and, in writing in role, refers constantly to their thoughts and feelings:

> 'I was confused. Most people thought it was their imagination, but I knew it was real. I saw her, I will never forget that moment, and I'll always wonder what she was and where she was from'.

Even in the piece of writing based on *Fire, Bed and Bone*, where the Henrietta Branford text contains few mental state verbs, and where other case study writers show only a slight increase in mental state verbs, Grace's piece registers an extraordinary 18. She is a writer who has a very strong sense of inner states of mind in her invented characters.

Mental state verbs are a very important indicator that writers are beginning to get inside the heads of their characters and to appreciate that fiction is not all about actions and events out in the world. D.H.Lawrence once said:

> *'It was really George Eliot who started it all…it was she who started putting all the action inside. Before, you know, with Fielding and the others, it had been outside.'* (E.T. 1935)

In modern writing much of the action does 'happen inside'; these young writers were beginning to realise the power they had to explore the inner as well as the outer worlds of fiction.

3. T-Units

In choosing to include T-units as a measure of growing maturity in writing, we were very conscious of the problematic nature of this indicator. We were aware that a measure of syntactic complexity was not necessarily a measure of quality of writing. Lengthening T-units do not necessarily indicate that a child's writing is getting 'better', although it is true that children do write longer T-units as they get older. Different types of writing may produce different lengths of T-units (and, as it happened, our samples illustrated this quite dramatically).

A T-unit is made up of a main clause together with all its dependent clauses and coordinated clauses. Here is an example of a particularly long T-unit from Harry's first sample 'Down the Drain':

> *Kevin saw everything and ran as fast as he could (which is not very fast because of the size of his legs) back to his mum and dad, told them everything, and darted back to the house.*

This was one of the longest T-units in all the samples (37 words).

We thought that this measure might reveal something about changes in the children's writing and so we carried out a T-unit analysis of the sample texts. This produced some interesting findings. In most cases, average T-unit length was relatively constant through the three sample pieces. Children seemed to write in characteristically different T-unit lengths: for instance, Harry's T-units were characteristically longer than most other children's, while Grace's and Yossif's were shorter. These three children's average T-unit lengths did not vary a great deal. (In the tables, T-unit range is shown, rather than average T-unit length.)

Harry was a particularly interesting case study because his writing seemed to show different influences from those of the other children. Habitually he wrote texts which were surrealistic in character and which were strongly action- and plot-oriented. The narrative drive of these stories, in which there were few reflective pauses and everything contributed to the build-up of the action, was striking and the stories communicated considerable energy and momentum. This was reflected in the length of his T-units, which in the first and second samples averaged 13.9 and 12.2, much the longest of any other child in the sample. Harry obviously relished the build-up of language in his stories:

> *Later they faced many more dangers, including spike pits, flaming volcanoes, falling rocks, and maybe one of the most savage, deadly, torturous things you could imagine, tickle boxes.* (Sample 2, 1 T-unit, 28 words).

In his third sample of writing, however, an extract from a more conventional mystery story based on the story of the Marie Celeste, which was written according to a plan being developed by the whole class, Harry's style changes, becoming in several ways less assured, and his average T-unit length is considerably shorter.

Sophie's work showed marked changes in T-unit length. In her earliest sample, the average T-unit length was 11.1, and in her last sample it was 10.5. But in her middle sample, based on *The Green Children*, the T-unit length fell dramatically, to 6.1. This was a striking change, but seemed fully explicable in the light of the text she was basing her writing on. Kevin Crossley-Holland's style in this book is plain and speech-based, sentences are short and simple. The average T-unit length of a sample page from *The Green Children,* when analysed, proved to be 6.6, not so very different from Sophie's average. It seemed clear that Sophie, in modelling her style on that of Crossley-Holland, was responding to these very short T-units. A very similar effect was found in Joe's samples, whose T-unit averages were 10.8 and 10.1 in his early and late samples, but only 7 in the *Green Children-*related sample. We must again conclude that this writer was mirroring, perhaps not even consciously, Crossley-Holland's style.

These examples demonstrate that T-unit length is interesting, not because of what it shows about progress in writing (overall the children's mean T-unit lengths did not rise across the three samples) but because of what it can reveal about a child's stylistic competence and responsiveness to the style of different authors and genres.

4. Non-right-branching sentences

Non-right-branching sentences are sentences where the main verb or main clause is delayed, because the sentence begins with a subordinate clause or phrase:

> *In an abandoned boat behind a house, lived a family of small people.*
> (Harry)
> *As Guy and I walked through the sunlight, we started to spin around...*
> (Emily)

This type of sentence is characteristic of writing rather than speech, and in particular of more literary writing; it is a piece of deliberate shaping which has the effect of delaying the point of the sentence, in a way which sometimes gives a dramatic effect. Of all the case study children, Emily and Harry used the most non-right-branching sentences in their three samples (Emily: 3, 3, 2; Harry: 4, 3, 0). Yossif, the least experienced writer in English, did not use this type of sentence until his last sample (based on *The Green Children*) which contained 3 such sentences. This is an interesting finding, as this retelling is a major breakthrough for Yossif, who has remembered much of the wording and many of the cadences of the Crossley-Holland text. The sudden appearance of non-right-branching sentences in this sample seems to signal that Yossif can now adopt, under the influence of this text, a much more literary style.

Scorable indicators
5. Narrative voice

To see the extraordinary leaps that some children made in the course of the research period one has only to compare Grace's early chatty first person narration, close to speech and somewhat breathless:

> *My name's Niome I'm going to tell you a very weird story. I was sitting down in the class I had finished all my work I was reading a very boring book so instead I looked out of the window like most children in the class do.*

With her final sample, in role as the hunting dog from *Fire, Bed and Bone*, where the narrative voice is so much more assured and measured. Here the role of the mother dog is sustained throughout and the rhythm of the prose reflects the shifts of her troubled thoughts:

> *I want Fleabane to join me. I want him to leave the wild. But what if he doesn't want to? What if he wants to stay here in the wild where he has been brought up? I guess he would call this home. I won't let it happen. I have lost both my other two puppies, I shall not lose Fleabane.*

We asked scorers to pay particular attention to the children's ability to *maintain* the narrative voice and viewpoint that they were adopting in the piece of writing. In the case of writing in role, it was clear that this also reflected their ability to sustain the role and write from within a chosen character. Where the role they had assumed was that of an adult (or a more mature persona, such as the hunting dog), this was reflected in their writing, which was notably more confident and controlled.

Of the six case study children, three were judged to have made significant progress on this measure, but three made less progress. These were all children from School E, where in the Summer term the teachers chose not to use the second 'standard' text, *Fire, Bed and Bone*, but instead spent a significant part of the term working with their classes on a long story in chapters, based on the legend of the Marie Celeste. This writing task made considerable, organisational demands on the children and also obliged them to work within a tightly predetermined framework. Perhaps because of this, the children's writing in this third term seemed less confident, both in terms of the narrative voice they adopted and in respect of other measures.

6. Sense of a reader

Some of the children's work showed a startling improvement in this area. Yossif's scores on this measure, for instance, advanced steadily throughout the year, as he became a more confident writer of English, learning to use it to tell stories for a listener or reader. From the beginning of the year it was clear that Yossif readily took up the role of the storyteller:

> *Once upon a time there was an old man that wanted to have a child he then*
> *a wood boy and after painted the wood boy the man went to sleep.*
> *In the night a angel appeared and give the boy that called Pinocchio life and*
> *Pinocchio went to wake up his dad*

In this piece of writing Yossif is sequencing the story with care and introducing important information *(the boy that called Pinocchio)* for the reader. But he has not enough command of written English to control the ensuing dialogue or to do more than recount the bare details of the narrative. By the Summer term, however, in retelling *The Green Children*, Yossif has internalised so much of the language and rhythm of Crossley-Holland's text that he can not only retell the story but introduce his own variations on the original, laying out the text in the same style and maintaining the storytelling tone and sense of a reader which makes this such a good text for reading aloud:

> *I ran away because I was scared of the people Guy found me and put a*
> *flower in my hand.*
> *He made me warm, comfortable and confident.*
> *We went back home and we danced altogether.*

Other children also made outstanding progress on this measure, notably Sophie, whose scores rose from 2, to 4, to 6 in the final piece of writing based on *Fire, Bed and Bone*. In her first piece of writing, she bounces through the story in straightforward recount mode:

The aeroplane landed we all got off the plane and made our way to the villa. The next morning we all put on our swim suits grabbed the pool key and a towel and we dived in the lovely swimming (pool) outside our villa. A strange man appeared at the swimming pool gate put his hand through the gate got our pool key and ran off with it.

But in her final piece of writing, Sophie, in role as Humble the Cat, slows the pace of her writing, which – like that of Henrietta Branford – is designed in this chapter to set a scene and create an atmosphere, while at the same time introducing essential information to the reader. Her progress is striking; this piece seems to be the work of a much more mature writer:

I heard the Wolves again last night, howling at the tops of their voices, long and loud big and bold.
I lay with shivers all over my body
I went out to my secret hunting field just now, I stayed out there for ages. I came in through the window, like the ghost of the cat next door, whose life was meant to end.
I've come in for warmth and comfort by the fire and up against the dog.

It should be noted that these two measures, 'narrative voice' and 'sense of a reader', were closely related and sometimes overlapping; assessing the children's writing in relation to them was a question of shifting focus rather than assessing completely different aspects of the writing.

7. Literary turns of phrase

All of the children's work showed that they made more use of literary turns of phrase in their writing as the year went on. But, as previously suggested, literary turns of phrase are not always a sign of good writing. In the case study children's texts it was often clear that such phrases and expressions were a sign of self-conscious literariness. When Emily, for instance, writing as the green girl, described a journey through the tunnel between two worlds, her writing became highly coloured, and her choice of expressions was sometimes unintentionally funny:

Guy felt like an ice cube with his arm round me, Guy and I took another step when all of a sudden I felt the warm breeze slicing through my skin and the green breeze swooping over me.

Children in Emily's school were strongly encouraged to use similes and metaphors in their writing and to seek out striking verbs and adjectives. The focus on the surface texture of writing often seemed to detract from the meaning of what they wrote.

8. Echoes

We decided to judge how far children's writing was echoing the work of the texts that they had read only in relation to the 'standard' texts that we introduced into the project schools. However, this measure was helpful in that it enabled us to track children's growing ability to draw on a literary source and to take on the style and tune of a text they knew well. By far the most striking examples of this came in the third term in the work of the children who read and worked on *Fire, Bed and Bone*. The children who wrote in relation to this text did so very confidently and responsively, picking up on the rhythms and patterns of Henrietta Branford's prose. The example from Sophie's writing in role as Humble the Cat, quoted in section 6 above, provides ample evidence of this.

Conclusion

The data analysis gave some objective means of pinning down our subjective impressions of the aspects of children's writing which improved in the course of the year, and enabled us to relate some of these improvements to the texts they had been reading. It confirmed the important part that these texts had played in moving children on in their writing. The exercise enabled us to demonstrate the value that writing in role had for most of the children, and how it had enabled them to move into areas of language that they might not so easily have had access to in writing in their own personae. It enabled us to recognise the importance of T-units as one measure of syntactical maturity in writing, while also clearly showing that growing maturity in writing need not always correlate with longer T-units.

In general we think that these indicators, both countable and scorable, have been shown through this small-scale study to be of some value in assessing children's progress and development as writers. But we hope that it is also clear that these are *research* indicators, rather than features which children can be directly taught to use in order to improve their writing. There is currently much anxiety about children's attainment in writing, yet some of the means of improving writing which are being promoted in schools are not always likely to achieve their intended aims. Our experience in this project suggests that the direct teaching of particular features of prose – for instance, an emphasis on the use of adjectives or of similes – is less likely to produce good writing than is a close focus on the meanings that children want to express, a discussion of their texts especially at the draft stage, or – more indirectly – the regular reading and discussion of literature of quality.

General Conclusions

What we learned

Our study took as its starting point the way in which teachers, children and literary texts come together in classrooms, and the kinds of benefits that there can be when teachers and children draw on and learn from these texts as they work on writing. We need in conclusion to ask ourselves whether the time and effort involved in the project was worth while and what we learned from our investigations.

We think that we have been able to establish a clear link between children's involvement with literary texts and their development as writers. We have shown these influences at work, both in the case studies of individual children and in the analysis of samples of their writing. Some of the tools used in this analysis have proved particularly useful in pinning down what kinds of changes indicate progress in writing.

We found children learning many things about how writing works through the attentive reading of literature and its discussion in their classrooms. Their writing during the year has offered ample evidence of their growing ability to write from inside a fictional situation, to pick up on literary styles and rhythms, to imagine a reader, and to work to influence a reader's response.

All of the case study children improved measurably as writers, as judged by their teachers' assessments on CLPE writing scale 2, in the course of the project year.

All case study children, CLPE Writing Scale 2 Oct 98 - July 99

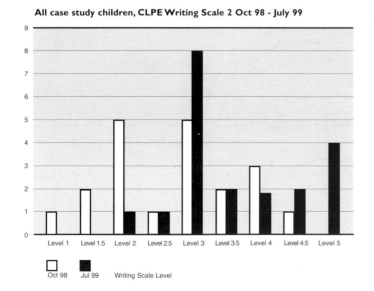

□ Oct 98   ■ Jul 99   Writing Scale Level

At the beginning of the year, half of the 18 case study children were assessed at levels 1 and 2 on writing scale 2, but by the end of the year the great majority (13) of children were assessed at levels 3 and above. This was a major shift and signalled a growing ability in most children to structure their writing, to write for a reader, and to choose their language and shape their texts more consciously. The progress of the six 'core' case study children was tracked in more detail through the data analysis process described in chapter 7. The outcomes of this exercise showed the progress that most children had made in the course of the year and also indicated those cases where children had made exceptional progress. Sophie, for instance, was assessed as having moved up two levels on writing scale 2.

Two of the other children who made exceptional progress were the bilingual pupils in our core case studies. Grace, the fully fluent bilingual pupil, improved markedly as a writer, as judged in relation to most of the indicators used in our data analysis. Her ability to sustain a narrative voice, and to maintain a sense of a reader, for instance, developed strikingly during the year. Grace's progress is in line with other findings about the relationship between children's linguistic background and their achievements in literacy (for instance the ILEA Research and Statistics Branch found that fully fluent bilinguals were among the highest scorers on the CLPE Reading Scale 2, [ILEA,1990]). Yossif, the inexperienced bilingual child in our sample, made excellent progress during the year, moving up from level 2 to level 3 on the writing scale, and improving dramatically in relation to the data analysis indicators. These findings underline the importance to children for whom English is an additional language of the kind of opportunities for learning made available in these project classrooms, and the particular value of literary texts in their learning of English.

Drama and role in writing development

This research project was conceived of, from the start, as one where the Project Coordinator would be an active participant in classrooms, as well as an observer. She would support teachers, especially in their work of implementing the National Literacy Strategy. The interventions she made, and particularly the introduction of two texts for study in project classrooms, generally proved positive experiences for teachers and children alike. We observed teachers' growing assurance as they saw children becoming more involved in the texts they were introducing, and as they saw them drawing on these powerful reading experiences in their writing. During the year, our observations of teachers' pedagogical approaches enabled us to begin to define what was happening in those classrooms where the teaching of writing was most effective.

One of the our key findings relates to the way in which drama can provide a strikingly immediate route into a fictional situation and help teachers and children to explore texts in an active way. We are convinced that the work on *The Green Children* was a watershed in the project; in most classrooms it led to writing which was thoroughly imagined and qualitatively different from what had gone before. This finding has implications for the place of drama in the English curriculum, and points to the value of enabling children to 'live through' fictions by involving them in different forms of enactment.

Similarly, at various points in this book we have drawn attention to the value of writing in role in children's writing development. Where children are writing in role, out of a fictional situation which they have been able to explore and discuss thoroughly, they are able to access areas of language and feeling that they might not normally be thought to be aware of. Writing in role seemed to be a way of developing and building on children's insights into the human experiences that fictions are based on. Often in this kind of writing children seemed to be 'trying on' mature experience, thinking their way into the responsibilities, cares, joys and griefs of adulthood. The writing in role offered them the opportunity of becoming, in the words of Vygotsky's description of dramatic play, 'a head taller'.

Both drama and writing in role were used in all the schools in the project as ways of entering imaginatively into the worlds of literary texts. The texts themselves provided the impetus for this work. The 'standard' texts that were introduced into the project schools offered children all the satisfactions of story but also allowed them to experience different ways of telling a story. We chose books which would have a dramatic impact when read aloud; both texts were by well-known children's writers and both were stylistically interesting.

At the end of the project, when we came to reflect on the year at more length, we were taken aback to realise that we had offered the project schools two books which were first-person narratives (told in very different voices). This was not a planned thing; we had simply judged these books to be powerful texts which would speak to most children. But by drawing attention in this way to the *version* of the story that is being told, to issues of viewpoint, stance, and voice, we had obviously highlighted a central question in fiction, the relationship between the teller and what is being told. As children went on to explore these stories from different imagined viewpoints they became part of a dialogue with the text and with the author, entering the world of the story, and taking on a narrator's voice and role.

By the end of the research year we were in a position to reply to our research questions as follows:

1. Research Question 1
What do children take from their reading of literary texts, and how do we know?

Our study tracked the way in which children's writing was influenced by literary texts in a number of ways:
a) Through case studies of particular children we looked closely at the influence of children's reading on their writing. We observed the progress of their writing during the whole year of the project, drawing on a wide range of writing samples.
b) By introducing two particular texts to all the classes in our study we were able to study the effect of these texts on children's writing right across our cohort and to arrive at generalisations about what they were taking from these texts.
c) We used samples of writing from three points in the project year to carry out a detailed analysis of our case study children's progress and the linguistic, stylistic and narrative changes in their writing.

Some of our findings have already been reported in the data analysis chapter (Chapter 7); this chapter summarises the main findings from all of our sources of evidence.

i) Moving into new areas of language
Perhaps the main effect of children's reading of literary texts was that it encouraged them to write differently, moving out of what might be termed their 'home style' into new areas of language. Frequently they did this by taking on the language of the text that they had been reading, and echoes of that text could then be found in their writing. We found children picking up on the rhythms and patterns of texts in ways that were easily trackable (eg picking up on T-unit length). All children, even those with special needs, seemed capable of picking up in this way on the language of a text and of adopting a more literary style, *especially if they were made familiar with the text through their teacher's reading aloud*.

ii) Writing in first person in role
Some of the work that children did in response to the standard texts we introduced involved children in writing in first person, but not as them-selves. It was evident from our samples that this kind of first person writing extended children's range as writers. Writing in first person was something that children did readily in any case; such writing, because it is

close to speech, seems more accessible to children. But writing *in first person and in role* produced quite different kinds of texts from their normal first-person writing. This experience helped children to assume different voices and enter areas of language that they did not normally use.

iii) Further observations on writing in role
In general, taking on a different viewpoint and writing in role seemed to be a powerful stimulus for children's writing. As children wrote in role, usually as a character within a story, they were learning to see the events of a narrative from a particular viewpoint and to write from a different perspective from their own. This led them to write from more 'inside' the story, to identify with very different characters, and to explore the mental states of these characters more fully.

iv) Becoming more confident managers of narrative
As children became more sophisticated writers of narrative, they learned to explore the world of a story more fully, and to keep a reader in mind. Overall, data analysis showed case study children gaining more control over their narratives and imagining their invented worlds in more detail. In the course of the project year their samples showed them taking on a narrative voice more confidently and developing a heightened sense of a reader and of a reader's needs.

Research Question 2
How far do certain classroom practices support children in learning about writing from literary texts?

We drew on a number of different sources of information in order to address this question:
a) We surveyed teachers' views of their practice in teaching writing by means of a questionnaire, and followed this up with individual interviews.
b) Classroom observation enabled us to look closely at the ways in which teachers drew on literary texts in teaching writing.
c) The individual case studies enabled us to trace the effects of certain pedagogical approaches on children's progress in writing.
d) Finally, by introducing drama as a way of exploring Kevin Crossley-Holland's *The Green Children*, we were able to observe and document the impact of this kind of teaching approach on children's subsequent writing around the text.

We identified the following six approaches as being particularly effective in supporting children's learning:

i) Reading aloud was an important feature of most of the classrooms in our study

The teachers in these classrooms believed strongly in the value of continuing to read aloud to older children and regarded this as an important way in which they could bring texts alive for them and engage them with literature. In some classrooms where children were inexperienced as readers and writers, a particularly strong emphasis was put on *re*reading. Although sometimes children had copies of the text being read aloud, quite often they did not. Reading aloud seemed to be a particularly helpful way of foregrounding the tunes and rhythms of a text in a way that subsequently influenced children's writing. In most of these classrooms children were visibly engaged in reading aloud sessions. Reading aloud was a powerful prelude to the subsequent discussion of texts.

ii) Discussions around a text helped children to articulate aesthetic responses to the writing

Reading aloud sessions were generally followed by and accompanied by discussions of the text. In the majority of classrooms these discussions were very skilfully handled by teachers, who were able to involve most of the class in responding to the text in some way. Children's initial personal responses were not cut off but were welcomed and then built on. Characteristic of the most effective practice was the way in which teachers moved children via these personal and affective responses to texts towards more aesthetic and critical responses, leading them to look more closely at what writers were doing.

iii) Drama work around texts led to strongly imagined writing in role

The drama work around *The Green Children* led to powerful writing in role in most of the classes in the project. One important feature of the drama work was the delaying of the introduction of the text itself until some aspect of the fictional world had been prefigured through drama. This had a big impact on the children, who seemed to relate much more closely and personally to this text because they had already 'lived through' some of its events and situations.

Following the drama work and the reading of the text, most children wrote in role as a character within the story. This writing in role was almost universally well done and sometimes marked a step forward in their work. Children seemed to have been helped to enter the world of the story by the role play within the drama. This piece of writing sometimes led to a shift in the case study children's writing; for instance children filled in more imagined detail around the narrative, in a way that had obviously been encouraged by the drama. Writing in role seemed to be, as already reported, a real aid to children's progress as writers.

iv) Some approaches to planning writing were especially helpful to children

Classroom observation suggested that the most effective teachers helped children to plan their writing in ways that were supportive but not overly formulaic. In general, in these classrooms, where children were offered ways of planning it was through 'open structures' which did not require them to over-plan. Sometimes 'planning' was simply done by encouraging children to reflect on and reread a text (such as the first chapter of *Fire, Bed and Bone*) which then became a starting point for their own piece of writing (for instance writing about the same situation from a different viewpoint).

v) Building in response and collaboration

Effective teachers put a great deal of emphasis on encouraging children to work on their writing together, for instance through the use of response partners or writing partners. Lessons were structured in such a way as to allow time for children to read their texts aloud to a partner, and to respond to each other's writing. The use of pairs was more common than the use of small groups for this kind of collaborative work on writing.

In the two classrooms in the study where the children's writing was particularly strong, there was less emphasis on the display and publication of children's work, and more emphasis on the sharing and discussion of their drafts and completed texts. In these classrooms a more responsive and exploratory attitude to writing was encouraged through the regular discussion of children's work in progress. 'Publishing' was more likely to take the form of public reading.

vi) Effecting 'positive transformations' in the Literacy Hour

Teachers in the project were all implementing the literacy strategy but most had some reservations about its effectiveness in relation to the teaching of writing at KS2. There was a general feeling that there was not enough time for extended writing within the Literacy Hour and in the course of the year teachers made other provision for extended writing, often establishing writers' workshops outside the hour on one or two occasions in the week. In addition, teachers continued to put emphasis on reading aloud to children, as well as on reading with a shared text. Some teachers felt there was a danger of the literacy strategy leading to a superficial approach to text work, with different texts becoming a focus in successive weeks. These teachers therefore chose to look at a few texts in more depth.

Research Question 3
Are the experiences which help children to develop as writers the same as those which help them to develop as readers?

Our third question was more difficult to answer. Our work on writing was so time-consuming that there was not enough time to look as closely at children's progress in reading during the project year. But although we amassed less evidence of children's progress in reading in the course of the project year, we did gather some. In particular we collected lists of the case study children's reading and interviewed them about their reading. We interviewed teachers about children's progress as readers as well as writers, and gathered evidence of their judgements of children's progress on the PLR reading and writing scales. We collected some reading samples from teachers in the project to put alongside the many samples of writing that we were gathering.

This evidence suggested strongly that children's reading was developing alongside their writing and that their progress in writing was informing their progress in reading. This was indicated by, in particular, teachers' observations on children's reading samples towards the end of the year that they were:

'enjoying the style of a text'

'able to identify that the narrative was in the first person and eager to discuss the thoughts and feelings of the character'

'involved with the text – "becomes" main character'

'very keen to talk about the different structures of poems'

'discuss(ing) the use of phrases to engage the reader'.

These kinds of comments provide insights into children's growing sense of how texts are made and their awareness of authors at work. With more time in classrooms we would have liked to document more fully the way in which children's progress in reading might be related to their growing confidence and competence as writers.

Research Question 4
What kinds of literary texts are particularly supportive to children learning to write?

In the course of the project year we observed teachers introducing a wide range of texts to children, and we discussed their selection with them. In addition, by engaging in a selection process to choose two texts to introduce to all of the classes in the project, we identified some features of texts which would support children as writers. We interviewed children about their reading and writing, and asked them what they felt they were learning about writing from their reading. We also gathered lists of books that were read with all the classes in the project and lists of books read by individual case study children. Through this kind of observation we formed a view about the kinds of texts which were especially supportive to children as apprentice writers.

i) Traditional tales

Texts with strong clear narrative structures, such as traditional or folk tales, were helpful to all children, and especially to children for whom English was an additional language. In several of the classrooms visited in the project children had been introduced to books of traditional tales such as *Cric Crac Stories, Hansel and Gretel, Psyche and Eros, Cinderella* and *Aesop's Fables*. We agreed with Carol Fox's view that folktales have a particularly important role to play in children's narrative education, providing a bridge from oracy to literacy for young children. Stories like these demonstrate particularly clearly the patterns and structures of narrative, and we found children remembering and using these patterns in their own writing.

ii) Poeticised speech

Kevin Crossley-Holland's *The Green Children*, one of our 'standard' texts, was a first person narrative with a strong oral quality, and a plain yet poetic style. It seemed to exemplify literary language as 'poeticised speech' (Olson, 1996), yet it was simple enough to be accessible to the whole ability range and to children who were learning English. We chose this text for all these features, and for its very strong and involving story. We found children echoing the style of this text in a very marked way in their own writing. Their engagement with this story in the drama workshops, and in the subsequent writing around the text, made them thoroughly familiar with its tunes and rhythms.

iii) Emotionally powerful texts

Several of the texts to which children were introduced in the course of the year dealt with powerful emotional experiences. For instance, *The Green Children* could be read as a story about cultural and racial difference, and about prejudice. *The Lion and the Unicorn* is a story about a child evacuee in the second world war, and explores his feelings of loneliness, fear and inadequacy. *The Wreck of the Zanzibar* tells the story of painful divisions in a family, and of a small community in the Scilly Isles struggling for survival. *Fire, Bed and Bone* is a book with many important themes; it is set at the time of the Peasants' Revolt, and raises issues of social equality and political action. The dog-narrator is preoccupied with trying to hold together a 'family' which includes her own pups and her human owners.

Texts with these kinds of emotionally powerful themes communicated immediately with children in the classes we visited. They moved children and led to valuable discussions of the human situations they dealt with, discussions during which children talked in very mature ways about their responses and reactions. Although it is not so easy to measure or track the effect of this kind of experience on children's writing, it is likely that emotionally powerful texts of this kind helped children to adopt other points of view, and to explore the inner states of characters, more readily. To show this, and to demonstrate that not only the case study children wrote well in response to such texts, we have included a selection of examples of writing about *Fire, Bed and Bone* as Appendix 4.

Conclusion

None of these texts would have had so much impact on the children, we were convinced, if they had not been mediated to them by the teacher and brought to life through skilful reading aloud. The project teachers' conviction of the importance of reading aloud, in both the teaching of literature and the teaching of writing, was endorsed by the writer Susan Price in a conference at CLPE which marked the end of the project. Price emphasised the value of folk stories, in particular, in learning written language: 'I've learned more from folk story and folk ballad than I've ever learned from any other kind of language'. She was convinced of the power of traditional stories to help children as writers, emphasising that 'the more these stories are told to children, the more they begin to see how a story is built up'. She stressed how much she herself had learnt about narrative from becoming familiar with folk stories and their structures: 'I learnt it not by thought or by study but by constant reading and listening to folk story'.

The teachers' skilful reading aloud made these authors' voices resonate in classrooms. As they read to them, they were developing what Ted Hughes (1997) calls 'the audial imagination'. Hughes, in discussing how we remember poetry, suggests that the 'audial memory' picks up on the patterns of meaning and sound in a text, experiencing them almost as a 'current of syntactical force'. 'What is essential', he writes, in relation to the memorising of verse, 'is to keep the audial faculty wide open, and not so much look at the words as listen for them – listen as widely, deeply and keenly as possible, testing every whisper of air in the echo-chamber of your whole body'. The giving of voice and breath to a text, instead of leaving it inertly as marks on a page, is an essential way of communicating the full range of its force and meaning.

By their readings, teachers therefore showed children how the texts could sound, and also underlined their meanings. And it was clear that the most effective teachers did the same for children's own writing when they read it back to them, using all of their interpretative skills to do so. As James Britton remarks, working on a text 'above all involves listening to it'. In these classrooms children's ability to listen to their own texts thoughtfully and critically was being strongly developed.

So many interesting and imaginative texts were generated during the project year in response to the texts being read, that it is difficult to select one to end this report. Yet it does seem right that the last item should be a piece of children's writing in role which exemplifies some of the qualities of imaginative inwardness discussed above, and elsewhere in this book. Here then again, in conclusion, is Grace writing in role as the mother dog from *Fire, Bed and Bone*:

FIRE, BED AND BONE

Glancing at the dark stagnant heavens
Watching a gazing star,
pass by.

Watching the swishing tree,
swaying in the night like a
Hand reaching out for me.

The wind howling,
It was
Talking.

Hearing rain hitting the rocky path way,
hitting it like a
ball bouncing off the ground.

I lifted my ears,
I could hear every drop.

Lying on the soft hay.
Listening to the glowing sparkling fire,
ticking away.

I feel the night breeze,
the window is open.

Mumble climbs through the open window,
she curls up beside me,
soft as smoke.

She has come for the
warmth.

The children fidget in their sleep.
Only Alice the baby is awake,
Listening to me.

Rufus snores in his sleep,
Grindecobbe grunts.

All is still, I can no longer,
Keep my eyes open.
I need to rest.
Tomorrow,
Is the day.

APPENDIX ONE

The Green Children:
Learning through drama

Summary of a report by
Susanna Steele and Fiona Collins

Before exploring *The Green Children*, the folk tale by Kevin Crossley-Holland, through more formal approaches, each of the research classes took part in a drama workshop that would prepare them for reading this new text. Two experienced drama practitioners, Susanna Steele and Fiona Collins, worked for a morning, in three schools each, with children and their teachers. The framework for the sessions was planned jointly, but the implementation reflected the individual approach of each practitioner. In all of the schools there was little experience of drama as a learning medium, so there was the additional aim of introducing a range of drama skills and techniques in relation to the reading and writing to follow. The lessons were planned so as to introduce the children to the language of the text, and to give them a first-hand experience of an imagined world, which they could link to their own experience.

Introduction

The triggering of an affective response is essential to the study of literature and it can be elusive for many children when the text is approached only in formal ways. Working with drama prior to reading a text can develop an engagement with the characters and events that can inform, sustain and enrich children's commitment both to investigating the language, form and structure of the text and their subsequent writing. Drama offers an interactive way of working that enables children to use their own knowledge, understanding and experience in conjunction with the events in the narrative. The emphasis is on collaborative work using individual, group and whole class strategies that enable children to bring their understanding to the text initially in an active rather than a discursive way.

The preparation for a piece of work enables a honing of ideas and attitudes and a selecting of what it will be appropriate to present. The process of drama entails three interdependent elements: making, performing and responding. The discussion and negotiation that take place between children establishes the focus for both the form and the content of the work. Whether they are working individually, in groups, or as a whole class children need to know what is expected of them. As drama-in-education is not free-flow role-play but focused work, each task needs to have clearly defined aims and structures that support children into working creatively and imaginatively within clearly set parameters. The structures that the children will use need to be planned in relation to their age and experience in drama work. In presenting everyday encounters between characters as an improvisation, children will draw on the transactional language appropriate for such a meeting. However, if what is to be explored is the inner thoughts and feelings of characters, then other strategies can be employed which will require the expression of these, 'thought tracking' for instance, where it is the inner voices that are spoken.

The move from preparatory discussion to enactment marks the point at which the children move into the 'here and now' mode of drama. Enactment requires children to 'know' where they are by being able to visualise the setting; to have an understanding of the characters and to imagine how they would respond in the situation; and to use language and silence, gesture, movement and expression, the language of theatre, to convey their intended meaning. In taking on the roles of the characters in the story, the children are not required to become the characters, but to use their understanding and experience of the real world within the context of the imagined reality of the text, exploring possibilities inherent in the encounters that take place. Drama enables children to participate in meaning making by giving them first-hand experience in the imagined world.

Priority is often given to the value of enactment in developing children's language. Whilst children can gain confidence in expressing ideas during drama work and are able to draw on a range of language registers, the visual aspect of drama is also of key importance. Meaning is not carried solely through language. It is also carried visibly. The physical relationship between characters, expressions and gestures contribute layers of meaning that are not necessarily available through spoken language. In presenting a 'freeze-frame' of a significant moment of an event, for instance, what can be shown can exceed what it is possible to express through language.

By observing each other's work and talking about what is being represented, children come to understand more broadly how it is possible to respond differently to the same event. The quality of teacher intervention at this point, both within and outside the drama, is crucial in extending the children's ability to understand and reflect on what they have created. It is through reflective discussion on what is seen as well as on what is heard that children can come to more complex understanding of both characters and events.

Susanna Steele at Schools A, C and E

In each of the schools the session began with the children being encouraged to create their vision of a village and what might happen there as a way into the story of the Green Children. At School A there was very little sense at first of rural or agricultural life, but in subsequent discussions the children were able to describe what the landscape of the village would look like. The working groups had a strict, self-chosen gender divide and all were focused and on task. In their freeze frames the boys created three pubs and a blacksmith's, all of which included violence, while the girls created riding stables and a tourist centre. The boys included a gunfight such as they see on TV. It was the only time during the work that they used violence and it was not surprising that it came at this point. The activity did not give them any motivation or action to portray. However, the freeze frame strategy provided containment and the events portrayed were not developed into action. If we are to work authentically with children's understanding then we have to accept what they offer and work with them from that point of entry. In the discussion of the freeze-frame incidents, the normality of village life was discussed, including the possibility that sometimes fights break out in village pubs when people have too much to drink. There was very little sense of rural or agricultural life immediately brought into play but in subsequent discussion the children were able to describe what the landscape around the village would look like and this did include fields, animals, crops and woodland.

At School E the children introduced crops, fields, 'greenery', thatched roofs and wooden houses as part of their understanding. They also talked about quietness and the lack of pollution in contrast to city life. They worked in mixed gender groups. Their freeze-frames showed haymaking, pheasant shooting, picking fruit and the local library. The discussion also included the landscape and the sounds and smells of a village. At School C the children worked in single gender groups and drew on their knowledge of village life in Bangladesh. Their comments were specific and authentic, drawing on experience of village communities based within their own culture. There was too little space for much movement, but the children concentrated well.

In each school, the understandings that the children offered were the point of entry for the drama teacher who then shifted the scene to what lay around the village, imaging in particular the forest of the story. The children were asked to stand as trees and to think about what would be going on around them in different seasons and at different times of the day and night, and to call out softly what they might see. This involved a move away from the 'social realism' of most drama lessons to the creation of an imagined world that is nonetheless recognisable as a place where they could still play.

At School C, where there were many bilingual learners, the children were encouraged to think of all the different colours of green that could be seen in the forest. Although for them this was a challenging task, they handled it very capably. In many cases they had images of what they wanted to say but had not yet met the English word. For example, 'frog green' was followed by 'the thing that a frog sits on green'. Lily pad green was introduced and taken up by many children later in the session. In this school the drama work had not sufficiently connected the children to the imagined world of the Green Children for them to explore that world through enactment, but it may have enabled them to respond differently to their own world. But the children created a sound basis for the introduction of the text. They worked in pairs to storyboard the narrative, drawing on their first hearing of the book and the drama work they did prior to the reading. This gave them the opportunity to clarify their understanding of the events of the narrative before going on to look at the text more closely.

By break time at School A and School E the children's commitment to the alternative world had been established. In both schools, when the book was then introduced, the children recognised at once the connections between the text and the drama work they had done. The words of the text had been brought within their realm of knowing and a bridge built between the world of the text and the way a writer makes a world from language and imagination. The next stage of the drama brought the Green Children to the Suffolk village where they were ill-treated. In groups the children were asked to discuss how they thought the village would react when they first saw the Green Children. That the school children understood the nature of this transition was clear from the expressions of their feelings about it. In further improvisations, the range of their responses prefigured those they would meet in the text. They also became aware of the possibility of differing points of view. This capacity to perceive events from different perspectives is important if we are to ask children to write in role or in the first person about the same event. Subsequently, the children wrote in role as one of the Green Children looking back at the other world that was now inaccessible. In both schools, the children engaged readily with this writing task, working with great concentration well into the lunch hour.

Fiona Collins at School B and School D and a second class in School E

The drama work began with the creation of a community that the children could feel they belonged to and would be sorry to lose. It was important for the children to make an investment in the story world and so experience effectively the exile of the Green Children. When the class was fixed in a whole group freeze-frame, (a situation which needed strong concentration from the children), several were asked to 'speak their thoughts' and thus demonstrate the reaction of the villagers to the strangers. To increase the tension the villagers were told to keep secret what they noticed about the Green Children. In each school this was undertaken with seriousness and commitment. When the secrets were later shared in role or discussed out of role, the children introduced many new elements, ranging from sinister (someone fell sick after touching one of the Green Children) to lyrical (a sweet sound accompanying the speech of the Green Children).

From this point the drama and its written outcome differed in each school. In School D the children were to write a letter in role to describe the colourful world they had entered. Many of the letters were pleas for help and rescue and expressed the fear of a child who is lost. The class teacher was impressed with a pupil who never wrote, but who now showed that the drama had engaged her with the text of the story. At School B the children had partners with whom they engaged in further enactment as writer and recipient of letters composed orally. At School E the children had the text read to them a third time during which they learned about Ralph of Coggeshall, who wrote a version of the story seven hundred years ago. The drama teacher then became Ralph, who wanted to find out from the villagers about the strange children. The villagers could choose whether or not they told him their secret. After some whole group discussion in role the children continued this activity in pairs. There was an interesting debate about the ethics of the treatment of the children after one girl had told 'Ralph' that the Green children were caged in case they were dangerous. In all three schools, the drama was rich in detail and the written pieces thoughtful and extended.

Assessment

An important aim was that the children should develop a sense of owner-ship of the world of the text, and this was achieved in all the schools. It was an aspect which was prioritised in the drama, and this successfully enabled the children to build up a clear inner image of the green world, aiding their commitment to the drama and also contributing later to the quality of their written work. They gained a heightened awareness of the language of the text, and the work undertaken in several of the schools on compiling a 'green' lexicon showed evidence of this awareness in the children's talk and writing. In the improvised dramas there was also evidence of children 'latching on' to particular expressions or phrases in Crossley-Holland's com-plex text and taking ownership of them, using them to establish and create character in their own role work.

The children were offered a range of ways of responding to the text of *The Green Children*, both in dramatic enactments and in writing. The diversity of roles they undertook helped them to become aware of the possibility of writing from a number of different viewpoints. This work also encouraged them to find a voice for their responses and to synthesize their own actual experiences with those they engaged with, thus extending their under-standings of events and feelings. In the writing directly related to this exercise the children were intent on conveying both the sense and their feeling for the events they narrated. The teachers were introduced to drama work. It was also an opportunity for them to see their classes with other professionals. This gave them a chance to reflect on and re-evaluate their expectations of the children's responses to a text.

APPENDIX TWO

Questionnaires and Pro-formas

The Links between the Study of Literature and Writing Development
CLPE Research Project:1998/9

Teacher Questionnaire

Name

LEA

School

Year Group

---

1. Are there any particular features of the classroom environment which you think are supportive in promoting writing as an enjoyable/desirable activity?

---

2. Are there certain kinds of literary texts which you think are supportive in the teaching and learning of writing? (List any particular texts which you have used in particular contexts)

---

3. What kinds of language activities make explicit to children the links between reading and writing? (Describe any which you have found to work well)

---

4. Are there any kinds of teacher responses to children's writing, which you have found encourage young writers to reflect on their *own* texts, and increase their knowledge of the writing process?

---

5. Describe the best ways you have found of supporting a child's writing development?

---

6. Which do you consider to be the most effective ways of monitoring children's progress and development in writing to help you to plan their next learning opportunities?

---

7. Who and/or what do you consider to be the most important influences on a child becoming a writer?

---

8. How would you define an "experienced" writer? (List the aspects or features you would take into account which would enable you to identify such a writer.)

Val Cork
Project Coordinator

My Reading/Writing History (Pupil Questionnaire)

Name

School

Class

What kind of reading material do you like to read? (think of favourite authors, favourite texts, particular story genres, eg. fantasy, adventure, science fiction, historical stories, poetry, etc.)

When you read, do you ever write at the same time?

When you play, do your games ever involve writing?

Where do you like to write best? (at home and at school)

What kinds of writing do you like to do? (think of stories, letters, bookmaking, poems, factual accounts, diaries, leaflets, posters, etc.)

Are there any particular subjects or topics that you like to write about?

Are there any people who have really helped you with your reading and writing?

Which parts of writing do you most enjoy? (think about getting ideas, planning, drafting, redrafting, talking about your writing with a friend or your teacher, making a best copy, publishing your work for an audience to read, reading your writing aloud, etc.)

Are there any particular aspects of writing that you don't enjoy or that you find difficult?

What helps you most with your writing?

What do you do when you have difficulty with some aspect of your writing?

Are there any particular things in the classroom that you use to help you when you have difficulties?

Is there anything you don't have in your classroom which you would like to have that would be helpful to you as a writer?

How do you think you learn best to be a writer ?(who or what might help you?)

Does reading help you with your writing?

Are there any special texts that you have read which have been important to you as a reader or as a writer?(think about texts you have read as a class, on your own or with parents/carers or friends)

How would you describe yourself as a writer? (What are you best at and is there anything you need to work on?)

Would you like to add any further comments?

Classroom Observation Pro-forma

School

Date

Class Teacher

Provision

Range/quality of texts
Titles/author/genre
Book corner: promotion of specific texts

Teacher reading aloud to whole class (texts and children's composed texts)

Opportunities to reflect on and discuss texts (including children's composed texts)

Opportunities for shared reading/shared writing (whole class)
Teacher modelling the process of writing

Opportunities for collaborative writing(group)

Opportunities for independent writing (children's own choice of writing)

Opportunities to revise/redraft writing. Use of response partners

Opportunities for publishing work/bookmaking

Opportunities for children to see their work on display/reading texts created by each other

Opportunities for dramatising texts

Range of resources used by children for supporting independence

Use of I.T.: individual/paired work,composing/transcribing/editing,etc

Particular intervention strategies employed by teacher

KS2 Writing Project
Children's Writing Samples – Proforma for analysis

Structure	Genre
Influences of texts read	Cohesion and consistency
Characterisation and dialogue	Language and style
Sense of reader/audience	Viewpoint
	Retellings

Writing Samples Key Stage 2 (writing in English and/or other community languages)

Date			
Title /type of writing (Draft/finished work)			
Context • How the writing arose • Degree of confidence and independence • Nature of support given			
Process • How the child went about the writing • How far the child discussed and developed the writing			
* Compositional aspects How far the child is: • developing ideas through writing • able to handle this particular kind of writing • writing with a reader in mind • drawing on experience of reading in structuring this text • organising this text coherently • choosing language thoughtfully			
* Transcriptional aspects: How far the child is: • using punctuation appropriately to mark meaning • drawing on a range of strategies in spelling eg known words, plausible phonetic spellings, visual patterns, knowledge of word structures and meanings • using organisation structures eg paragraphs, headings • using a fluent handwriting style			
Child's self-assessment and learning aims			
Plan the next steps for this child as a writer (eg developing confidence, range of writing, compositional and transcriptional aspects)			

*Use the points as a guide. Comment on those relevant to the child and writing context
© CLPE 1998

Reading Samples Key Stage 2 (reading in English and/or other community languages) *to include reading aloud and reading silently*			
Date			
Title of book/text W Well known F Fiction K Known P Poetry, rhymes U Unknown I Information T Teacher chosen C Child chosen			
Sampling procedure used: M Miscue Analysis I Informal (Individual/group)			
Overall impression of child's reading degree of confidence and independence way in which the child read the text aloud (eg fluency, expression) choice of text			
* Strategies used when reading the text aloud: drawing on previous experience using semantic/syntactic/grapho-phonic/illustration cues predicting using analogy self-correcting using several strategies or over dependent on one using strategies appropriate to this kind of text (eg information text)			
* Response, understanding and analysis How far the child is able to: make links with personal experience and other texts, indicating preferences explore literary meanings eg retell, predict, read pictures/diagrams hypothesise and make inferences, using evidence critically reflect on author intention and style, interpret wider meanings discuss patterns and features of texts			
Child's self-assessment and learning aims			
Plan the next steps for this child as a reader (eg developing confidence, strategies, range of texts, response and understanding)			

*Use the points as a guide. Comment on those relevant to the child and reading context
© CLPE 1998

The links between the study of literature and writing development at KS2/CLPE Research Project 1998/99 (Final questionnaire)

1   Has the CLPE Project made a difference to your practice this year? If so can you define how it has affected your practice?

2   What aspects of your teaching do you think have most helped children in your class to learn about writing?

3   Do you have any evidence that the literary texts read with the class this year have influenced children's writing for the better? What kind of evidence?

4   Which literary texts do you think have most powerfully influenced children's writing and why?

5   Have these same texts and experiences made a difference to children's progress as readers do you think?

6   What would you now look for, in assessing children's progress in writing, that you might not have been so aware of before the project began?

7   Has the literacy hour supported your work within the project this year? Are there any ways in which it has constrained your work?

Val Cork
Project Coordinator

CLPE Writing Scale 2   September 1997

(For children between the ages of nine and twelve)   **From Inexperience to experience**

1 Inexperienced writer	2 Less experienced writer	3 Moderately Experienced writer	4 Experienced writer	5 Exceptionally experienced writer
Experience as a writer may be limited: may be composing orally with confidence but be reluctant to write or avoid taking risks with transcription. Needing a great deal of help with developing own texts (which are often brief) and with the writing demands of the classroom. Relying mainly on phonetic spelling strategies and memorised words, with few self-help strategies. Seldom using punctuation to mark meaning.	Increasingly willing to take risks with both composition and transcription. Writing confidently in certain genres (eg simple narratives) and trying out different forms of writing, drawing on experience of the models available. May find it difficult to sustain initial efforts over longer pieces of writing. Mainly using language and sentence structures that are close to speech. Spellings of familiar words are generally correct and attempts at unfamiliar spellings reveal a widening range of strategies. Using sentence punctuation more consistently.	Shaping writing in familiar genres confidently, drawing on experience of reading. Widening range of writing and taking on different forms more successfully. Aware of audience and beginning to consider appropriateness of language and style. Learning to revise own texts with support and to link and develop ideas coherently. Spellings of words with regular patterns are mainly correct and attempts at unfamiliar words show a growing knowledge of visual patterns and word structures. Using sentence punctuation appropriately.	A self-motivated writer who can write at length and is beginning to use writing to refine own ideas. Developing own style and range as a writer but needing support with the structuring of more complex narrative and non-narrative forms. Likely to be reflecting on writing and revising texts for a reader, choosing language for effect or to clarify meanings. Using standard spelling more consistently and drawing on effective self-help strategies. Increasingly able to use punctuation, including paragraphing, to organise texts.	An enthusiastic writer who has a recognisable voice and uses writing as a tool for thinking. Making conscious decisions about appropriate forms and styles of writing, drawing on wide experience of reading. May show marked preferences for writing in particular genres. Able to craft texts with the reader in mind and reflect critically on own writing. Using mainly standard spelling. Managing extended texts using organisational structures such as paragraphing and headings.

Data analysis scoring sheet

NAME	No. 1 Breaks in time sequence	No. 2 Mental state verbs	No. 3 T-unit length (as range)	No. 4 NRB sentences	No. 5 Narrative voice	No. 6 Sense of a reader	No.7 Literary turns of phrase	No.8 Echoes

APPENDIX THREE

Texts used in Data Analysis

Sophie: EARLY SAMPLE

An Adventure in Spain

"Hurry up" I shouted "We'll miss the plane"
 "Sorry we're coming" said Georgia and Hollie giggling. We climbed up
on to the plane and we all sat down tiredly. Georgia, Hollie, Millie and
Baby Allysia were all fast asleep. The aeroplane landed we all got off the
plane and made our way to the villa. The next morning we all put our
swim suits on grabbed the pool key and a towel and we dived in the
lovely swimming pool outside our villa. A strange man appeared at the
swimming pool gate put his hand through the gate got our pool key
and ran off with it.
"Let's follow him," shouted Georgia we grabbed our towels. I grabbed
and put her on my back and ran too up with the others. We saw the man
go into a villa right beside ours. "I'm going back and telling Daddy" said
Millie so we all made our way back to the villa and told my Uncle David
all about it. David phoned the Police and came round and broke into the
villa grabbed the strange looking man gave us the key and they went off.
"Everything's back to normal" I said.
"But where's Millie?" said Georgia "oh no" I said, "Here I am" she said as
she jumped up from behind the bench!

Sophie: MIDDLE SAMPLE

Writing in role as the Green boy.

As soon as I opened my eyes colours dazzled. I could not open my eyes
properly. The colours started to fade. I could see strange creatures staring
down at us. I dug my nails into my sister. "What are they" I asked. She
told me she thought they were children. The oldest child sang us some
soft words. I could see some berries in a leaf nest. Well I thought they
were berries but they were not green. There were birds hanging. They
had lost their song. They were not green. One of the creatures fell over a
tree root. I looked harder, I realized that we must be lost. I started to cry.
I could feel little bits of air wave over my face. It felt strange.
My sister sat up. "Who are you? Why aren't you green? Where is this
place?" she said. She looked scared. Little bit of water began to trickle
down my nose. My sister told me to follow the creatures I didn't want to,
all I wanted was to go home.

Sophie: LATE SAMPLE

Chapter one written by: Humble the cat

I heard the wolves again last night, howling at the tops of their voices,
long and loud, big and bold.
I lay with shivers all over my body.

I went to my secret hunting field just now, I stayed out there for ages.
I came in through the window like the ghost of the cat next door, whose
life was meant to end.
I've come in for warmth and comfort by the fire and up against the dog.

Alice is fidgeting in her cradle she can smell mouse on me.
The dog lies near the fire with her belly facing the centre of the sparks.
I hear noises and turn my head, I thought it might have been Alice, but it was
the Dog wandering over to Alice's cradle, wobbling with her belly so big.

I lie watching Alice lift her small red fist up to stroke the dogs soft furry
ear. I hear more movements. It is the twins, coughing and moving from
side to side, at their parents' feet, as children do when they are sleeping.
Only Alice is awake, she's lying still, silent and calm; she does not fear the
Wolves. Their loud howling voices come to her from far outside the
house, which is the only world she knows.
The strange howls echo through my ears, I snuggle up to my tail hoping
the dog will come and lie against me.

The dog heaves her belly round and is starting to hobble towards me, so
she can lie down by the fire. It shan't be long for the dog she can hardly
move with her belly stopping her.

Its cold outside, the snow lies thickly across the fields, it's hard to hunt,
but I shall manage tomorrow after a rest.

Harry: EARLY SAMPLE

Down the drain

get me out ───────────────────────────── HELP!

In an abandoned boat behind a house lived a family
of small people, Kenny and Kevin are twin brothers
and their mum and dad are called Louis and Rose.

One day Kenny and Kevin got bored and decided
to go and explore the house, little did they know
luck was not on their side.
Kenny was daring and thought he would run
around the fish tank but he slipped and sank.

Kevin saw everything and ran as fast as he
could (which is not very fast because of the size of
his legs) back to his mum and dad, told them
every thing and darted back to the house.

By the time the news sunk in Kevin was
already on the side of the tank, trying to calm
down his brother.

When his mum and dad arrived the fish tank
had been emptied and Kenny had gone down
the drain, Kevin was about to jump down
after him when Rose called him and told
him not to be so stupid but nothing could
stop this kid, his brother had gone down
and he was going too.

Louis and Rose watched in disbelief but
they decided they had to go down too.
When they got to the bottom Kenny and
Kevin had already made friends with a rat called Chip.

After a lot of discussion Chip agreed to
give them a ride, but after a couple of
hours Chip was too busy showing them every
thing he didn't see the pipe and BANG!
Chip was out cold.

Kevin noticed a pipe they could push Chip up
and maybe even escape, after ages of pushing
they came out of a shower and landed in a bath.

Almost straight away they were on the
window sill and jumping out with Chip, they
ran across a massive garden and they found
an oak tree, which they all decided would be
a good place to rest and to see to Chip's
injuries, and they have lived there ever since.

Harry: MIDDLE SAMPLE

No time to lose.

"Its mine" "No its mine" Phil and Lil where off on another argument
about one of their toys but this time it was serious they didn't know that
in a couple of seconds their life would change forever.

"Uh oh"! The Reptar doll flew across the air and smashed against the
wall with the head rolling along the floor.

They were just about to argue about whose fault it was but thank god for us evil Reptar was released with Reptar the Great not far behind. Immediately Phil, Lil and Reptar the Great knew there was big trouble, "I will destroy all" roared evil Reptar but Reptar the Great knew that if they could find the idol of Reptars all would be saved.

As quick as anything they were somehow transported to the Temples of Doom in Zorgan.

"We must find the idol" said Reptar "but beware we will face many dangers".

They found this out almost straight away because only ten paces in was a raging fire pit, "We have no choice but to jump" said Phil but quickly adding "do we?"

But Reptar and Lil were already over and with no hesitation Phil joined them.

Later they faced many more dangers including spike pits, raging volcanoes, falling rocks and maybe one of the most savage, deadly, torturous things you could imagine – tickle boxes. After many more treacherous, annihilating dangers like these they found the wondrous, amazing, sparkling, golden, marvelous, magnificent idol of Reptars, but celebration was cut short as soon as they removed the idol "Guys" shouted Phil "there's a bloody boulder that looks like it could squash us any second, RUN"!

So they ran like maniacs back to the teleporter where they were taken back to the house and placed the idol back in the toy where the two Reptars were kept forever.

Harry: LATE SAMPLE

Chapter 1: The great voyage

The old crumbling dock could barely hold the colossal ship known as the Marie Celeste the greatest ship on earth with a crew of 32 all of them were in pub but the Captain, Benjamin Briggs soon commanded them to get to work.

Tom Hawk was a Navigator on the great ship he and the rest were working like ants to prepare for the voyage to Genoa in Italy with a cargo of beer to trade.

Tom held the silver sword tight, although it was only three inches and could not protect him from any real danger as the sun shone 'REFLECTED A SIGN OF HOPE INTO HIS HEART".

His brother James was a bit apprehensive as his best mates had lost their lives on a voyage and he didn't want to join them at least not yet so Tom knew telling him that the sword would bring them good luck.

"Get back to work," said Briggs he was their boss everyone hated him he was the complete opposite but they had to obey his orders.

The boards of the docks began to creak and everyone spun to see who it was and a mysterious figure as black as the night advanced towards the ship and said "I wish to remain anonymous as my name and identity does not of convenience to you, I have come to ask may I be a member of your crew?" but with a hasty reply he had the answer no "then your ship will be cursed in a great storm" and with that he left.

"Never mind 'im" said Briggs 'the sea is as calm as a kitten lets set sail" Tom didn't like the sound of what the wizard had said but there was no turning back the ship was already a mile from port and the sky was as grey as unpainted metal.

Emily: EARLY SAMPLE

Bang,
Kevin's car had just broke down....
In the middle of nowhere
in the middle of the night....

He turned on the radio, wanting to listen to some music to calm his nerves, "NEWSFLASH there is a murderer in the city woods"
"That's silly" replied Kevin.

Kevin stepped out of the car and a little shiver went down the back of his spine, he trembled as he walked slowly to the woods, pulling his collar up to cover his neck. He shivered with fear. The trees came down on him like hands reaching to get him, as he walked through the woods, his heart was beating faster than the West wind he carried on slowly until he heard a scream, just then in the tinkle of his eye he saw a wallet lying on the floor it had loads of money in it he saw a man lying on the floor Kevin went over to him he said he has broke his leg and that there is a murderer in his house, now Kevin is getting braver because he has someone with him as they made their way back to the house they heard the hooting of an owl, they get back to the house they walked slowly up stairs they heard some footsteps in his bedroom they tried to make no noise so they went in the bedroom and it was, who is the murderer nobody knows. Why did they come nobody knows.

Emily: MIDDLE SAMPLE

THE RETURN

This is what happened....

Guy and I had been searching for days which seemed like years for the tunnel which led me here, to this multi-coloured world. Eventually Guy and I gave up and decided to go home, well my foster home, when I thought I heard the voice of my lost brother telling me the way home, he said to follow the sunlight, I thought my mind was playing games with me, but I was wrong, I asked Guy if he would come with me "It might be the way to the tunnel" "Why" he replied "I feel it in my heart" he smiled, I took his hand as we walked through the sunlight, we started to spin around and something made us shut our eyes, then all of a sudden we stopped we opened our eyes and found ourselves in front of the tunnel. Guy and I looked at each other and jumped with joy until we lost our energy. I whispered " thank-you brother" Guy clung his arm around me as we walked into our worst nightmare.

As we walked through the tunnel we heard the dead souls telling a story of 2 worlds changing colour I was listening very carefully when there was a big clang between the 2 worlds, at that moment I was feeling very scared because there was water dripping like the howling of wolves and it was dark, damp and very cold, Guy felt like an ice cube with his arm around me, and I took another step when all of a sudden I felt the warm breeze slicing through my skin and the green sunlight swooping over me. Guy and I stepped into the green world, for some strange reason one half of me felt happy and the other sad because I wished my brother was here so he could have made home as well.

The landowner Rose, came over and told me about my brother dying and how he was the most precious gift to our people. " This is what happened", began Rose, "when your brother died, Airha, a curse was put on our green land and the only thing that can cure it is your love with Guy, you must prove your love to each other."

Guy and I gazed into each others eyes and saw our future together, he bent down and picked a Rose-bud and he swept it into my hands. I felt the petals and smelt the greenness. As I smelt it, the petals unfurled and a bright light shone in my face from the stigma. The rose which was once green turned ruby red, "THE LAND IS SAVED" exclaimed Rose....

Emily: LATE SAMPLE

The Storm

Jack felt lonely, as his friends had disturbed him, so he decided to write in his diary. He felt a bit tired so he lay on his bunk with a glass of water next to him; the boat gently started to rock like a babies cradle it got more and more heavy and the glass fell to the ground with a big crash. Jack jumped with shock, he jumped down from his bunk and started to pick up the glass and went to throw it into the bin when he got thrown to the wall, his heart was beating so fast, he grabbed onto the window ledge, he made it and looked out of the window it was his worst nightmare amongst the tempest clouds they parted and the suns rays shone through the ferocious sea dogs charging towards the boat it was his worst nightmare....

Big bang, everybody screamed then a flash of lightning struck the boat big waves drowned people on deck the captain shouted "all board the deck there are life boats waiting for women and children first and then men". Jack thought women and children first his mum would be boarding the lifeboats he had to say goodbye he wanted her touch to die with him. He struggled. I don't know how Jack was supposed to get to deck, he couldn't though even get up, suddenly he saw water sliding through the bottom of the door like a lift shooting down floors and floors of a building.

Yossif: EARLY SAMPLE

Pinocchio

Once upon a time there was an old man that wanted to have a child, he then a wood boy and after painted the wood boy the man went to sleep. In the night a angel appeared and give the boy that called Pinocchio life, and Pinocchio went to wake up his dad,"said who are you", I'm Pinocchio how you can be a real boy no you are wood boy but a angel give me life.
The old man had one cat and one fish then the old man went to sleep, the fish went too, the cat as well the old man said to Pinocchio to tomorrow you will go to school like all

Yossif: MIDDLE SAMPLE

Roasted Peanuts Don't Grow!

Once there was a nephew, and his uncle Guro was the uncle and Tsuro was the nephew. A long time ago they had an argument. They were arguing about when Tsuro was shooting rocks at the bee's nest. Tsuro told the bees that his uncle throw the rocks.

The bees came out to sting Tsuro then they bit Guro until he collapsed. That was two harvests ago. They each planted peanuts for harvest, harvest arrived Guro had 2 bags of peanuts as well as Tsuro.

Guro roasted the two bag of peanuts. Tsuro only roasted one bag and left one bag.

Now came the sowing time winter the rain came and went this is time to plant peanuts on the soil. Guro never knew much he decided to sell all the roasted peanut.

Tsuro's peanuts were growing.

They were growing through the soil growing healthy green peanuts. 'Tsuro will you expect to the roasted peanuts to grow?'

His uncle was disappointed that his nephew's peanuts grew and his don't grow. His nephew walked him back and in sympathy he said, "uncle roasted peanuts don't grow."

Yossif: LATE SAMPLE

The Green Children

This is what happened. One of our lambs skipped into a cave and we went to rescue it. It was scary and dark and we saw eyes and hands looking and trying to grab us. We heard bright bells.

When we came out of the cave the ringing was sunlight. We saw faces but they were not green, there was a tall girl and another girl dangling two birds, which had lost their songs. There was a boy who buckled and bumped his brains and his bottom.

And a little boy who was holding berries. My little brother pinched me and I said, "they are children I think!" and then they fore fingered us. The tallest girl came out and I asked her "who are you! And then she turned her back to us. She beckoned us to follow her through the woods, when we came to a house then a woman came out of the house.

The mum looked and circled us after that she brought us some pigeon pie... rabbit mince...peacock-in-a-roll I have never seen or heard those things words before, and the food smelt and tasted wrong. I said we will wait until we go back home.

Then one young man passed through the door with some beanstalks. The young man split open one for me to see what was in side there was a froth in the bean I ate them anyway they tasted all right.

After we ate was ready to go back home. The cave disappeared we couldn't find our way back home it brought sorrow to our faces. Then my brother began to cry and he threw what he had in his hand. The children soon began to us some words. After seven weeks my brother wasn't eating or speaking to me. The mum sang some words to my brother.

My brother soon lost his song, I was lonely then and I soon learnt their language. They brought me to a festival everyone wanted to buy me but Guy said no.
They asked how much these she cost.
They said; 'she's not for buy or sell' just because she's green and you are white.
They asked how much does she cost.
They said she's rotten that's why she's green.
I ran away because I was scared of the people Guy found me and put a flower in my hand.
He made me warm, comfortable and confident.
We went back home and we danced altogether.

Joe: EARLY SAMPLE

The mystery man with a cricket bat

It was a frosty, snowy night passing by to midnight, the cold flakes were up to John's ankles. John Silver old wrecked car had broken down at the side of the road next to a path through a wood. John sat in his car thinking how he was going to get back to his girlfriend's house so he could get some sleep before morning. Slowly he fell to sleep, he slept longer than he thought He put the radio on "Someone has been murdered in Anfield woods in Shropshire the murderer has not been found and neither has the man that was murdered". John looked at the sign next to the path it said, Anfield woods Shropshire. He looked around perturbed anxious to get out of his car. He was terrified he looked at the watch it was exactly midnight aaarrrrrrrhhh, some one screamed from in the woods. He got out his car stepping slowly in the snow and walked towards the sign (that said Anfield woods, Shropshire) he looked at a sign on a tree it had a picture and said murder beware (there at that moment he took first his steps into the woods) onto some flaky leaves that made a crackle noise when he crunch them. He began to feel worried and pushed the branches out of his way and got caught on a prickle bush that ripped his trousers, There in the distance he saw a wallet and a coat just sticking out from around a bend. It was his lucky night he thought to himself John walked in and out of the creepy bushes to the wallet and coat. He finally got there, John began to pick up the wallet and was just about to put it in his inside coat pocket when he looked beside the path, the snow was red and a hand and a leg was sticking out of it John picked most of the snow feeling horrified. He looked at what was under the snow, he was petrified. It was a dead man that had been stabbed by some-one. He stepped one or two steps back and dropped the wallet. He ran like mad jumping over bushes and over logs winding himself around the bends till the end of the path. At the end there was a row of houses. John knocked on one a few times no one was there He knocked on the next someone answered the door. He came out and stood on the dirty mat in front of the door and asked John in a deep crusty voice 'why have you come here at this hour?' "Come with me with a coat or a blanket." He came with a coat and something under it. John didn't ask him what they were running too fast to talk. John went ahead and couldn't see the man behind him. He got to the stabbed man and waited for the man idling behind him, he came and threw the coat to John. He wrapped the blanket around him, suddenly the man that brought the coat had a cricket bat in his hand. He brought the bat up ready to hit John. John got up with his hands in front of his head and started to run, Lucky for John the man was slow he was too slow to follow and turned back. John got two ten pence pieces and phoned the AA and his girlfriend from a telephone booth that he found up the road he broke down on.

Joe: MIDDLE SAMPLE

The Return

This is what happened.... The last brick was placed, a strike of lightning forked the sky and roaring thunder followed, snow started falling heavily as I ran back to Guy. I told him "Its happened, its happened I must go back and you have to come too" Guy and I ran fastly to the middle of the woods where the statue stood "Its here" I cried "What's here" guy replied. I didn't answer, I just ran in the cave dragging Guy with me. The snow, thunder and lightning suddenly stopped we were in the cave and the door closed.

The cave suddenly shook and made a huge sound like a yawn, it was moving.... Then it bashed against the green world, the door re-opened, It was my world, but, there was something not right, not right at all.

This is what happened....
A curse had appeared and it is all my fault, I had left the land. It was winter although it was June. Snow fell everyday. Sunrise and sunsets had past .... But still it was covered in snow. Half a year had passed, I still haven't found my relatives. Guy and I were becoming too cold to live as was too much of a contrast. Freezing cold ice hanged from mine and Guys wrinkly bodies. That night we both slept but Guy didn't wake up. The lush green grass and Olive green weeds were appearing and our land was coming back. The trees stood still and I went back, back to my family and I left Guy still in a wood to breathe the fresh air. The curse was ended.

Joe: LATE SAMPLE

Chapter 1: The Ship

The mist overcame the bright beaming sunshine as Tommy Ryan saw the ghostly ship. The ship peeked out from behind the trees, so big, so bold, and so bright. Each step Tommy took, he got an extra feeling to go back. The boat looked curious, guilty and like a crime. Tommy was near the innocent boat, his mind told him to go back but he knew to go on.

Men were stealing from people, one tried to steal Tommy's but he just smacked them and clipped them around the ear and said get lost! And they ran a mile and a half away from him. But that's going off the point. He was at the great ship standing, staring at the stair that were leading on to the story.

The boat was called the Enigma and if you read on you will see why. This was the first time he'd taken this boat and the first time the boat had taken him.

A man asked him to start queuing up and of course he skip the queue to the front. Give us your tickets he said and then they boarded Tommy being first. ★The ship was called the ship of mysteries and indeed it was ....Read on.......

★ Everybody was loading their baggage on to the boat one by one like rats ready to slaughter the cats.

Grace: EARLY SAMPLE

Look who's talking

My names Niome I'm going to tell you a very weird story. I was sitting down in class I had finished all my work I was reading a very boring book so instead I looked out of the window like most children in the class do. Any way I was chewing my pencil at the same time. Then suddenly a little voice came from my pencil saying, "Hey how would you like it if someone was writing with your feet and chewing your hair off." "Who said that", I shouted look down. Then I saw my pencil talking. I screamed the whole class looked at me. The teacher sent me to the corner. That day was so embarrassing I even wanted to cry. But I couldn't. Everybody was asking me why I was screaming. Denise just kept on bullying me as usual. I only told my best friend Jake do you know what he did he just laughed at me my best friend I didn't dare tell anyone else. The next day I put my school pencil away and used a different pencil. The same voice came from my pencil-case. But this time it said "Get me out of here I'm suffocating in this thing". Me and my mum Joe had a talk that day she just thought I was crazy, and took me to the doctors. My pencil talked again this time everyone heard it. I told them I said that me and the pencil were friends forever. Sometimes people thought I was crazy because I always talked to myself Well that's what they thought anyway. I didn't always use the pencil in case it broke. I didn't want that to happen. I wonder how he can talk well I bet I'll never find out. Hey I wonder if he can do my homework. It will save me time.

About 2 years later my pencil case fell and someone stepped on it the talking pencil snapped in half that was the worst day of my life. (well I think so anyway.) In my bedroom I had a picture of him on it, it said

IN MEMORY OF
PENCIL, MY BEST
PENCIL.
I'll never forget him.

Grace: MIDDLE SAMPLE

The Green Children

My name is Joseph and I have a story to tell. You might not believe me, but I didn't believe it myself when I first saw it. Even though I'm old, *this* story has never came out of my head. I remember it as if it was yesterday. I was very young when it all happened.

It was a normal day when everybody would go to the fair, buy something, or go on terrifying rides. Bargains going on and children breaking things and messing about. I owned a stall back then, at the fair, the fair was visiting the village Woolpit. I even remember what kind of day it was. The blazing sun shone down on us. The ground was hot like fire, it burnt my feet, until everything went quiet, there was a big crowd of people all staring at one thing. I struggled to get through the tremendous crowd. A normal boy was approaching us with a strange green creature standing right next to him? Everyone was shouting things out, and pointing their fingers. What was it? Nobody knew. I had come with my Grandma, and she had already fainted. The green creature came closer, and closer, I noticed it was a child. But before I could say anything else, the green child ran away. I couldn't see her anymore, she was camouflaged with the olive green grass, and the silky green leaves, that was the last time I saw her. I was confused. Most people thought it was their imagination, but I knew it was real. I saw her, I will never forget that moment, and I'll always wonder what she was and where she was from.

Grace: LATE SAMPLE

Fire, Bed and Bone

I gave Fleabane a bath. I could see he was still tired, so I let him sleep. I had a feeling that we had a long day ahead of us. While Fleabane was sleeping I crept out of the den, and looked over to the old Farmhouse. I remembered my fire, bed and bone. Fleabane has lived life as a wild dog. I taught him how to hunt for food and sense well with his nose. I'm very proud of him.

The next day, I went to visit Rufus and Comfort in the stable. I saw their faces. Dirt mounted on them. They want to go home as much as I do. I could tell. They looked terrible. I hate the Miller. He did this. He told on Rufus and Comfort. He doesn't care. One of these days he'll get something he deserves. I wish we could be a family again. We will be a family again.

I'm worried about Fleabane. I am worried he might join a pack. I don't want him to join a pack. I want my fire, bed and bone back. I want Fleabane to join me. I want him to leave the wild. But what if he doesn't want to? What if he wants to stay here in the wild where he has been bought up? I guess he would call this his home. I won't let it happen. I have lost both my other two puppies, I shall not lose Fleabane. He's all I've got now. What shall I do?

I went to see the children yesterday morning. They were safe and sound. I was really worried about Alice, (the baby) the most. They were amazed at how big Fleabane had grown. After we had seen them, we went back home. I though of how we used to be safe, and happy. Now we had lost all of that.

Fleabane wanted to sleep. I lay down. I watched him fall asleep, but I couldn't stay awake and I fell asleep myself.

He was growing every day, Sooner or later he would live his own life. I loved Fleabane and I don't want to lose him. I'll make sure of it.

That night I couldn't sleep. I could sense danger. I looked around suspiciously. I saw nothing. I looked again. I knew there was something wrong. I walked out of the den, leaving Fleabane asleep. I looked over to the old Farmhouse. I saw a lady and a man entering. Rufus and Comfort? I thought. Or wasn't it.

APPENDIX FOUR

Fire, Bed And Bone:
A selection of other Children's Texts
from Project Schools

Pupil A

I miss my lifestyle, by the fire with my bed and bone. I like hunting and showing Fleabane how to hunt in the wild but I wish I could teach him how to hunt in the day and in the night I could take him home so we wouldn't have to hunt for food. In the winter it is very hard to survive. Most animals are hibernating. I am not used to this. I was born in the wild, but all my life I've been a domestic dog. I feel like hen tonight. But if I hunt it down, the village men will hunt us as well. They will kill us.

I can see in Fleabane's eyes, that he is hungry. I've been looking but I can't find anything, why is this happening to me? What have I done to deserve this? Even when Humble sees me he spits at me. I'm sorry to say this for myself, but maybe it wasn't the best thing to give birth to Fleabane because everything was going right before I gave birth to him. I wish I could sit by the fire with my bed and bone. The things I used to do. It's very hard to cope with a different lifestyle. I would give anything to do it again even for one day. I must set out to hunt some food.

That night I set out to the woods. I was determined to find something. I was looking high and low. Then into the distance I saw rabbit. There would be a lot of meat out of that one, I thought to myself. But I had to think of a way to get it because if it saw me it would run away. There were some paths covered with trees. I passed there crawling with every inch I took. I didn't want anything to go wrong. I was nearly there. I felt like running. But then again if I did, and it ran away Fleabane would be disappointed. So I went really slowly. The rabbit went into the middle of the path. I had to run. I got him where I wanted. I ran with every bit of energy I had. This would be very rewarding. I got out my jaws and used my sharp, canine teeth. I let out one big crunch. And it was dead. I had caught my prey. I crunched it and went towards home.

Home, I thought, home was the place where I had my fire bed and bone. I was going back. I had to take the risk.

Pupil B

Rats playing in the kitchen
munching and making noise.
Fire sparkling brighter
than the glowing sun.
Ticking stars reflecting
into a diminutive puddle.
The tumbling of horses
and a moon so bright
it is beaming into my eyes.

Foxes cry and run about
on the crackly, mist-green
and copper brown ground.
Bats fly through the smoke
and smell of the ashes
of the dying fire.

My belly is aching with pain,
it is torture.

Pupil C

As the noise grew louder I quickly woke the other two, but it was too
late the boar had charged into the hollow and flung me effortlessly to one
side. Serlo growled and got ready to pounce as the boar came charging at
him, Serlo locked his jaws round the back of the neck of the ferocious
boar. As I started to come round I could see Serlo getting thrown about
from left to right, so I threw myself at the beast and bit his hind leg. I
could see Blackthorn trying bite the pig's tail, then I heard a loud grunt
then silence. Blackthorn had got underneath the boar and had bitten its
stomach.

I was getting old now and wanted to go back to Comfort. As I
approached Ede's old house I could hear Comfort laughing. When I got
inside I saw Comfort, Watt, Will, Alice, the baby and another man.
Comfort came running to me and embraced me. Comfort had married
Rufus's cousin, he looked so much like Rufus and he treated me like
Rufus. I was home again! With fire, bed and bone

Pupil D

I remember Fire, Bed and Bone.
I was safe. Comfortable. Fleabane knows the country around now. He is wild. He is wild. He knows how to catch his own food. Fleabane still has a lot to learn, although he knows what to kill and what not to kill.

Rufus and Comfort still live in the stables near the great house. They're weak and can barely speak. They barely get anything to eat. They're held up by chains. The only memory they have of our life before is Alices sweet smelling hat that I brought from Edes house. They have been in the stables since winter it is now spring and the different coloured flowers blossom, and the buds burst to make lovely flowers and overtime you walk past them the scent makes you want to stop and smell more. But Rufus and Comfort cannot smell them nor see them. It's pitch black in the stable and no one or nothing can get in. I have to look in through a chink big enough for one eye.

Watt, Will and Alice are fine and healthy. They were amazed at how Fleabane had grown. It was a nice to be in a warm home again. It reminded me of the times before my family split up. Before Rufus and Comfort were arrested and Squill and Parsnip were alive. We begged for food but Ede scolded us. "I've got enough mouths to feed as well as you two"

That night was a cold one.

Fleabane was asleep as soon as we got in from hunting. I soon dozed off but not for long. I sensed danger and my hackles rose. I got up and sniffed the air. I looked over at Fleabane, he was asleep. I was worried I didn't want to lose Fleabane as I did Parsnip and Squill. I strolled over to him and bent closer just to hear him breathe, and I rested my paw on his paws. I knew he was safe now but my hackles were still aroused. But I managed to get to sleep puzzled with questions running through my head.

The next night our tummies full and our eyes drowsy, we lay down our heads for a good nights sleep.

Within a few short minutes I smelt smoke I looked towards the farmhouse, and saw a light, smoke belted from the chimney.
A man opened the door and looked out.

RUFUS & COMFORT –
HOME

Or was it?………………………..

Pupil E

I called for help but no one answered. Then an unknown dog walked in with a snarl on his face. We ganged up on Lupus. He kicked the unknown dog clean across the room. Fleabane pounced at Lupus's neck.

While I latched on to Lupus's legs, Vetchen ran out through the pantry door. Fleabane caught Lupus's nerve, then he went crashing to the floor.

I went to help the injured dog, licked the wound but he growled. He told me his name. 'Watt" he yelped

We went into the pantry where we found the door open. As we ran towards the open air for freedom, the tempting smell of hare came wafting into my nose, Freedom or hare? Hare.

We stopped and searched. While we searched Vetchen came in with a stick. Out of the blue I saw the hare behind the door. I charged at the hare and latched onto its ears with my strong jaws. I banged my left leg on the door to warn Fleabane and Watt. Fleabane and I got out safely, but Watt got caught by Vetchen. She grabbed the scruff of his neck and slammed the door shut.

Out in the yard we looked back one last time before we ran to the cave.

I miss my fire, bed and bone.

Pupil F

I am a creature of different worlds
I know the tops of trees
I know all the little places where mice hide.
I know where baby birds hide in the tall trees.
I know where Rats run in and out of rubbish.
I know where the cool, shimmering shining water
flows; and the fat silver fish hide,
I know if my soft comfortable cosy bed is in
front of the fire.
I know where the most daring and dangerous
places are I dare go there.

Pupil G

Writing as Fleabane

I lie freezing in an empty barrel. I run out of the barrel forgetting the chain. I run so fast the chain pulls me back into the barrel, my ear catches on a nail and I yelp in pain. I can feel the hot sweaty blood dribbling down my face.

The wolves barked last night as they spoke to me of freedom, but I didn't want to think of freedom all I wanted was my mother.

My mother used to tell me that humans were good, that they gave you a bed and a nice warm fire to sleep next to. I do not believe that.

Pupil H

The sound of Rufus's snore kept me awake
lying by the golden fire it ticks.
My back is torturous
I am in agony.

Ripples trickle along the
flowing water,
Where toads and frogs jump
Outside the world is stagnant.

Wolves howl and mumble
quieter and quieter until we
are silent again
Silent as usual silent as ever.

The children cough and fidget
in their sleep.
Only Alice is awake,
Her small red fist flies in the dark.

Outside Grindecobbe grunts
in her sty.
She is awake too.

Humble creeps in through the window
the scent of mouse on her floats under my nose.
Her soft fur rubs my skin,
as she curls around me.

Humble meows in her sleep
She is probably dreaming

I will dream of
tomorrow.

Straw dries outside in the barn
Crispy and flaky
The scent is carried by the gentle draft
which floats through the window.

Mice in the pantry play
and scamper.
Their beastly stink
blocks my nose.

Shadows creep up the wall
and tower over us.
Shadows surround the house
I know it is the trees.

The shadows are a
black as a ravens wing.
flying in the midnight
sky.

The sky is lit with
a hundred stars
all shining in the night.

But the moon is the vastest
with beams like
thunderbolts.

The stars are like a thousand
Candles in the sky light heaven
All shining brightly through the long
winters night.

Pupil I

It's cold tonight I've never know it to be so cold my mother wouldn't
believe what's happened to me. Blood is covering my ear I shouldn't have
tried to escape. My paw is infected from a sharp thorn my mind won't let
me stop thinking about my mother, the more I think of her the more my
life seems to get worse. My neck is chafed from the rope digging into me.
If I knew humans were like this I would never have come to them.
My paw is in pain I can feel it. I freeze as the boys come dashing out of
the house. I duck as deep as I can when one boy flicks a stick from side
to side as if he is about to hit me. I often wonder if my life is supposed
to be like this.

Pupil J

Lying there ashes spitting on my fur
as they die down slowly
crackling from the windows
as a small draft come in
and sways in my fur.

Humble curling up towards me
stroking her luxurious tail against my aching back.

Chickens scuttling about
rats tapping their tiny feet in the pantry.

The calling of the owls as 'tis just coming morning
The bright moon shining shining on me
as the crystal snow falls.

Rustling of hay as horses run around.

Glistening stars like diamond rings
shining in the dark

The swaying of the trees as a
small draft blows in the leaves

The vast cradle Alice lies in
her tiny red face that is
like the burning fire next door to me

BIBLIOGRAPHY

REFERENCES

Barrs, Myra (1988) 'Maps of Play' in Meek, Margaret & Mills, Colin, eds, *Language and Literacy in the Primary School* London, Falmer Press

Barrs, Myra (1992) 'The tune on the page' in Kimberley, Keith, Meek, Margaret & Miller, Jane, eds: *New Readings. Contributions to an understanding of literacy* London, A & C Black

Barrs, Myra & Thomas, Anne, eds (1991) *The Reading Book* London, Centre for Language in Primary Education

Barrs, Myra, Ellis, Sue, Hester, Hilary and Thomas, Anne (1988) *The Primary Language Record Handbook* London, Centre for Language in Primary Education

Barrs, Myra, Ellis, Sue, Kelly, Clare, O'Sullivan, Olivia and Stierer, Barry (1996) *Using the Primary Language Record Reading Scales* London, Centre for Language in Primary Education

Bartlett, E (1979) 'Curriculum, concepts of literacy, and social class' in L Resnick and P Weaver, eds, *Theory and Practice of Early Reading (Vol. 2)* Hillsdale, New Jersey, Lawrence Erlbaum Associates

Bartlett, F (1932) *Remembering* London, Cambridge University Press

Britton, James (1982) *Prospect and Retrospect, Selected Essays of James Britton*, edited by Gordon M Pradl. London, Heinemann Educational

Bruner, Jerome (1986) *Actual Minds, Possible Worlds* Cambridge, Ma, Harvard University Press

Bussis, Anne M, Chittenden, Edward A, Amarel, Marianne and Klausner, Edith (1985) *Inquiry into Meaning. An Investigation of Learning to Read* Hillsdale, New Jersey, Lawrence Erlbaum Associates

Byatt, A S (1990) *Possession – a romance* London, Chatto & Windus

CLPE (1996) *Primary Language Record Reading Scales* in Barrs, Myra, Ellis, Sue, Kelly, Clare, O'Sullivan, Olivia and Stierer, Barry *Using the Primary Language Record Reading Scales* London, Centre for Language in Primary Education

CLPE (1997) *Primary Language Record Writing Scales 1 & 2* London, Centre for Language in Primary Education

Cliff-Hodges, Gabrielle, Drummond, Mary Jane & Styles, Morag, eds (2000) *Tales, Tellers and Texts* London, Cassell

DES (1975) *A Language for Life* (The Bullock Report) London, HMSO

DfEE (1998) *National Literacy Strategy Framework for Teaching* London, Department for Education and Employment

DfEE (1998) *National Literacy Strategy Literacy Training Pack* London, Department for Education and Employment

DfEE/QCA (1999) *National Curriculum for English* London, DfEE & QCA

Dombey, Henrietta (1992) *Words and Worlds: Reading in the Early Years of School* Sheffield, National Association for the Teaching of English

Ellis, Sue & Barrs, Myra (1996) *The Core Book* London, Centre for Language in Primary Education

E T (1935) *D. H. Lawrence. A Personal Record* London, Jonathan Cape

Fox, Carol (1993) *At the Very Edge of the Forest: the influence of literature on storytelling by children* London, Cassell

Genette, Gerard (1980) *Narrative Discourse* Oxford, Blackwell

Goelman, Hillel, Oberg, Antoinette & Smith, Frank, eds (1984) *Awakening to Literacy* Portsmouth, NH, Heinemann Educational

Graham, Judith – personal communication

Graham, Lynda (1999) *Changing Practice through Reflection: the KS2 Reading Project Croydon* Croydon, Davidson Professional Centre

Hall, Nigel (1989) *Writing with Reason* London, Hodder

Harding, D W (1963) *Experience into Words* London, Chatto & Windus

Hollindale, Peter (1997) *Signs of Childness in Children's Books* Stroud, Thimble Press

Hughes, Ted, editor (1997) *By Heart. 101 Poems to Remember* London, Faber & Faber

Hunt, K (1965) *Grammatical Structures Written at Three Grade Levels* NCTE Research Report no.3. Urbana, Il, NCTE

ILEA Research and Statistics Branch (1990) *Reading Experience of pupils: validation survey of Reading Scale 2 from the Primary Language Record. RS 1285/90* London, Inner London Education Authority

Iser, Wolfgang (1978) *The Act of Reading* London, Routledge

Labov, W (1972) *Language in the Inner City* Philadelphia, University of Pennsylvania

Lightfoot, Martin and Martin, Nancy (1988) *The Word for Teaching is Learning. Essays for James Britton* Oxford: Heinemann Educational

Mallett, Margaret (1997) *First Person Reading and Writing in the Primary Years* Sheffield, National Association for the Teaching of English

Manguel, Alberto (1996) *A History of Reading* London, HarperCollins

Medwell, Jane, Wray, David, Poulson, L & Fox, G (1998)
Effective Teachers of Literacy Exeter, University of Exeter

Meek, Margaret (1988) *How Texts Teach What Readers Learn* Stroud, Thimble Press

Neisser, Ulric (1967) *Cognitive Psychology* Appleton-Century-Crofts

Nelson, Nancy & Calfee, Robert, eds (1998) *The Reading-Writing Connection.*
97th Yearbook of the National Society for the Study of Education. Part II
University of Chicago Press

O'Donnell, R C (1974) 'Syntactic differences between speech and writing' in
American Speech 49; 102-10

OFSTED (1999) *The National Literacy Strategy: an evaluation of the first year of*
the *National Literacy Strategy* London, OFSTED

Olson, David (1996) *The World on Paper. The conceptual and cognitive implications*
of writing and reading Cambridge University Press 1996

Ong, Walter (1982) *Orality and Literacy* London, Methuen

Pradl, G (1982) *Prospect and Retrospect: selected essays of James Britton* London,
Heinemann Educational Books

Pradl, Gordon (1988) 'Learning Listening' in Lightfoot, Martin & Martin,
Nancy (eds): *The Word for Teaching is Learning, essays for James Britton* Oxford,
Heinemann Educational/Boynton Cook

Rosenblatt, Louise (1978) *The Reader, the Text, the Poem: the Transactional Theory*
of the Literary Work Carbondale, Il, Southern Illinois University Press

Rubin, Donald (1998) *Writing for Readers: The Primary Audience in Composing* in
Nelson, Nancy & Calfee, Robert, eds (1998) *The Reading-Writing Connection. 97th*
Yearbook of the National Society for the Study of Education. Part II
University of Chicago Press

Scholes, R (1989) *Textual Power: Literary Theory and the Teaching of English*
New Haven, Yale University Press

Smith, Frank (1984) 'The Creative Achievement of Literacy' in Goelman, Hillel,
Oberg, Antoinette & Smith, Frank, eds *Awakening to Literacy* Portsmouth, NH,
Heinemann Educational

Sperling, Melanie (1998) *Teachers as Readers of Students' Writing* in Nelson,
Nancy & Calfee, Robert, eds (1998) *The Reading-Writing Connection. 97th Yearbook of*
the National Society for the Study of Education. Part II
University of Chicago Press

Torrance, Nancy & Olson, David R (1985) 'Oral and literate competences in the early school years' in Olson, David R, Torrance, Nancy & Hildyard, Angela, eds, *Literacy, Language, and Learning. The nature and consequences of reading and writing* Cambridge, Cambridge University Press

Vygotsky, Lev (1978) *Mind in Society: the Development of Higher Psychological Processes* Cambridge Ma: Harvard University Press

Watson, Victor (1993) 'Multilayered Texts and Multilayered Readers' in Styles, Morag & Drummond, Mary Jane, eds *The Politics of Reading* University of Cambridge Institute of Education & Homerton College

CHILDREN'S BOOKS

Ahlberg, Janet and Allan: *The Jolly Postman, or Other People's Letters* Heinemann 1986, Viking 1999

Aiken, Joan: *The Moon's Revenge,* illus. Alan Lee Red Fox 1990

Asbjornsen, Peter Christen & Moe, Jorgen: *East o' the Sun, West o' the Moon,* illus P J Lynch Walker 1991

Benjamin, Floella: 'Akim the Mermaid' in *Floella's Folk Tales,* illus. Jennifer Northway Hutchinson 1984 Beaver Books 1986

Berry, James (ed): *Classic Poems to Read Aloud* Kingfisher 1995

Branford, Henrietta: *Fire, Bed and Bone* Walker 1997

Burningham, John: *Come Away from the Water, Shirley* Cape 1977 Red Fox 1992

Burningham, John: *Granpa* Cape 1984

Byars, Betsy: *The Midnight Fox* Faber 1970 Puffin 1976

Collodi, Carlo: *Pinocchio* First published in Italy 1882 Puffin 1974

Crossley-Holland, Kevin: *The Green Children,* illus. Alan Marks Oxford University Press 1994

Crossley-Holland, Kevin: *The Old Stories,* illus. John Lawrence Colt Books 1997 Dolphin 1999

Dalton, Annie: *The Afterdark Princess* Mammoth 1992

Doherty, Berlie: *Daughter of the Sea* Hamish Hamilton 1996 Puffin 1998

Doherty, Berlie: *Street Child* Hamish Hamilton 1993 Collins 1995

Foreman, Michael: *War Boy. A Country Childhood* Pavilion 1991 Puffin 1991

Frank, Anne: *The Diary of a Young Girl*
First published in Holland 1947 Pan Books 1954 Definitive edition Viking 1997

Grahame, Kenneth: *The Wind in the Willows*, illus. E H Shepard
Methuen 1908 Mammoth 1989

Hallworth, Grace: *Cric Crac. A Collection of West Indian Stories*
Heinemann 1990 Mammoth 1994

Hughes, Shirley: *The Lion and the Unicorn* Bodley Head 1998 Red Fox 2000

King-Smith, Dick: *Lady Daisy* Viking 1992 Puffin 1993

Magorian, Michelle: *Goodnight Mr Tom* Kestrel 1981 Puffin 1983

Mooney, Bel: *The Stove Haunting* Methuen 1986 Mammoth 1998

Moore, Christopher: *Ishtar and Tammuz. A Babylonian Myth of the Seasons*,
illus. Christina Balit Frances Lincoln 1996

Morpurgo, Michael: *The Wreck of the Zanzibar,* illus. Christian Birmingham
Heinemann/Mammoth 1995

Nichols, Grace, ed: *Can I Buy a Slice of Sky?* Blackie 1991 Knight 1993

Norton, Mary: *The Borrowers* Dent 1952 Puffin 1958

Pearce, Philippa: *Tom's Midnight Garden*
Oxford University Press 1958 Puffin 1976

Rowling, J. K. *Harry Potter and the Philosopher's Stone* Bloomsbury 1997

Scieszka, Jon: *The True Story of the Three Little Pigs,* illus. Lane Smith Viking/Puffin 1989

Tennyson, Alfred Lord: *The Lady of Shalott*, illus. Charles Keeping
Oxford University Press 1989

Thompson, Colin: *Ruby* Julia MacRae 1994

Twain, Mark: *The Prince and the Pauper*
First published 1881 Abridged edition Puffin 1983